Religion
in the Public Sphere II

Religion
im Öffentlichen Raum II

FORUM MISSION
Volume   9/2013
Band   9/2013

D1730727

Religion
in the Public Sphere II
Religion
im Öffentlichen Raum II

FORUM MISSION
Volume   9/2013
Band   9/2013

Published for
Association for the Promotion
of Mission Studies/
Verein zur Förderung der
Missionswissenschaft

Brunner Verlag

Publisher:
©Verein zur Förderung der Missionswissenschaft (gegründet 1967)
www.forummission.ch

Editors:
FORUM MISSION, RomeroHaus, Kreuzbuchstrasse 44, CH-6006 Luzern, Switzerland
e-mail: red@forummission.ch
Josef Meili SMB, M.A.; e-mail: josefmeili@bluewin.ch
Dr. Ernstpeter Heiniger SMB; e-mail: epheiniger@bluewin.ch
Dr. Paul Stadler; e-mail: pablomm@hispeed.ch

Administration:
Brunner AG, Druck und Medien, Arsenalstrasse 24
CH-6011 Kriens, Switzerland; e-mail: verlag@bag.ch

ISBN   978-3-03727-046-2
ISSN   1661-4216

Cover/Umschlag: Eva-Maria Christen
English Translations: Susan Räber-Wilkinson

Table of Contents/Inhaltsverzeichnis

Notes/Beiträge

Book Reviews/Buchbesprechungen

Book Note/Buchhinweis

Editorial

From recent International News:
- Date: 12 March 2013
- Place: Jerusalem, Wailing Wall (or Western Wall)
- Event: Public Prayer of a group of women (from the "Women of the Wall", an organization founded by Anat Hoffman in 1988)
- Passing of the event: peacefully
- Surprise effect: no arrests for the first time since months. According to Tamar Zandberg, one of the three Knesset members present at this prayer, it was due to their presence that the Police refrained from intervention this time.

(Reported by Monika Bolliger, Jerusalem, in: *Neue Zürcher Zeitung Online* (www.NZZ.ch – 13.3.2013)

The Mission Statement of this organization explains the reasons why women have gathered at the Wall for prayer for the last 25 years:

"Our central mission is to achieve the social and legal recognition of our right, as women, to wear prayer shawls, pray, and read the Torah collectively and out loud at the Western wall."

(Source: www.womenofthewall.org.il – accessed 13.3.2013)

This event and its history illustrate one aspect of the particular situation of Religion and State in Israel. The problem seems to reside in the fact that Orthodox Judaism has a prominent position in the State of Israel although there is no constitutional reference to it. This is but one of the numerous variations of the presence of religion in the public sphere, an example that shows how State and Religion can be intertwined in a particular manner and eventually become offensive to secular minded citizens.

In the neighbouring Arab world, religious influence in politics is variably strong dependent on the respective ruling parties and constitutions. The epitome of such tendencies is a theocratic state that exists in some countries with various shades.

Since the revolutionary movements that started to sweep the Maghreb and Middle East two years ago, eyes are drawn to Egypt because of its political and symbolic significance for the Arab world. Today, Egypt is politically far from being settled although a new constitution was signed into law by President Mohamed Morsi on 26 December 2012. Fashioned in the spirit of religiously-bound parties (Muslim Brotherhood, Noor-Salafists, Wasat-Islamists), it was passed in a referendum held 15–22 December with 64% support, but with only 33% electorate participation. Since then, public protests have not stopped among others by those who disapprove of the new constitution, opposing it for the lack or inadequate recognition of human rights (particularly those of women) and true democracy.

It might be an inadmissible generalization to state that in the history of humanity religions (particularly institutionalized ones) have a record of an ambiguous and contradictory involvement in the public sphere. At times they were constructive agents of cultural progress, peace, and the fostering of human values or ethics, at others, they were caught up in conflicts and criminal deeds, in struggles for power and influence in the political, national, or international arenas of the time. Often religions kept silent in the face of crimes committed by totalitarian and dictatorial regimes. Religions stand for the best as well as for the worst humanity has produced thus far. Adherents of a particular (institutionalized) religion are faced with the contradictory history of their religion in two respects: the use and abuse of power within and without. Power within is visible in the structures (e.g. hierarchy) and leadership of a religion; power without is felt in the way the representatives appear and act in the public sphere. How do they implicitly or explicitly exert influence on the public? What is their message to their constituency, to society, and to the world at large? What do they stand for, endorse, support, defend, combat, foster, criticize? What kind of initiatives do they take? How do they communicate with the public, and what are the means (e.g. symbols of authority, attire, rituals, etc.) they use to reach audiences?

As everyone knows, the media is omnipresent in modern societies. Traditional religions as well as new religious movements (e.g. Pentecostal communities) have become attractive objects for the media, but do not hesitate themselves to take advantage of the general mediatisation by running their own media (Radio and TV stations, newspapers, publications, films) and using the new personalized social media (Face-book, Twitter, etc.). To create events: this has become imperative for religions that seek to be present in the public sphere. Other events, such as an abdication, election, death, visits of religious leaders, are widely covered in the media in similar ways as political representatives, royals or exponents of the entertainment sector. To mention a few examples:

– The Dalai Lama, both spiritual leader and head of the Tibetan exile-government (since 1950 respectively 1959), resigned from his office as head of state in 2011. His successor, Lobsang Sungay, was elected by Tibetan exiles around the world in April 2011 and installed as prime minister of the Tibetan exile-government on 8th August of the same year. – In 1989, the Dalai Lama was awarded the Nobel Peace Prize for his non-violent struggle for the liberation of Tibet. His involvement for Peace, Dialogue and Human Rights attract numerous religiously and non-religiously minded people around the globe. They respect him as spiritual leader who is committed to the promotion of basic human values or secular ethics (see: www.dalailama.com).

– Shenouda III, Pope and Patriarch of the Coptic Orthodox Church of Alexandria (Egypt) and described as a noted leader, died on 17th March 2012. He was succeeded by Anba Tawadros II (Theodoros), elected on 4th November and enthroned as 118th Pope of Alexandria and Patriarch of the See of St. Mark on 18th November 2012.

– Rowan Williams, Archbishop of Canterbury, stepped down from the position as of 31st December 2012 and was followed by Justin Welby, Bishop of Durham, elected on 4th February and enthroned at Canterbury Cathedral on 21st March 2013.

– On 11th February 2013, Pope Benedict XVI not only surprised his Church but also a world-wide audience with the announcement of his (historical) decision to abdicate as of 28th February. Jorge Mario Bergoglio, archbishop of Buenos Aires (Argentine) was elected his successor and took the name Francis after St. Francis of Assisi. This event in two distinct sequences within a month triggered off a worldwide media hype. This may be attributed in part to the fact that some 1.2 billion people belong to the Roman Catholic Church and thus make it the largest religion in the world.

To set the record straight, many religions (especially those propagating their faith and spreading throughout countries and continents) have always been generously involved in humanitarian, charitable and developing projects through their own aid agencies and in cooperation with partner organizations. Guided by spiritual and religious motives, these activities were and are, in truth, not without exception, totally unselfish. As the history of Christian Mission impressively shows, the implementation of such projects was to a certain extent compromised by the affinity or the submission to colonial strategies, economic and political interests.

Despite having been part of fateful cooperation, religions continue to be committed to the human cause in many ways – such as promoting human rights, advocacy work on different levels including UN-agencies. Depending on their socio-political conscience, alertness and courage, religious bodies dare to speak up in public, e. g. against violation of human rights, oppression, exploitation, corruption and injustices. In the prophetic tradition, they use the public sphere to advice and to appeal, to admonish and to reproach, to accuse and to warn, to oppose and to resist.

Whether religions are entitled to claim space in public may be a matter of public discourse in secular, secularized or individualized societies tending to relegate religion to the marginal zones of civil life. In reality, religions have probably been visibly present in the public sphere since they emerged, and if they are officially banned from it, there they are nonetheless present "in absentia".

In conclusion, may we recall two major programmatic projects that continue to have an impact on the public sphere. In 1989, the Christian churches in Europe took a far-reaching initiative by organizing the First Ecumenical Assembly (EEA1) in Basel (Switzerland) on "Peace with Justice". From this event a programme emerged under the headings "Justice-Peace-Environment". It led to an increasing awareness in many churches of their responsibility for the construction of a just and peaceful world and the preservation of creation. This reflects a deep concern of many contemporaries to secure a place to live for the generations still to come. – The second initiative was the founding of the World Council of Churches (WCC) in 1948 in Amsterdam. Nine Assemblies were held since then in different continents on pertinent issues, followed by important programmes, one of the most effective being the "Programme to Combat Racism". The 10th WCC Assembly will take place in Busan, Republic of Korea, from 30th October to 8th November 2013 on the theme "God of life, lead us to justice and peace".

We would like to share with the readers of Forum Mission the hopes raised by the first and promising words the new Pope Francis uttered in the public sphere as he addressed the people waiting for him at St. Peter's square after his election:

"E adesso, incominciamo questo cammino: Vescovo e popolo … un camino di fratellanza, di amore, di fiducia tra noi." – "And now, let us begin this journey, the Bishop and the people … a journey of brotherhood in love, of mutual trust."

May these hopes come true!

The Editors
Josef Meili, Ernstpeter Heiniger, Paul Stadler

Articles
Artikel

Bedrohung oder Bereicherung?
Religionen im öffentlichen Raum

Edmund Arens

Summary

Not only nowadays religion is perceived as threatening. Already Rousseau and Feuerbach as well as radical 21st century secularists consider it as destructive for the living together. However, religions are present in the public sphere in various ways: through official representatives, fundamentalist sections but also through prophetic-critical movements. Religions are challenged to introduce their faith and ethical-political ideas in the public discourse. While «public religions» introduce their visions and prophetic criticism into the process of the formation of the public mind they reduce their potential of threat and contribute to the vitality of the society.

«Die Religion ist ein erstaunliches Phänomen, das widersprüchliche Rollen im Leben der Menschen spielt. Sie kann zerstören oder beleben, betäuben oder wachrufen, versklaven oder emanzipieren, Fügsamkeit lehren oder die Revolte.» Das schrieb der iranische Soziologe und Reformer Ali Schariati.[1] Die amerikanische Ausgabe des Buches, dem dieses Zitat entnommen ist, trägt den bemerkenswerten Titel: «The Power of Religion in The Public Sphere»[2]. *Power* kann beides bedeuten: inspirierende, bereichernde Kraft, aber auch bedrohliche Macht. Damit sind wir beim Thema «Religionen im öffentlichen Raum».

Ich beginne mit einigen Bemerkungen zur öffentlichen Wahrnehmung von Religion. Sodann komme ich auf religiöse Präsenz in der Öffentlichkeit zu sprechen. Am Schluss folgen Ausführungen über öffentliche Religionen.

---

[1] Zit. nach Craig Calhoun, Nachwort: Die vielen Mächte der Religion, in: Eduardo Mendieta/Jonathan VanAntwerpen (Hg.), *Religion und Öffentlichkeit*, Berlin 2012, 170–195, 170.

[2] Judith Butler/Jürgen Habermas/Charles Taylor/Cornel West, *The Power of Religion in the Public Sphere*, ed. and introduced by Eduardo Mendieta/Jonathan VanAntwerpen, New York 2011; dazu meine Besprechung in: *Theologische Revue* 107 (2011) 340–341.

1. Öffentliche Wahrnehmung von Religion

In der öffentlichen, vor allem durch die Massenmedien vermittelten Wahrnehmung gilt Religion heute häufig als gefährlich und bedrohlich. Die Medienöffentlichkeit richtet sich gern auf die radikalen Ränder, die eskalierenden Konflikte sowie die religiös motivierte Gewalt.

Das Konflikt- und Gewaltpotenzial von Religion hat bereits vor 250 Jahren der Schweizer Philosoph Jean-Jacques Rousseau prägnant auf den Punkt gebracht, wenn er in seinem «Gesellschaftsvertrag» schreibt: «Man kann unmöglich mit Leuten in Frieden leben, die man für verdammt hält ... Man muss sie bekehren oder verfolgen.» Ähnlich äussert sich Mitte des 19. Jahrhunderts der Philosoph Ludwig Feuerbach in seinem Werk «Das Wesen des Christentums». Laut ihm liegt das Verdammen Anders- oder Ungläubiger gerade «im Wesen des Glaubens», und der Glaube geht «notwendig in Hass, der Hass in Verfolgung» über.

Auch für heutige Religionskritiker ist das für das Zusammenleben destruktive Potenzial von Religion offensichtlich. Säkularisten sehen in Religionen wegen deren unerbittlicher Wahrheitsansprüche eine Belastung für das demokratische Zusammenleben. Der amerikanische Philosoph Richard Rorty nennt Religion einen «conversation stopper», eine Gesprächsabbrecherin, welche das freie Gespräch abschneidet. Darum muss der Glaube strikt Privatsache sein; deshalb haben Religionsgemeinschaften in der Öffentlichkeit nichts zu suchen. Aushängeschild der gegenwärtigen radikalen Religionskritik ist der britische Biologe Richard Dawkins.[3] Er bezeichnet den Gottesglauben als einen sozial schädlichen Komplex gefährlicher Viren, den er für unvernünftig, ethisch verwerflich und pädagogisch höchst gefährlich erklärt. Die Geisteskrankheit des «Gotteswahns» ist ihm zufolge verbunden mit Absolutismus, Homophobie, Pädophilie, Fundamentalismus und Kindesmissbrauch.

Jedoch nicht nur notorische Religionskritiker denunzieren die Bedrohlichkeit von Religion für die moderne Gesellschaft. Auch von religionswissenschaftlicher Seite wird auf das Konflikt- und Gewaltpotenzial

---

[3] Vgl. Richard Dawkins, *Der Gotteswahn,* Berlin 2007; dazu: Edmund Arens, Ein Zelot des Atheismus, in: *Orientierung* 72 (2008), 13–14.

von Religionen aufmerksam gemacht. Der amerikanische Religionswissenschaftler und Soziologe Mark Juergensmeyer etwa stellt eine «Globalisierung religiöser Gewalt»[4] fest. Er verweist auf die Ausbreitung religiös motivierter Gewalt in Gestalt von Rebellionen, Glaubens-, Bürger- und global ausgerichteten Kriegen in diversen Religionen. Der deutsche Religionswissenschaftler Hans G. Kippenberg befasst sich ebenfalls mit «Religionskriegen im Zeitalter der Globalisierung»[5]. Er deutet Gewalt gegen Anders- bzw. Ungläubige als religiöse Gemeinschaftshandlung, welche von religiösen Gemeinschaften getragen werde.

Dass religiöse Spannungen und Konflikte ein weltweites Problem darstellen, hält auch der indische Jesuit Michael Amaladoss im neuen «Forum Mission» fest. Gegenüber einem negativen Säkularismus befürwortet er einen positiven Säkularismus. Dieser ermögliche Religionen eine aktive Rolle im Rahmen der Öffentlichkeit und fördere so deren dialogische, friedensstiftende Potenziale.[6]

Jedenfalls ist das Droh- und Konfliktpotenzial von Religionen im Fokus einer Medienöffentlichkeit, welche auf Skandalisierung setzt und insofern die schlimmen Missbrauchsfälle in der katholischen Kirche zusammen mit islamistischen Selbstmordattentätern, christlich-fundamentalistischen Holocaustleugnern und Koranschändern als Repräsentanten bigotter, bizarrer bzw. brutaler Religion vorführt.

2. Religiöse Präsenz in der Öffentlichkeit

Religionen sind im öffentlichen Raum auf vielfältige Weise präsent. Ihre Vertreter gebrauchen diesen Raum zum einen zur Selbstdarstellung und zur Repräsentation religiöser Machtansprüche. Wallfahrten und Prozessionen waren früher Demonstrationen etwa katholischer Macht, welche die Herrlichkeit der Kirche, ihres himmlischen Herrn und ihrer irdischen

---

[4] Vgl. Mark Juergensmeyer, *Die Globalisierung religiöser Gewalt*. Von christlichen Milizen bis al-Qaida, Hamburg 2009.

[5] Vgl. Hans G. Kippenberg, *Gewalt als Gottesdienst*. Religionskriege im Zeitalter der Globalisierung, München 2008.

[6] Vgl. Michael Amaladoss, Religion in the Public Space, in: *Forum Mission* 8/2012 – Religion im Öffentlichen Raum I, 16–27.

Herren anschaulich machten. Papstreisen oder Weltjugendtage sind heute aufwendig inszenierte Darstellungen des Katholischen. Bei solchen Grossereignissen handelt es sich um herausragende öffentliche Inszenierungen, in denen sich die offizielle Kirche in der Öffentlichkeit und als Öffentlichkeit repräsentiert und rituell inszeniert. Damit markiert sie zudem gegenüber anderen Assoziationen und Institutionen in der Zivilgesellschaft auf der öffentlichen Bühne immer auch massenmediale Präsenz. Diese Ereignisse haben freilich nicht nur eine repräsentierende, sondern auch eine mobilisierende Seite. Es sind dies Performances, welche das Fussvolk buchstäblich in Bewegung bringen und zu Massenaufläufen verleiten.

Den öffentlichen Raum nehmen zum anderen dissidente, prophetische, protestierende Gruppen und Bewegungen in Anspruch. Auch ihnen geht es um Mobilisierung und die Artikulation ihrer Anliegen. Dies kann geschehen durch das Öffentlichmachen von Diskriminierung und Ausgrenzung, durch den öffentlichen Protest gegen Unrecht, durch das «gegenöffentliche» Ritualisieren, Inszenieren und Dramatisieren verdrängter Konflikte «auf der öffentlichen Bühne»[7]. In «Forum Mission» wird dieser Aspekt eindrücklich im Beitrag von Joseph M. Wandera[8] beleuchtet. Am Beispiel des charismatischen muslimischen Strassenpredigers Khalid Balala zeigt Wandera den Kampf um den öffentlichen Raum in Kenia auf; zugleich bringt er den Streit der zwischen öffentlichem Protest und Anpassung lavierenden anglikanischen Kirche einerseits und der autoritären Staatsmacht andererseits aufs Tapet.

Zur repräsentativen, mobilisierenden und prophetisch-kritischen religiösen Präsenz im öffentlichen Raum kommt im Falle eines normativ anspruchsvollen Verständnisses von Öffentlichkeit noch eine diskursive Dimension hinzu. Wenn Öffentlichkeit mit Jürgen Habermas der zivilgesellschaftliche Raum der Konfliktaustragung und Verständigung zwischen

---

[7] Vgl. Jeffrey C. Alexander, *The Civil Sphere*, Oxford-New York 2008; dazu: Edmund Arens, Kritisch, kirchlich, kommunikativ. Fundamentaltheologie als öffentliche Theologie, in: Christoph Böttigheimer/Florian Bruckmann (Hg.), *Glaubensverantwortung im Horizont der «Zeichen der Zeit»* (QD 248), Freiburg-Basel-Wien 2012, 432–453, 436 ff.

[8] Joseph M. Wandera, Muslims, Anglicans, and State, and the Contest for Public Space in Kenya, in: *Forum Mission* 8/2012 – Religion im Öffentlichen Raum I, 93–115.

gesellschaftlichen und religiösen Gruppen, einander widerstreitender Überzeugungen und Handlungsorientierungen darstellt, dann sind Religionsgemeinschaften ebenso wie Säkulare gefordert, ihre Glaubensauffassungen und ethisch-politischen Vorstellungen in den öffentlichen Diskurs einzubringen. Ob religiöse Gruppen und Gemeinschaften dazu bereit sind, hängt entscheidend davon ab, ob sie die «Welt» fundamentalistisch als durch und durch korrumpiert auffassen sowie als feindliches Gegenüber begreifen. Bei allzu grosser Fixierung auf die jeweilige religiöse «Binnenöffentlichkeit»[9] bleibt die Bereitschaft zur öffentlichen Beteiligung und Beratung auf der Strecke. Wer wie der Papst auf seiner letzten Deutschlandreise einer «Entweltlichung» der Kirche das Wort redet, begibt es in gefährliches und zudem morastiges Fahrwasser. Hans Waldenfels weist in seinem Beitrag in «Forum Mission», in welchem er fragt, worin für Papst Benedikt «bei der Abkehr von der ‹reinen Weltlichkeit› dann die ‹Weltoffenheit›»[10] bestehe, dezent darauf hin – meines Erachtens etwas zu dezent. Mit Néstor da Costa ist gerade umgekehrt die Frage zu stellen: «¿Una sociedad civil dentro de la Iglesia Católica?»[11] Gibt es/ braucht es eine Zivilgesellschaft innerhalb der katholischen Kirche?

3. Öffentliche Religionen

Den Begriff der «öffentlichen Religionen» hat der in «Forum Mission» mehrfach zitierte spanisch-amerikanische Religionssoziologe José Casanova in Umlauf gebracht und bekannt gemacht.[12] Ihm zufolge ist öffentliche

---

[9] Vgl. Erwin Koller, Religion im öffentlichen Raum, in: *Forum Mission* 8/2012 – Religion im Öffentlichen Raum I, 179–199, 194 ff.

[10] Hans Waldenfels, Entweltlicht in der Welt. Die Religion in der heutigen Welt, in: *Forum Mission* 8/2012 – Religion im Öffentlichen Raum I, 28–45, 37; vgl. Edmund Arens, Weltkirche statt entwirklichter Kirche. Wendet sich Rom wieder vom «aggiornamento» ab?, in: *Erwachsenenbildung* 58 (2012) H. 3, 114–117.

[11] Néstor da Costa, Religión y espacio público. Una mirada latinoamericana, in: *Forum Mission* 8/2012 – Religion im Öffentlichen Raum I, 80–92, 90.

[12] Vgl. José Casanova, *Public Religions in the Modern World*, Chicago 1994; dazu die Beiträge von Néstor da Costa, Joseph M. Wandera sowie Erika B. Seamon in «Forum Mission» 8/2012; vgl. auch: Edmund Arens, *Gottesverständigung*. Eine kommunikative Religionstheologie, Freiburg-Basel-Wien 2007, 145–152.

Religion zum einen Resultat einer Entprivatisierung des Religiösen und zum anderen einer Entstaatlichung der Religion. Das Heraustreten aus der Privatsphäre meint, dass Religion den ihr von Seiten der Aufklärung, des Liberalismus und Laizismus zugewiesenen Bereich verlässt. Das Öffentlichwerden beinhaltet zugleich eine Absage an alle Formen von Staatsreligion, also die Aufgabe jedes Monopolanspruchs, der sich aus der exklusiven Verbindung mit dem Staat ableitet. Bei der öffentlichen Religion tritt an die Stelle der Beschränkung auf den Privatbereich bzw. der Beanspruchung staatlicher Privilegien und politischer Macht deren Verortung in der Zivilgesellschaft. Letztere wird zum öffentlichen Raum, in dem Religionen ihre Anliegen, Beiträge, Perspektiven und Potenziale in die gesellschaftliche Öffentlichkeit einbringen und im Diskurs mit anderen zivilgesellschaftlichen Akteuren zur Geltung bringen.

Als öffentliche Religionen kommen zum einen die christlichen Kirchen in Frage. Fulbert Steffensky spricht in «Forum Mission» mit Bedacht von der «öffentlichen Kirche»; sie ist für ihn gerade keine angepasste, liberalisierte, sondern eine durch «ihre Fremdheit, ihre Besonderheit und ihre Klarheit»[13] kenntliche Kirche. Auch andere Glaubensgemeinschaften kommen als öffentliche Religionen in Frage, insoweit sie nicht nur um das persönliche Heil ihrer Anhänger und Mitglieder besorgt sind, sondern zugleich das gesellschaftliche Zusammenleben und Wohlergehen, das Gemeinwohl und damit die soziale Gerechtigkeit und Solidarität im Blick haben.[14]

Öffentlich wird Religion dann, wenn eine religiöse Gemeinschaft dem von ihr vertretenen und gelebten Glauben eine gesellschaftliche Bedeutung beimisst und dies in ihrer Glaubenspraxis bekundet. Das beinhaltet die Bereitschaft, sich an den gesellschaftlichen Auseinandersetzungen um Grundfragen menschlichen Lebens und Zusammenlebens zu

---

[13] Fulbert Steffensky, Religion und Öffentlichkeit. Einige unsystematische Bemerkungen zum Thema, in: *Forum Mission* 8/2012 – Religion im Öffentlichen Raum I, 116–131, 125.

[14] Zum Islam vgl. Reinhard Schulze, Islam im öffentlichen Raum oder Der Islam als öffentliche Religion, in: Mariano Delgado et al. (Hg.), *Religion und Öffentlichkeit*, Stuttgart 2009, 141–166; Armando Salvatore, *The Public Sphere. Liberal Modernity, Catholicism, Islam*, New York 2010.

beteiligen. Über die Teilnahme an öffentlichen Auseinandersetzungen wird ein «public encounter»[15], eine öffentliche Begegnung mit anderen möglich. Dies kann längerfristig zu Lernprozessen und zur Verständigung der verschiedenen Religionen miteinander führen. Beteiligung am öffentlichen Diskurs und Begegnung mit anderen sind zudem wirksame Heilmittel gegen exklusivistische Selbstüberhöhung und fundamentalistische Selbstabschottung. Begegnung, Dialog und Diskurs verhindern die Verhärtung und vermindern das Bedrohungspotenzial religiöser Gemeinschaften sowie das bei säkulären Menschen verbreitete Gefühl der Bedrohung durch Religionen.

Öffentlichen Religionen geht es darum, die in ihnen überlieferten Glaubensüberzeugungen, moralischen Einsichten und Wertvorstellungen zu bewahren, sichtbar zu machen und öffentlich darzustellen und damit zugleich ihre Vorstellungen vom guten Leben und gerechten Zusammenleben in den gesellschaftlichen Diskurs einzubringen. Öffentliche Religionen bringen ihre Auffassungen von sozialer Gerechtigkeit und Gemeinwohl, Solidarität und Anerkennung, Fürsorge und Verantwortung füreinander sowie für andere in ihrer eigenen gemeinschaftlichen Praxis zum Ausdruck. Durch ihr «public commitment» und ihr «advocacy work»[16] erweisen sie sich als wichtige Akteure im Raum der Zivilgesellschaft. Zudem bringen sie ihre Forderungen, Visionen und prophetische Kritik in gesellschaftliche Meinungs- und Willensbildungsprozesse ein. Mit ihren prophetischen Interventionen sowie ihren moralischen Optionen tragen öffentliche Religionen zur Vitalisierung der Zivilgesellschaft bei. Sie mobilisieren moralische Ressourcen, derer auch eine moderne pluralistische Gesellschaft und ein säkularer Staat bedürfen. Wie Erika B. Seamon völlig richtig am Beispiel der USA herausstellt, hält gerade die gesunde Spannung zwischen religiöser Gesellschaft und säkularem Staat

---

[15] José Casanova, Civil Society and Religion, in: *Social Research* 68 (2001), 1041–1080, 1076.
[16] Josef Meili/Ernstpeter Heiniger/Paul Stadler, Editorial, in: *Forum Mission* 8/2012 – Religion im Öffentlichen Raum I, 7–14, 13.

respektive säkularem Recht «American democracy and religious liberty intact»[17].

Öffentliche Religionen und öffentliche Kirchen stehen in Verbindung mit öffentlicher Theologie. An einer solchen wird international intensiv gearbeitet, zum Beispiel in Brasilien, wie aus dem Beitrag von Afonso Maria Ligorio Soares[18] ersichtlich wird. Öffentliche Theologie geschieht im Global Network for Public Theology oder im International Journal for Public Theology. Meiner Auffassung nach geht es nicht um eine «Theologie der Öffentlichkeit», wie sie Erwin Koller in «Forum Mission» im Anschluss an eine in Bielefeld erdachte und in Zürich verfeinerte publizistische Theorie der Öffentlichkeit skizziert.[19] Zur Reflexion von Religion und Religionen im öffentlichen Raum eignet sich eher eine öffentliche Theologie, welche sich in der wissenschaftlichen, der kirchlichen und der gesellschaftlichen Öffentlichkeit verortet und entfaltet.[20]

---

[17] Erika B. Seamon, A Healthy Tension? The Encounter of Religious Society and Secular Law in American Political Life, in: *Forum Mission* 8/2012 – Religion im Öffentlichen Raum I, 132–154, 151.

[18] Vgl. Afonso Maria Ligorio Soares, Religião e Coisa Pública no Brasil: tensões e negociações, in: *Forum Mission* 8/2012 – Religion im Öffentlichen Raum I, 155–178, 169 ff.

[19] Vgl. Erwin Koller, Religion im öffentlichen Raum, 193 ff.

[20] Vgl. David Tracy, *The Analogical Imagination. Christian Theology and the Culture of Pluralism*, New York 1981; Dirkie Smit, Notions of Public and Doing Theology, in: *International Journal of Public Theology* 1 (2007), 431–454; Edmund Arens, Kritisch, kirchlich, kommunikativ; ders., Vom Schrei zur Verständigung. Politische Theologie als öffentliche Theologie, in: Thomas Polednitschek et al. (Hg.), *Theologisch-politische Vergewisserungen. Ein Arbeitsbuch aus dem Schüler- und Freundeskreis von Johann Baptist Metz*, Münster 2009, 129–138.

Edmund Arens studierte kath. Theologie und Philosophie an den Universitäten Münster und Frankfurt. 1982 Promotion, 1989 Habilitation für Fundamentaltheologie an der Universität Münster; seit 1996 Professor für Fundamentaltheologie an der Universität Luzern. Neuere Veröffentlichungen: Gottesverständigung. Eine kommunikative Religionstheologie, Freiburg 2007; (Hg.), Zeit denken. Eschatologie im interdisziplinären Diskurs, Freiburg 2010; (Hg.), Gegenwart. Ästhetik trifft Theologie, Freiburg 2012.

Bergstrasse 13, CH-6004 Luzern, Schweiz; edmund.arens@unilu.ch

La place de la religion dans une société à démocratie tâtonnante Cas de la RD Congo (2011–2012)

Josée Ngalula

Summary

The author analyses the case of the Democratic Republic of Congo (DRC/RDC) in the period from 2011 to 2012. In the then highly tense situations of the public debate on the position of religion in a society groping towards democracy, the author observes that the Catholic Church reacted to this as if by reflex by shaping her evangelization through three fundamental attitudes. Firstly, by calling for conversion by means of public declarations of denunciation, demanding change of behaviour, and calling for prayer for the country. Secondly, by allying evangelization and human promotion in getting involved in institutions emanating from civil society in order to prepare the citizens to comply correctly with their civic duties. And thirdly, by positioning herself in the dynamics of actions taken in times past by Cardinal Lavigerie in order to battle against the complexities of the slave-trade, i.e. public manifestations and an appeal at the international level. Finally, the author asks the question whether such an appeal could not also be a missionary strategy.

Introduction

La place de la religion dans les sociétés africaines postcoloniales a connu plusieurs cas de figures, dont les deux extrêmes sont les suivants: d'une part la persécution des institutions ecclésiales à cause du témoignage prophétique en faveur des pauvres et des opprimés; et d'autre part, la présidence de l'Eglise (comme membre de la société civile) des hautes institutions comme les parlements de transition ou les commissions nationales électorales. Comme l'ont montré les nombreuses études théologiques et missiologiques sur le sujet, le rôle actif des églises dans la longue transition des sociétés africaines vers les indépendances d'abord, et la démocratie ensuite, a suscité quelques initiatives originales.[1]

C'est dans cette perspective que je propose un coup d'œil sur le débat public relatif à la place de la religion chrétienne, dans une société où la démocratie tâtonne encore. Je prends le cas de la RD Congo, où ce débat a été houleux durant la période pré et postélectorale, de 2011 à 2012. Je m'intéresserai spécialement aux initiatives prises par les institutions ecclésiales pour gérer ce débat public: s'est-on limité aux stratégies classiques héritées de l'époque coloniale ou a-t-on inventé de nouvelles stratégies de présence du christianisme sur la place publique face aux enjeux de l'heure? Mes réflexions ici ont une allure de témoignage.

I. Débats autour des élections

Au début de 2011, la RD Congo se préparait à organiser des élections législatives et présidentielles dans un climat de tensions sociales sur toute l'étendue du pays, de climat de guerre et d'insécurité au Nord-Est du pays. Et juste avant les élections, la Constitution du pays a été révisée, pour accommoder les choses selon les goûts et projets de la majorité au pouvoir: faire un seul tour des élections, et non pas deux tours comme prévu par la Constitution. Cet acte grave de changement brusque de la Constitution sans avoir consulté la volonté de tout le peuple provoqua un débat public houleux. L'archevêque de Kinshasa, le cardinal Laurent Monsengwo, qui avait été autrefois président du Parlement de transition (comme membre de la société civile), tint une conférence de presse, dans laquelle il expliquait pourquoi un tel changement dans la Constitution était un acte grave pour l'avenir de la paix en RD Congo, et pour rappeler les débats politiques dont il avait été témoin dans l'histoire du pays et la raison pour laquelle la Constitution avait opté pour deux tours. Il s'en suivit un débat très passionné dans les médias sur la place de la religion dans l'espace public, spécialement dans un état laïc. Les opinions furent carrément

---

[1] Voir notamment *Eglise et démocratisation en Afrique. Actes de la XIXe Semaine Théologique de Kinshasa,* Facultés Catholiques de Kinshasa, 1994; Hizkias Assefa and George Wachira, *Peacemaking and Democratisation in Africa: Theoretical Perspectives and Church Initiatives,* Nairobi, East African Educational Publishers, 1996, 242 p.

divisées en deux camps. D'un côté une position soutenant que la Bible ayant déclaré «A César ce qui est à César», les évêques catholiques et les chrétiens en général n'ont pas à s'ingérer dans la marche de ce pays, car l'objectif de la religion est seulement de prier. De l'autre côté, une opinion soutenant que si on accepte que la religion s'ingère dans les soins de santé pour soigner le peuple malade, dans l'éducation pour la promotion de la population non instruite, il est cohérent qu'elle s'ingère aussi dans les manigances des politiciens lorsqu'ils posent des actes ou prennent des décisions qui troublent la paix sociale. Ce débat dans les médias divisa même les chrétiens catholiques et autres dans leurs paroisses, lieux de travail et familles!

Face à cette situation, la conférence épiscopale nationale des évêques catholiques du Congo (CENCO) adopta une vieille méthode, en vigueur déjà depuis l'époque coloniale: écrire une lettre pastorale adressée aux catholiques et hommes de bonne volonté, pour faire entendre la voix, les peines et les espoirs de la population, et pour inviter les dirigeants du pays à remplir correctement leur devoir. En effet, en février 2011, elle publia un document intitulé: Année électorale: «que devons-nous faire?» (Ac 2,37). *Exhortation du Comité permanent de la Conférence Episcopale Nationale du Congo (CENCO) aux fidèles catholiques, aux hommes et aux femmes de bonne volonté.* La position exprimée publiquement fut sans équivoque:

> *Dans la perspective des prochaines échéances électorales, la Constitution a été révisée. La CENCO en prend acte, mais elle ne saurait s'empêcher de relever que la Constitution, gage du consensus national laborieusement obtenu et retrouvé, approuvée par référendum, a été révisée de manière précipitée et expéditive. En effet, la Constitution modifiée a été votée et promulguée en moins de deux semaines, en fin d'une session extraordinaire du Parlement à l'ordre du jour de laquelle elle n'avait pas été inscrite initialement alors qu'elle aurait pu intervenir en toute sérénité, plus tôt, sur base d'une large concertation et d'un débat public et parlementaire ouvert. Cette procédure a suscité beaucoup d'inquiétudes dans l'opinion nationale. Ce qui a amené certains à s'interroger sur la visée réelle de la révision constitutionnelle. Nous craignons que cette révision ne prélude à d'autres qui conduiraient au retour du monopar-*

tisme, à la fin de la démocratie et à l'instauration d'une nouvelle dicta-
ture. Nous avons été fortement affectés et indignés par la virulence de la
réplique du Gouvernement et ses propos désobligeants à l'égard de Son
Eminence Laurent Cardinal Monsengwo. Nous estimons que son inter-
vention ne comprend rien qui mérite une réaction aussi acerbe et irrévé-
rencieuse. Le débat d'idées en démocratie n'autorise pas des attaques
personnelles. A cet effet, la CENCO invite la population et les acteurs
politiques à éviter tout discours discourtois et discriminatoire et à adop-
ter des attitudes et des propos capables de favoriser l'unité de la Nation
congolaise (n° 7–9).

La deuxième contribution est une exhortation morale à toutes les couches de la population, aux catholiques et aussi aux hommes de bonne volonté, pour

> *que tout se déroule dans le respect strict de la loi électorale, la vérité et*
> *la transparence, sans fraude ni manipulation, dans l'apaisement, à l'ex-*
> *clusion de toute dérive autocratique et de toute forme de violence d'où*
> *qu'elle vienne (n° 16);*
>
> *… à la population de redoubler de vigilance pour ne pas vendre sa*
> *conscience en échange de cadeaux et dons divers de la part de ceux qui*
> *les lui apportent en ce temps crucial, ni céder à la tentation du triba-*
> *lisme ou du régionalisme; elle devra s'impliquer d'une manière respon-*
> *sable dans le processus électoral. Aux professionnels des médias, confor-*
> *mément au code de déontologie de leur métier, de ne pas déformer,*
> *dénaturer ou fausser, par leur formulation, par insistance, grossisse-*
> *ment, omission ou manipulation, les opinions d'autrui, les titres ou les*
> *commentaires des articles qui doivent être traités avec impartialité et*
> *bonne foi. Au clergé, en particulier, de réserver la chaire de vérité à la*
> *prédication de la Parole de Dieu et de l'enseignement social de l'Eglise;*
> *de ne jamais accorder la parole aux acteurs politiques pendant les célé-*
> *brations eucharistiques pour battre campagne (n° 21).*

La deuxième vieille stratégie utilisée dans ce débat public est celle de prendre des initiatives pour baliser le terrain, d'une part en implorant le secours de la grâce divine, et d'autre part en préparant les personnes, en vue d'un avenir meilleur:

L'Eglise catholique, fidèle à sa mission évangélisatrice et au souci de promotion humaine intégrale qui en fait partie intégrante, accompagnera par la prière, la formation à l'éducation civique, ce processus électoral dont dépend l'avenir de la Nation congolaise (n° 22).

Effectivement, dans les paroisses catholiques sur toute l'étendue du pays, une prière composée par les évêques fut récitée chaque matin au cours de la célébration eucharistique, pour que les élections se passent dans la paix et que les votants voient l'intérêt de toute la nation et pas des considérations partisanes, qu'ils résistent aux offres de corruption. Cette prière fut récitée publiquement et quotidiennement sur l'ensemble du pays, à la fin de la célébration eucharistique, jusqu'à la tenue des élections en novembre 2011.

De plus, l'Eglise catholique s'unit à toutes les confessions religieuses qui le souhaitaient, pour la formation civique des citoyens durant les six mois précédant les élections. Ce fut une belle œuvre œcuménique et inter-religieuse, car plusieurs confessions chrétiennes ainsi que les musulmans de la RD Congo firent un programme commun d'éducation de la population à l'acte libre de choix de candidat, la répétition dans l'urne, etc.

A la veille des élections, de nouveaux débats surgirent sur la place publique et dans les médias. Un premier débat, assez discret mais très significatif, eut lieu quelques jours avant les élections, l'épouse du chef de l'Etat, qui était candidat à sa propre succession, déclara avoir eu une «révélation divine» lui demandant d'intercéder pour le peuple congolais comme Esther le fit dans l'Ancien Testament. Par conséquent, elle donnait «l'ordre» (comme Première Dame) à tous les responsables des confessions religieuses pour venir la rejoindre à cette prière qui allait être publique et qu'elle allait diriger. L'Eglise catholique et quelques églises protestantes n'y allèrent pas. L'Eglise catholique répondit officiellement que selon ses habitudes, l'intercession pour le pays se faisait au cours de la célébration eucharistique, et qu'elle était en cours depuis plusieurs mois. L'absence de quelques confessions religieuses à ce rassemblement provoqua un débat houleux dans les médias et on accusa les confessions religieuses absentes d'être «contre le chef de l'Etat». On publia dans les médias une série des versets bibliques qui «prouvaient» que ces confessions religieuses ont l'obligation de se soumettre aux autorités civiles, et en refusant d'aller, elles «péchaient» contre Dieu. Mais on oubliait que le chef de l'Etat était un candidat à la présidence parmi tant d'autres et que, pour des confessions religieuses, prendre part à cette prière allait influencer les votes de leurs membres, car c'était comme une campagne électorale camouflée derrière la prière avec la première dame.

Un deuxième débat, encore plus houleux, eut lieu juste après les élections (qui s'étaient passées dans une grande désorganisation). Au moment où on publiait progressivement les résultats provisoires, la majorité de la population était sous le choc car le jour-même des élections, on avait affiché, à la fin de la journée, les résultats pour chaque bureau de vote: ce qui était publié progressivement comme résultat ne correspondait pas à ce que leurs yeux avaient vu! La manière dont la compilation était faite affichait des anomalies qui créèrent une très grande tension dans la population, et ce au point que les chefs des grands partis politiques devaient supplier leurs membres de rester calmes et de ne pas basculer dans la violence. La tension sociale devenait de plus en plus vive et la situation risquait d'exploser. Les autorités civiles réagissaient en déployant la police partout, pour intimider la population. Devant cette situation, l'archevêque de Kinshasa convoqua alors la presse et lui donna une déclaration publique appelant officiellement le chef de l'Etat et le président de la Commission électorale de tout mettre en œuvre pour que les résultats proclamés soient conformes à «la vérité des urnes et à la justice». Cela déclencha, dans les médias publics et privés, un tollé d'insultes sur sa personne ainsi que tous les chrétiens qui osaient s'ingérer dans les débats publics qui ne traitaient pas de la religion. Et même certains catholiques qui étaient membres du parti politique du chef de l'Etat déclarèrent qu'ils allaient quitter l'Eglise catholique, car elle osait se mêler de la politique, ce que Dieu ne lui a pas demandé (sic).

Un troisième débat, un peu moins houleux, mais d'une grande envergure quand même, eut lieu après la proclamation des résultats définitifs des élections. Les évêques catholiques se rassemblèrent pour évaluer le processus électoral, car, à travers les commissions paroissiales et diocésaines «justice et paix», l'Eglise catholique avait mis des observateurs sur l'ensemble du pays. Les évêques catholiques écrivirent une déclaration officielle affirmant que les irrégularités, fraudes et corruptions observées durant tout le processus électoral rendaient et le processus lui-même et les résultats problématiques. Il y eut une nouvelle vague d'insultes sur les autorités de l'Eglise catholique dans les médias, et cette fois-ci on alla même loin: les partis politiques qui se sentaient attaqués par la déclaration de la conférence épiscopale demandèrent aux catholiques membres de leurs partis d'aller insulter publiquement les évêques dans les médias, et de «prouver» que, d'après l'évangile, les évêques ne sont pas habilités à être les seuls porte-parole de l'ensemble de l'Eglise! Il y a donc une nouvelle donnée ici: ce sont les membres de l'Eglise qui se dressent contre l'autorité, non plus seulement pour dire que la vie de foi ne doit pas s'occuper des situations et débats politiques, mais aussi pour affirmer que les autorités de l'Eglise n'ont aucune compétence pour parler publiquement au nom de toute l'Eglise! Ce fut un moment très dur pour l'Eglise catholique.

Retenons, dans ce premier point, que l'Eglise catholique a utilisé une stratégie plutôt «classique» depuis le début de l'évangélisation du Congo: déclarations publiques de dénonciation, prière pour le pays et participation à des institutions relevant de la société civile pour préparer les citoyens à remplir correctement leurs devoirs civiques.

II. Tensions publiques autour de l'insécurité, provoquée par le pillage des richesses du pays

Les richesses de la RD Congo ont été objet de la convoitise internationale et de pillage organisé depuis le XIXe siècle, avec Léopold II. La colonisation et la période de la dictature de Mobutu ont plus ou moins camouflé et atténué institutionnellement ce pillage. Mais il va reprendre avec plus d'envergure avec la découverte du coltan, minerai précieux pour les nouvelles technologies du XXe siècle. Du coup, les multinationales occidentales, avec la complicité de certains pays occidentaux et africains (producteurs d'armes), ainsi que des complicités à l'intérieur même du Congo, vont créer des bandes armées alimentant une grande instabilité au Nord-Est du pays, climat favorable pour un pillage systématique des ressources naturelles. Depuis presque 15 ans, des voix des ONG et des Eglises s'élèvent pour dénoncer cette situation et exiger des changements.

En un premier temps, l'Eglise catholique a utilisé une stratégie classique: la dénonciation publique. Pour le faire, il fallait avoir des données objectives, comme c'est le cas pour les ONG qui participent au débat public sur cette question. C'est ainsi que la CENCO a décidé de créer, en son sein, une «Commission épiscopale ad hoc pour les ressources naturelles». Se servant des structures paroissiales et diocésaines des «commissions justice et paix» à travers tout le pays, cette commission permet d'avoir, au jour le jour, des données très précises sur l'exploitation illégale et le pillage des richesses du pays. Ces données ont permis d'amorcer, en 2010, un plaidoyer pour que soit votée une loi dissuadant et sanctionnant les multinationales d'origine américaine engagées dans l'exploitation illégale des richesses du Congo. Et ce, en synergie avec la conférence épiscopale américaine, pour sensibiliser les sénateurs et parlementaires.

Et durant la période qui nous préoccupe ici, c'est-à-dire 2011–2012, un grand débat a eu lieu (et continue) lorsque, au Nord-Est du pays, un mouvement dénommé «M23» a conquis une partie très riche du territoire et pris des populations en otage. Et il y a beaucoup de paroisses catholiques dans ce territoire occupé, ce qui fait que les évêques catholiques avaient connaissance de tout ce qui se passait, donc de la profondeur de la souffrance de la population. Or durant les trois mois qui ont suivi l'occupation de ce territoire, le gouvernement central de Kinshasa a semblé banaliser la situation, qui était extrêmement grave pour l'avenir du pays. Des pays voisins étaient y impliqués indirectement, avec un agenda affiché de balkaniser le pays, et le gouvernement central ne semblait pas y voir une urgence. Les évêques catholiques réunis en assemblée ordinaire au moins de juillet 2012 publièrent une déclaration dans laquelle ils dénonçaient publiquement qu'il y avait un projet de balkanisation du pays et annonçaient qu'ils allaient faire une série d'action «fortes» pour que cette tentative de balkanisation échoue. La première fut d'informer les autres confessions religieuses: les musulmans, les juifs, les confessions chrétiennes protestantes, pentecôtistes, de réveil et les confessions libres. Il s'en suivit une déclaration officielle forte de l'ensemble des confessions religieuses présentes sur le territoire de la RD Congo, qui dénonçait un plan de balkanisation, condamnaient explicitement les pays voisins impliqués, l'inertie du gouvernement central, etc. Il y eut de nouveau un débat dans les médias, sur l'intervention de la religion dans les affaires politiques, les uns condamnant les confessions religieuses, les autres les félicitant.

Après cette déclaration officielle, les chefs des confessions religieuses formèrent un comité pour rédiger une pétition, la faire signer dans toutes leurs institutions, pour qu'elle soit portée jusqu'au niveau de l'ONU et de toutes les grandes puissances impliquées dans l'exploitation des richesses de la RD Congo. En plus de cette pétition, chaque confession religieuse allait organiser des activités complémentaires, selon ses habitudes propres. Pour l'Eglise catholique, une marche de prière avec des affiches «non à la balkanisation du Congo» fut organisée simultanément dans tous les diocèses le 1er août 2012. C'était impressionnant de voir des milliers de gens défiler au même moment à travers tout le pays, la procession précédée par la croix du Christ portée par un enfant, et une incessante prière dans la bouche pour que le projet de balkanisation échoue. Dans certaines provinces, les autres confessions religieuses s'étaient jointes à cette marche solennelle.

Pour l'Eglise catholique, ce fut aussi la visite officielle, du 14 au 21 septembre 2012, d'une délégation des évêques dans le territoire occupé par le M23: bravant toutes les difficultés (y compris le fait qu'on avait refusé de leur donner une escorte pour leur sécurité), ils sont entrés dans le territoire, ont été dans une paroisse catholique, ont célébré l'eucharistie et mangé avec les fidèles, tout cela sous les armes de M23. Cette bravoure vint comme clore le débat: pour une fois, tous les journaux qui insultaient autrefois les confessions religieuses qui osent se mêler de la politique ont dit que, contrairement aux politiciens qui ne pensent qu'à leurs intérêts égoïstes, les confessions religieuses, elles, pensent aux pauvres. Un journal a même averti le public: «que les politiciens sachent que, chaque fois qu'ils négligeront ou bafoueront la justice dûe aux pauvres, ils auront les confessions religieuses sur leur chemin».

Et à la même période, la délégation des représentants des confessions religieuses était déjà en Occident pour remettre la pétition et faire un plaidoyer international pour que la situation change en RD Congo. En faisaient partie: des représentants de la Fédération des églises protestantes au Congo, des orthodoxes, des kimbanguistes, des églises indépendantes, de la communauté islamique, des méthodistes, de l'armée du salut; de la communauté anglicane, du réveil ainsi que quelques femmes membres de la société civile et quelques journalistes. Accompagnée de la pétition signée le 1er août 2012 sur l'ensemble du territoire congolais, dans les villages les plus reculés et les villes, cette délégation a fait le tour des capitales des pays (par exemple Etats-Unis, Canada, France) dont les multinationales et les gouvernements sont impliqués dans l'alimentation de l'insécurité qui traîne dans le pays depuis plusieurs années, et qui a atteint un sommet insupportable dans l'existence du M23. Ils ont sensibilisé les institutions religieuses, ainsi que les chrétiens et musulmans membres des parlements et sénats de ces pays, pour qu'ils fassent pression sur leurs gouvernements et sur les instances internationales. Ils ont déposé la pétition à l'ONU en septembre 2012.

Cela a porté au moins un fruit: après ce plaidoyer, la «communauté internationale» a déclaré publiquement son engagement à ne pas laisser bouger les frontières du Congo, alors qu'un certain nombre de pays occidentaux vendent des armes aux milices engagées dans cette balkanisation et les soutiennent, afin de profiter de l'exploitation illégale des richesses.

Mais le combat n'est pas fini: d'autres actions de plaidoyer sont en cours. Voici comment le secrétariat général de la Conférence épiscopale nationale du Congo (CENCO) a expliqué cette action sur son site officiel (www.cenco.cd):

> *Solidement implantée à travers tout le pays, l'Eglise catholique est un témoin privilégié de l'histoire mouvementée de la RD Congo. Pour elle, il existe une corrélation entre la présence de groupes armés et l'exploitation illégale des ressources naturelles dans le Kivu et que la finalité de cette insécurité récurrente est sans nul doute l'instauration d'un climat propice au morcellement, à l'émiettement, à la balkanisation de notre pays. En vue d'arrêter la guerre et toutes les souffrances qu'elle engendre (destruction des infrastructures sociales, déplacement forcé des populations, désintégration sociale), en vue de contrer les tentatives de balkanisation de ce pays, don de Dieu, hérité de nos aïeux, l'Eglise-famille de Dieu entend mener des actions de lobbying pour sensibiliser les opi-*

nions publiques et les décideurs au niveau national et international. [...]
La CENCO croit, prie et espère que ces actions sont le prélude d'une
grande prise de conscience que le Congo est notre patrimoine à tous et
que nous devons le sauvegarder. Nous savons que les défis que nous de-
vons relever pour un Congo uni et pacifié sont réels, ils sont graves, ils
sont nombreux. Ils ne seront pas faciles à relever. Mais, nous sommes
convaincus que, mûs par «l'espérance qui ne déçoit point» (Rm 5,5)
nous les relèverons. C'est donc le moment de la prise de conscience que
nous devons choisir de faire triompher l'espoir sur la peur, l'unité de
notre destin sur les conflits, le moment de choisir de défendre l'intégrité
de notre territoire. Les actions que proposent l'Eglise s'inscrivent dans
ce choix à opérer pour un Congo uni et prospère.

Conclusion

Défendre les droits humains, spécialement des pauvres et des exploités,
fait partie de la mission de l'Eglise. Pour la RD Congo, on est habitué, depuis l'époque coloniale déjà, aux dénonciations publiques, ce qui ne fait
pas plaisir aux politiciens. Cela a déjà produit plusieurs martyrs ces dix
dernières années, notamment deux évêques: Mgr Munzinrhwa et Mgr Ka-
taliko (évêques de Bukavu), tous deux assassinés pour avoir dit tout haut,
à leur époque, que les conflits armés à l'intérieur du Congo ont une cause
extérieure et alimentent le pillage clandestin et organisé des richesses naturelles du pays. D'où le débat public sur la place de la religion dans un
pays à démocratie tâtonnante, comme nous l'avons vu.

C'est pour défendre les droits de ce même peuple à bénéficier paisi-
blement des richesses de son sous-sol qu'une nouvelle stratégie va être
inventée: des manifestations publiques et le plaidoyer. Ces manifestations
publiques consistent en des marches accompagnées de prières, ce qui permet de différencier l'approche chrétienne et celle des ONG. Le plaidoyer
nécessite des données objectives et une expertise, et c'est pour cela que la
commission ad hoc des ressources naturelles de la RD Congo a été recréée.

C'est à dire que pour avoir un impact dans la société d'aujourd'hui,
avec toute sa complexité, les vieilles stratégies ont besoin d'être enrichies,
et pour le cas de la RD Congo ici, le plaidoyer est devenu incontournable,

vue les ramifications internationales des causes de l'insécurité et des guerres interminables dans le pays.

Notons que ce n'est pas la première fois qu'une action de plaidoyer est utilisée par les institutions ecclésiales comme contribution à un débat social. Il a déjà été utilisé dans les années 1888 par le cardinal Lavigérie, pour lutter contre l'esclavage. En effet, comme beaucoup d'humanistes de son époque, le Cardinal Lavigerie avait personnellement un sens très aigu de la dignité humaine. En France, l'esclavage était aboli par une loi de 1848, mais celle-ci s'appliquait difficilement dans les colonies africaines. Archevêque d'Alger depuis 1867 et fondateur des Missionnaires d'Afrique, il fut profondément indigné devant l'ampleur de la persistance de l'esclavage dans les colonies africaines et fut convaincu que seul le fait de donner une alerte à l'opinion publique européenne pouvait faire bouger les choses en profondeur. En plus d'une mobilisation des chrétiens pour la prière en faveur de l'abolition de l'esclavage, il s'engagea, 1888–1889, d'une manière intense en faisant un véritable plaidoyer pour l'abolition effective de l'esclavage sur le continent africain, en menant une campagne personnelle contre l'esclavage dans toutes les capitales européennes, y révélant les expériences déchirantes de l'esclavage en Afrique occidentale et dont ses missionnaires étaient témoins. Il utilisa les opportunités politiques, diplomatiques, sociales et médiatiques que sa position de cardinal lui offrirent. Il rencontra des personnages influents, fit des discours publics, des sermons dans les chaires d'églises renommées, donna des interviews, écrivit des articles, etc. Bref, un véritable lobbying, comme on dit aujourd'hui. Ce fut sa méthodologie missionnaire pour libérer les captifs des structures de péché de son époque. Et son plaidoyer porta progressivement du fruit.

Prière et plaidoyer: est-ce là des nouvelles stratégies missionnaires? Le débat vaut la peine.

Josée Ngalula est religieuse de saint André, de nationalité congolaise. Docteur en théologie de l'Université Catholique de Lyon, elle est professeure à Kinshasa. Elle enseigne la théologie dogmatique à l'Institut saint Eugène de Mazenod – Institut Africain des Sciences de la Mission – et aux Facultés Catholiques de Kinshasa. Elle est auteure de: *La mission chrétienne à la rencontre des langues humaines*, Kinshasa, Médiaspaul, 2003; *Ces femmes qui peuplent la Bible. Anthologie de références et thématiques sur les 250 femmes de la Bible*. Kinshasa, Mont Sinaï, 2005; *Du pouvoir de la piété populaire. Enjeux théologiques de la crise kimbanguiste entre 1990 et 2005*, Kinshasa, FCK, 2007.

ngalulajosee@yahoo.fr

Church – State Relationship in Colonial Sri Lanka[1]

Jeyaraj Rasiah

Zusammenfassung

Der Artikel erscheint begrenzt in seinem Bereich und scheint nur von geschichtlichem Wert zu sein. Indem er die wechselvolle Geschichte vom kolonisierten Sri Lanka nachzeichnet, legt er die verschiedenen Weisen der Beziehungen zwischen der Kirche/der Religion und dem Staat oder zwischen den kolonialen Herren und lokalen Herrschern dar. Der Artikel stellt auch die wichtige Frage, weshalb die lokalen Herrscher oder die ausländischen Herren der Religion gegenüber entweder feindlich oder beschützend gegenüberstanden und wie diese verschiedenen Weisen der Beziehungen, sei es feindlich oder freundlich, Religion beeinflusst haben. Die Analyse zeigt, dass Religion in den meisten Fällen für selbstsüchtige oder politische Ziele gebraucht wurde. Der Artikel kommt zum Schluss, dass Religion, wenn sie sich selbst bleibt, wie jeder lebende Organismus eine innere Dynamik zum Überleben und Sichverbreiten hat.

Introduction

For a general reader, the title of this article may seem rather limited and may even seem to have only a historical value as something of the past. However, this small Island nation with its recorded history of about 2,000–2,500 years seems to be an epitome of monarchical, colonial and self rule with varying degrees of Church-State relationship that is friendly or hostile. In general it is pointed out that in the friendly type of Church-State relationship the interference of one in matters of the other are mutually limited while in the hostile type, religion is confined to one's personal life and public display of beliefs are restricted.

---

[1] The historical data in this article is directly taken from my own contributing in Peter C. Phan, ed., *Christianities in Asia*, West Sussex: Blackwell Publishing Ltd., 2011, Chapter 3: Sri Lanka, 45–59.

Before the arrival of the Portuguese in then called Ceylon in 1505 and along with them the present day Christianity, the country was divided into three Kingdoms. Of these, two were Buddhist and the one in the North of the Island was Hindu. While there are evidences of the presence of Christians in the 6th and 7th C., the present day Christianity traces its origins to the arrival of the Portuguese in 1505, who ruled some parts of the Island till 1658.

The colonial history of Sri Lanka, over four centuries dominated by three different western powers had been described variously: Negatively as "a Portuguese period of colonial aggression, a Dutch period of indifference and harassment, and a British period of moderate imperialism; and more benignly as 110 years of Portuguese imperial patronage and Catholic evangelization, 150 years of Dutch Protestant neglect and commercial exploitation and 150 years of British religious toleration, Western education, and benign but self-interested economic improvement"[2]. It is this variegated Church-State relationship that we propose to trace below.

During the Portuguese Period
The first Portuguese Franciscan missionaries arrived in Colombo in 1546 as a delayed response to the request of the King of Kotte by the name King Buwanekabahu VII in the South in 1543. After the death of the King, as guaranteed by the Portuguese, his grandson succeeded him in 1551[3] who was later converted to Christianity. Understandably, in a traditional monarchical system where the subjects generally embraced the religion of the King, as a Tamil proverb says: "the subjects go the way of the King," when the King was converted to Christianity, along with the King, his household, his courtiers and many common people, altogether around three thousands, embraced Christianity. The same King, popularly known as Dharmapala, with the Christian name Dom Joao Periya Pandara bequeathed his kingdom to the King of Portugal in 1580. In 1597 with the death of the King, the Kingdom of Kotte ended and officially passed on to

---

[2] Samuel Hugh Moffett, *A History of Christianity in Asia Vol. II: 1500 to 1900;* American Society of Missiology Series, No. 36, New York, Maryknoll, Orbis Books, 1998, 336.
[3] Cf. *Ibid.* 39.

the King of Portugal. After bequeathing the Kingdom, the King also granted to the Franciscan missionaries properties of some of the Buddhist temples. This act of the King can either be seen as antagonistic towards his former religion and favouritism towards the new religion which he had embraced or repaying to the Portuguese for the protection and favours he has received from them. As for the Portuguese, even though by then they were aggressively pursuing a policy of gaining control of other divided kingdoms in the South of the Island and more interested in their trade of the spices, the missionary activities were assisted by them and the period may well be called a period of Portuguese imperial patronage and Catholic evangelization.

While the South was caught up in power struggle between the local Kings and the Portuguese for control, in the North, in the Island of Mannar which was part of the Hindu Kingdom of Jaffna, hundreds were converted to Christianity by a secular priest sent by St. Francis Xavier from India. The enraged King of Jaffna sent a company of soldiers, to deal with these converts, who put to death at least 600 of the newly converted, the first martyrs in the Island. A Portuguese expedition sent by the Governor of Goa in 1560 to avenge the slaughtering of Christians was beaten back by the King of Jaffna and the retreating Portuguese took control of the Island of Mannar and fortified it for a possible future invasion of Jaffna. The Jesuits who had gone with the army remained in Mannar and began organizing a Christian community there. Yet another Portuguese invasion of the kingdom of Jaffna in 1591 gave them foothold there and in 1618 Jaffna became a Portuguese possession. Now the Franciscans too entered the kingdom for missionary work. Thus, much under the Portuguese influence, if not control, gave ample scope for evangelization. The Jesuits were invited from India to Colombo in 1602 to open a college, and they were followed by the Dominicans in 1605 and the Augustinians in 1606. All these religious along with the secular clergy laboured hard with state patronage and some of the villages formally attached to Buddhist temples were given to these religious for their up keep. These evangelizing activities brought abundant harvest that by the end of the Portuguese period in 1658 it was estimated that there were about 100,000 to 150,000 Catholics in the Island served by about 100 missionaries. Once again it can be seen that the Portuguese who came into the Island for trade not only taking progressive control of the Island both in the South and in the North but also under their influence and patronage, Catholic evangelization was expanded and the Church was gradually established.

During the Dutch Period

The Dutch who arrived in the Island allied themselves with the King of Kandy, the only independent kingdom under the Portuguese, to drive away the former masters and to wrestle control of administration. They issued decrees after decrees calling for the allegiance of the Catholics. When these failed to win the alliance of the Catholics, the Dutch began rounding up priest and shipping them to India, forbade, under pain of death, concealment of priests, prohibited public or private assemblies of Catholics and the priest were forbidden to baptize. According to Catholic mission reports there were four periods of persecution between the years 1689 to 1729: the first in Jaffna, the second in Colombo and Negombo, the third in Jaffna and Mannar and the last in Colombo[4]. This is clear hostile interference, in religious matters, though not by the state but by the foreign masters who had other stakes in the Island.

However, these measures, rather than suppressing the Catholics helped them to grow in different ways. Further, the King of Kandy who latter fell out with the Dutch invited the Catholics to his kingdom and thus Catholicism survived the onslaught of the Dutch at least in some parts of the Island. Some Catholics, both Sinhalese and Tamils, who lived within Dutch territories of the Island, continued to be so while outwardly conforming to the Dutch regulations. Some others reverted back to Buddhism or became Calvinists or Baptist, at least externally. Thus other Christian Churches than the Catholic Church too entered the Island with the Dutch patronage.

The first Reformed Presbyterian landed in the Island in 1643 and between 1658 and 1661, they organized and established several Reformed

---

[4] Cited in *A History of Christianity in Asia Vol. II*, 224.

Christian communities in Jaffna. They did not build churches as they took away the Catholic churches and transformed them for worship on Sabbath and for schools during the week. The Franciscan church of St. Francis in Colombo became the official church of the Dutch[5]. Thus again here we see antagonism and favouritism not against another religion and towards one's own respectively but within the one Church of Christ itself but within churches.

During the same period a young Catholic priest from Goa, India, by the name Joseph Vaz, belonging to the Oratory of St. Philip Neri, disguised as a beggar, entered the Island in 1687 and made his way to Jaffna. After having worked there for sometime, haunted by the Dutch, he travelled to the kingdom of Kandy. After initial set backs, he was allowed full freedom to carry out his zealous ministry from there to other parts of the Island, even inviting members of the Oratory in Goa. Here it can be seen that even in one single person's missionary activity, the state players played different rolls. While Blessed Joseph Vaz was haunted by the Dutch, eventually he was given full freedom by the then King of Kandy to continue his missionary activities, including even inviting other missionaries from India.

Notwithstanding the harassment of the Dutch, Catholicism kept spreading far and wide in the Island due to the hard work of the Oratorians, based in the kingdom of Kandy. However, the freedom enjoyed by the Catholics in the kingdom of Kandy came to an end with the end of the Sinhala dynasty in 1739 when a Nayakkar, from South India, the brother of the then queen, took over the reigns of the kingdom of Kandy and banished the Oratorians from there due to the influence of the Dutch and the Buddhist revivalists. The Oratorians found refuge with a petty ruler in the Vanny region and continued their evangelizing mission. The banished Oratorians along with the Sinhala Catholics offered help to the Dutch in their failed attempt to invade the kingdom of Kandy. This brought greater freedom to the Catholics under the Dutch and the first baptismal registries of the Island date back to this period in 1763. These changed conditions also brought about changed attitude and life style of the Oratorians.

[5] Cf. *A History of Christianity in Asia Vol. II*, 226.

Though they continued to be venerated by the people, there were also accusations of many kinds levelled against them.

It would seem clear from these episodes that Christianity could not have taken roots in Sri Lanka, for that matter in many countries of Asia, without the patronage of the local rules or of the foreign masters. That seems clear enough. That is not all. What seems more important is to ask the question why were the local rulers or the foreign masters patronizing religion and to attempt an answer. Further what effect did this patronizing have on the religion?

To begin to answer the first question, in the case of the King of Kotte who bequeathed the Kingdom to the King of Portugal, and granted to the missionaries properties of some of the Buddhist temples, he would have felt obliged to the King of Portugal for making him King and further he was troubled by various attacks on his kingdom and he needed protection which was readily granted. Hence it would seem that his bequeathing the Kingdom and his support to the missionaries are simply favours returned. Yet, it is to be noted that without these, neither the Portuguese would have remained in the country nor Christianity would have set foot as it did. On the part of the Portuguese who came to the Island for trade and gradually got entangled with local power struggle, their patronage to Christianity was one of control of those who embraced the faith for the sake of the trade which was their main concern.

As to the King of Kandy who aligned himself with the Dutch at the beginning and called for alliance of the Catholics and later falling out with the Dutch and gave protection to the Catholics in the midst of persecution, the kingdom of Kandy having been the only independent kingdom when the Dutch arrived, it was a matter of self interest for the King to have a foreign power with him to protect himself against another foreign power. Yet again when he fell out with the Dutch, it was on his self interest to have the Catholic population with him that he invited them and allowed them freedom to practice their religion. Yet again the Catholics who lived in the Dutch territories offered help to the Dutch in their failed attempt to invade the kingdom of Kandy and the Dutch allowed them greater freedom. It was in their best interest to have the locals with them to harass the local King of Kandy. It could be argued from this that it was not the love of the religion that prompted the local rulers or the foreign masters to patronize Catholicism but their own self interests and repaying for favours received. Hence it may be safely concluded that, at least in these circumstances, during the colonial Sri Lanka, local or foreign patronage of religion was only a tool for political ends and self interests. Looking around the world, we are well aware that colonial Sri Lanka is not the only example.

Now to turn to the second question as to what effect did the patronizing of religion has on the religion? The Oratorians were by and large very successful in their evangelizing mission in the Island under varying circumstances, mostly hostile conditions. However, under the patronage of the Dutch for their own self interests, there had been various accusations of different kinds levelled against Oratorians. From this it could be argued that Catholicism survived and flourished under hostile conditions or even severe persecutions imposed on the people by the rulers and dwindled or lost its vitality when sponsored or patronized by authorities.

During the British Period

The English East India Company became the masters of the Maritime Provinces of Sri Lanka in 1796 replacing the Dutch East India Company. In 1802, due to various accusations against the Company, the British Government took over the Island from the Company and made it a Crown Colony with a Governor representing the British Sovereign. Finally in 1815 the English conquered the kingdom of Kandy, the last independent kingdom to have survived the Portuguese and the Dutch, and became the sole masters of the whole Island.

With the advent of the British, though Anglicanism was the state religion, the Catholics began to breathe freely; all restrictions previously imposed by the Dutch being removed in 1806. This religious freedom was further enlarged eight years later. Even in 1807 the government still recognized the Presbyterians of the Dutch Reformed Church as the "ecclesiastical establishment of the colony". As for the Buddhist the 1815 treaty which ended the independence of the Buddhist kingdom of Kandy guaranteed support to its national religion which was "declared inviolate and is to be maintained and protected." In 1853 the authorities dissociated themselves from governmental administration of Buddhist affairs. This paved the way for the Christian missionaries to move about with no hindrance administering to the faithful even though some have fallen back to Buddhism or Hinduism. Other missionary bodies such as the Baptists (1812), Wesleyan Methodists (1814), American Board of Commissioners for Foreign Missions (1816) and Church Missionary Society (1818) too arrived to carry out the evangelizing mission by setting up schools, hospitals, printing establishments and churches. This trend continued and other missions such as the Salvation Army (1883), the Seventh-day Adventists (1904), and Assembly of God (1923) too arrived to carry out their missions. The arrival of these missionary societies was not an unmixed blessing. While they set up several institutions to serve the people in their various needs, there had been bickering and squabbles within the Christian fold. This is partly due also to the privileged position enjoyed by the Anglican Church. There had been several attempts at different times aimed at unity and smooth functioning with varying success.

It may also be noted here in passing that the second half of the 19th century saw a Buddhist revival orchestrated by some monks educated in Christian schools who challenged the missionaries to debate and defeated them. About the same time, the arrival of members of the Theosophical Society from Europe and America who went around fostering Buddhism and beginning Buddhist schools favoured the Buddhist revival which has already begun by the locals.

As for the Catholic Church, Rome created Sri Lanka as an Apostolic Vicariate in 1836 with an Oratorian as the first apostolic vicar who was succeeded by other Oratorians. Later Colombo in the South and Jaffna in the North were established into two vicariates. With missionary activities unhindered by the state, religious congregations established schools for boys and girls and the Catholic hierarchy was established in Sri Lanka in January 1887, with Colombo as archdiocese and the dioceses of Jaffna and Kandy as *suffragans*.

After the establishment of the hierarchy a permanent Apostolic Delegate too was appointed for India and Sri Lanka, in the person of Msgr.

Agliardi, who was succeeded by A. Aiuti, who was followed by L. Zaleski who latter founded the papal seminary in Kandy for the training of local clergy, which continues to serve the Church till today. The 20th century saw many changes in the Island, the chief of which being the political independence in 1948 which gave greater impetus to the Church to become fully indigenous with presently 12 dioceses entrusted to the diocesan clergy helped by 18 clerical congregations, 4 non-clerical congregations, 28 apostolic women's congregations and 7 contemplative women congregations majority of whom are indigenous.

It seems evident from the above that when any religion is left without interference or hindrance, it has its inner dynamism like any organism to grow and propagate itself. On the contrary, we have also seen above that influence of the State either hostile or friendly in matters of religion affects religion in different ways. From the forgoing analysis, it would seem that during hostile influence, the Church in Sri Lanka somehow managed to keep alive and even grew to some extent. While on the other hand during periods of patronage, acquiring wealth and other material benefits, the Church becomes entangled in local politics and power struggle and loses its vitality to be a spiritual force.

However, it is to be noted here that a complete separation is not argued for. The Catholic social teaching in *Dignitatis Humanae* of the Second Vatican Council on Declaration on Religious Freedom asserts that all people are entitled to religious freedom and that such freedom should be recognized in the constitution. According to the Church's understanding, the Church-State separation is permissible. However, the Church does not accept a complete separation of religion and politics[6] since the Church holds that religion should guide and inform the conscience of the people thereby serving humanity. Further the Church also asserts that if for historical reasons, special civil recognition is accorded in the constitution of a country to one particular religion; it is necessary that at the same time the right of all citizens and religious communities to religious freedom should be

---

6 Zachary A. Calo, *Catholic Social Thought, Political Liberalism, and the Idea of Human Rights*, Birmingham, Samford University, 2004, 18–20.

acknowledged and maintained.[7] The Catholic Church's teachings on political matters are not meant only for the Catholics in a country but for all women and men of good will.

Since Independence

Since Independence in 1948, things have changed radically for over half a century. After three successive foreign dominations, when with the Independence the Sinhala Buddhist majority, through democratic elections, took the reigns of the Island, they brought with them the contention, not without foundation, that those who embraced the new religion were unduly favoured by the colonial powers. The Oxford-educated Anglican S. W. R. D. Bandaranaike became Prime Minister in 1956 on a wave of Sinhala Buddhist nationalism after converting from Christianity to Buddhism and promising to make Sinhala the only official language within twenty-four hours. The English educated from all communities were in positions of power and prestige where the Sinhala Buddhist majority educated in vernacular felt marginalized. Further, the popular sentiment was that while those who embraced the new religion owed their allegiance to a foreign power, the patronage offered to Buddhism was, slowly but steadily, withdrawn. Hence to redress this imbalance certain measures were introduced: In 1956 Christian nuns were prohibited from working in government hospitals, Christian Schools were nationalized in 1961, the constitutions of 1972 and 1978 accorded a privileged position to Buddhism and since 1966 up to the present certain unsuccessful attempts are being made to prevent conversion to another religion with the accusation that unethical means are being used to lure people from one religion to another. Recent years have witnessed a sharp rise in violence such as burning of Christian churches as reaction to perceived threat of conversion by certain Christian churches. These measures went hand in hand with a process of internal revival within the Buddhist community, by which they "became better organized, self-confident, and intellectually sophisticated." This

---

[7] John Courtney Murray and J. Leon Hooper, *Religious liberty: Catholic struggles with pluralism,* Westminster John Knox Press, 1993, 213–214.

paved the way for a certain type of "Buddhist nationalism"[8] and turned out to be a reactionary movement against all forces perceived as being opposed to Buddhism which included "missionaries" and the colonially favoured Christians of the past era of foreign domination creating insecurity in the minds of the minorities.

Whither Sri Lanka?

In a 2008 Gallup poll, Sri Lanka was ranked 3rd most religious country in the world with 99% of Sri Lankans saying religion is an important part of their daily life.[9] It would seem so going by the public display of different beliefs in the country. Sri Lankan society is multi-cultural and multi-religious as the statistics show. As of 2001 census, of the 18 million population 76.7% of Sri Lankans are *Theravada Buddhists*, 7.8% are *Hindus*, 8.5% are *Muslims* and 6.1% Roman Catholics and others are 9%. By ethnicity, Sinhalese are 82.0%, S.L. Tamils are 4.3%, Indian Tamils are 5.1%, SL Moors are 7.9% and others 7%.[10] It is to be noted here that some of the districts of the north where the majority Tamils are Hindus were not surveyed. However, it serves us to point out the multi-ethnic, multi-cultural and multi-religious character of Sri Lankan society. However, the Sinhala Buddhist identity which some nationalist groups and the all monks' party in the parliament want to foster argues against the very fabric of the Sri Lankan society.

While the majority Sinhalese are Buddhists and similarly majority Tamils are Hindus, Christians are from both ethnic communities. As seen, Sri Lanka can boast of having the four major religions of the world. Yet this variegated richness of the Island is being threatened at present. It cannot be denied that due to historical developments, Buddhism and Sinhala

---

[8] *Buddhist Nationalism and Sri Lanka's Christian Minority*. The Institute for Global Engagement, 2004: Available from *http://www.globalengage.org/issues/2004/12/srilanka-2.htm;* Accessed on 2 April 2006.

[9] *http://en.wikipedia.org/wiki/Religion_in_Sri_Lanka#cite_note-2011census-1.* Retrieved 18/2/2013.

[10] Cf. *http://www.statistics.gov.lk/PopHouSat/PDF/p7%20population%20and%20Housing%20 Text-11-12-06.pdf.* Retrieved 18/2/2013.

identity are fused together to a great extent. However, they should not be and cannot be identified as one. Christianity, though a latecomer to the Island, compared to Buddhism, Hinduism and Islam has existed for the past five centuries. Accepting and respecting such a plurality, will it be possible to construct a national identity comprising all Sri Lankans, irrespective of ethnic and religious affiliations, is a million dollar question. The history of the Island in general, and more so of the past half a century along with the signs of the times at present, seem to suggest the negative. Can the Church succeed in her mission of being a bridge builder and bring about peace and reconciliation? In order to do so the Church needs to go through a change of heart, shedding her own superiority and becoming a servant Church. She needs to acknowledge her own past sins and find new ways of being the leaven in a land blessed with four major religions of the world.

Fr. Jeyaraj Rasiah, S.J. is the Provincial Superior of the Society of Jesus in Sri Lanka. Prior to this appointment he served as the Director of East Asian Pastoral Institute (EAPI), Philippines for six years. He lectured on subjects of Philosophy and Theology at the Ateneo de Manila University, Loyola School of Theology and at the East Asian Pastoral Institute. He has a Masters degree in Philosophy from Jnana – Deepa Vidyapeeth, Pune, India and a Licentiate in Dogmatic Theology from Pontificia Universita Gregoriana, Rome, Italy. He obtained his Ph.D. in Philosophy from the University of Peradeniya, Sri Lanka. His researches include Bhakti literature and quest for Transcendence in the Indian religious traditions. He has been involved in the formation of religious in Sri Lanka conducting workshops, seminars and retreats.
For many years except during his stay in the Philippines he has been teaching at the National Seminary of Our Lady of Lanka, Ampitiya, Sri Lanka, both in the department of Philosophy and Theology as a Visiting Professor.

SEVSEVANA, Jesuit Provincialate Xavier Residence, Akkara Panaha, Negombo, SRI LANKA; provincialsj@sltnet.lk

Evangelium und Öffentlichkeit

Georg Schelbert

Summary

The Gospel is not an esoteric doctrine. It is basically meant for the public. This destination is emphasized by sayings of Jesus handed down in the different layers of the Synoptic Gospels (Q, Mk, Mt). The author comments them briefly. The public, the crowds and the leadership are the addressees, even the peoples, actually the whole of humanity. This aim is true also for the witness about Jesus that is presented in the Gospel of John. Secrecy or public appearance is explicitly the topic of chapter seven in the discussions with the brothers of Jesus. The alternative is according to the interpretation of the Gospel-writer the contrast between the high-handed hunt for honour among people and being honoured by people contrasting the will and direction of the Father. The honour of God may solely be the intention and aim of public doing deeds of justice, not personal honour, not human recognition. In religious disputations the question is only God's honour and not one's own profile.

In den Evangelien gehören die beiden Wirklichkeiten «Öffentlichkeit» und «Verborgenheit» von Jesus von Nazareth zu den Schlüsselstellen seines Auftretens.

Im Folgenden geht es um eine Erhebung dieser beiden Themen in der Lebenspraxis Jesu selbst und seinen damit verbundenen Anweisungen an jene, die ihm folgen, wie es die Synoptiker und das Johannesevangelium darstellen.

1. Öffentlichkeit bzw. Verborgenheit in den synoptischen Evangelien

Zwar wird Jesus in den Evangelien nicht als Herold/kêryx bezeichnet. Doch das Hauptverbum für sein Wirken ist im Evangelium nach Markus und Matthäus «kêryssein (als Herold) verkünden» (Mk 1,14.38.39; Mt 4,17.23; 9,35). Jesus wird als Herold der Frohbotschaft Gottes vorgestellt: «Nachdem Johannes überliefert worden war, ging Jesus nach Galiäa das Evangelium Gottes verkündend.»

Dieses Evangelium Gottes ist ein kurzer Heroldsruf. Er lautet:
«Erfüllt ist die Zeit;
und nahegekommen ist die Königsherrschaft Gottes.
Denkt um und glaubt an das Evangelium!»[1]

Zwei synonym parallele Indikative bilden die Botschaft und zwei synonym parallele Imperative – «und» ist kai epexegeticum – die Anweisung zu entsprechender Antwort und entsprechendem Verhalten («Denkt um, d.h. glaubt an das Evangelium!»).

Adressaten sind Menschen in Galiläa, Menschen in den Synagogen der Dörfer Galiäas (Mk 1,38 f.). Auf Grund der ihnen bekannten tradierten Verheissungen der Propheten sind ihnen Botschaft und Aufruf verständlich. Ein solches Verheissungswort ist Jes 52,7. Es enthält die Ankündigung kommender Herrschaft Gottes: «Wie schön sind die Füsse des Frohbotschafters: … Sion, dein Gott ist König geworden.» Der Septuaginta-Text verheisst: «Gott wird als König herrschen/basileusei». Jesu Heroldsruf verkündet den Anbruch der Königsherrschaft Gottes. Neben kêryssein hat Lukas ebenfalls aus jesaianischen Verheissungstexten als besonderes Wort für Jesu Verkündigung «euangelizesthai/frohbotschaften» gewählt (Lk 4,18/ Jes 61,1; Lk 4,43; 7,22). Das Zeitwort deutet schon den positiven Inhalt der Botschaft an. Während sonst im Griechischen das Substantiv «Evangelium» fast nur im Plural «Evangelia» vorkommt, so steht «Euangelion/Frohbotschaft» im Neuen Testament trotz der Vielzahl der schriftlichen Evangelien nur im Singular. Es ist das eine Evangelium Gottes, das Jesus verkündet und die Apostel und Missionare in seinem Auftrag (Mt 10,7).

Die Matthäus und Lukas gemeinsame Überlieferung (Q)
Adressat des Evangeliums ist die Öffentlichkeit Galiäas und Judäas. Es darf nicht und es wird nicht im Verborgenen bleiben. Eine Matthäus und Lukas gemeinsame Deutung eines geläufigen Sprichwortes durch Jesus auf Grund seiner Erfahrung, dass alles Verborgene an die Öffentlichkeit drängt, bringt dies zum Ausdruck:

---

[1] Alle Übersetzungen der Abschnitte aus der Bibel stammen vom Autor. Zu den einzelnen Bibelstellen siehe die verschiedenen Kommentare zu den Evangelien.

Mt 10,26	Lk 12,2
Sprichwort:	
«Fürchtet euch also nicht!	
Nichts ist verhüllt,	*«Nichts ist ganz verhüllt,*
was nicht enthüllt werden wird,	*was nicht enthüllt werden wird,*
und verborgen,	*und verborgen,*
was nicht erkannt werden wird.»	*was nicht erkannt werden wird.»*

Deutung:	
«Was ich euch im Dunkeln sage,	*«Darum, was immer ihr im Dunkel*
sagt im Licht;	*sagtet, wird im Licht gehört werden;*
und was ihr ins Ohr (geflüstert) hört,	*und was ihr ins Ohr geredet habt*
verkündet auf den Dächern.»	*in den Kammern, wird verkündet*
	werden auf den Dächern.»

Es ist eine Erfahrungstatsache: Verborgenes und Geheimes kann auf die Dauer nicht geheim bleiben. Früher oder später wird es bekannt und publik. Jesus bezieht diese Erfahrung in der matthäischen Fassung auf sein Wort. Sein Wort darf nicht geheim bleiben. Es muss öffentlich verkündet und bekannt gemacht werden. In diesem überraschenden Verständnis konnte das Sprichwort als Auftrag an die Jünger zu unerschrockener Verkündigung als Element der Aussendungsrede (Mt 10) Verwendung finden.

Die lukanische Form des Wortes kann einerseits als Warnung verstanden werden: Auch was die Jünger im Dunkel sagen, wird dem Sprichwort gemäss ans Licht kommen. Selbst das nur ins Ohr Geflüsterte und in verborgenen Räumen Geredete wird publik werden. So verstand es Lukas als Warnung vor dem ansteckenden Sauerteig der Heuchelei der Pharisäer (nur hier bei Lukas). Sie wird in Lk 11,37 ff. angeprangert. Sie besteht vor allem darin, dass Fassade und Wirklichkeit, Wort und Leben nicht übereinstimmen, sondern auseinanderklaffen. Dieser Gegensatz kann nicht lange verborgen bleiben.

Andererseits kann das Wort im Blick auf den Widerstand gegen die Missionare, ja auf ihre Beseitigung, als Trost oder Ermutigung verstanden werden. Es folgt wie bei Matthäus (10,26) die Warnung vor Furcht des Falschen: «Ich zeige euch, wen ihr fürchten sollt» (Lk 12,4 f.). Der Bote kann getötet werden. Nicht aber die Botschaft. Die Passivformen der Verben sind theologische Passiva: Gott wird dafür sorgen, dass sie bekannt und offenbar wird.

Markus und Lukas
Das Sprichwort verwenden Markus und Lukas im Anschluss an die Erklärung des Gleichnisses vom Sämann.

Mk 4,21 f.	Lk 8,16 f.
«Und er sagte ihnen:	*«Keiner aber,*
Kommt etwa die Leuchte,	*der eine Lampe angezündet hat,*
damit sie unter den Scheffel gestellt	*verbirgt sie mit einem Gefäss*
wird oder unter das Bett?	*oder stellt sie unter ein Bett,*
Nicht, dass sie auf den Leuchter	*sondern stellt sie auf einen Leuchter,*
gestellt wird.»	*damit die Hereinkommenden*
	das Licht sehen.»

Sprichwort:

«Denn nichts ist Verborgenes,	*«Denn nicht ist Verborgenes,*
wenn nicht, dass es offenbart wird,	*das nicht offenbar werden wird,*
und nichts wurde Verborgenes,	*und nichts Verborgenes,*
ausser damit es ins Offenbare kommt.»	*das nicht erkannt wird*
	und ins Offenbare kommt.»

Das Wort der Verkündigung ist für die Öffentlichkeit bestimmt. Nicht Verhüllung der Geheimnisse des Reiches ist Gottes letzte Absicht, sondern ihr Leuchten, wie der Zweck einer Lampe, einen möglichst weiten Kreis im Raum oder beim Hauseingang zu erleuchten. Es drängt wie jedes Geheimnis in die Öffentlichkeit.

Die Bergpredigt nach Matthäus (5,14 ff.)
　Vers 14
　　　«Ihr seid das Licht der Welt/phôs toû kosmou.
　　　Nicht kann eine Stadt verborgen bleiben,
　　　die auf einem Berg liegt.»

Vers 15

> «*Und nicht zündet man eine Lampe an*
> *und stellt sie unter den Scheffel,*
> *sondern auf einen Leuchter;*
> *und sie leuchtet allen im Haus.*»

Vers 16

> «*So soll euer Licht leuchten vor den Menschen,*
> *damit sie eure guten Werke sehen*
> *und euren Vater im Himmel preisen.*»

Das Wort der Verkündigung muss auch durch das entsprechende Leben bekannt werden. Es soll am Leben der Verkünder erkannt werden. Die guten Werke dürfen freilich nur mit der Absicht getan werden, dass Gott dadurch geehrt wird, in keiner Weise zur eigenen Ehre, wie den Pharisäern als Heuchelei vorgeworfen wird (Mt 23,5). Vgl. Mt 6,1–18: «Achtet aber darauf, eure Gerechtigkeit nicht vor den Menschen zu tun, um von ihnen gesehen zu werden, sonst habt ihr keinen Lohn bei eurem Vater im Himmel» (Mt 6,1).

Volk, Volksmenge als Publikum

In der Schilderung der Verkündigung Jesu werden immer wieder das Volk/ochlos bzw. die Volksscharen/ochloi als Adressaten, als Hörer seiner Worte und Zeugen seiner Taten genannt. Im ersten Teil des Markusevangeliums (1,14–9,50, Galiläa und Umgebung) geschieht es 27 Mal. Fünf Mal beschreibt sie Markus als grosse Menge (ochlos pleistos, polys). Bei den Speisewundern sind es 5000 bzw. 4000 (Männer). Das grosse Summarium vor der Wahl der zwölf Mitarbeiter (Mk 3,7–12) berichtet: «Und Jesus zog sich mit seinen Jüngern zum Meer zurück, und eine zahlreiche Menge von Galiläa begleitete ihn und von Judäa und von Jerusalem und von Idumäa und jenseits des Jordan und um Tyrus und Sidon, und eine zahlreiche Menge, da sie hörten, was er tat, kamen zu ihm.»

Die Erwähnungen finden sich vielfach auch in den Einleitungen zu Einzelerzählungen. Zwar erwähnt Mk 9,30 ff. (Durchreise durch Galiläa, Aufenthalt in Kapharnaum 9,33 f.) keine Volksschar. Doch die Einleitung zu Teil drei (10,3–14,36, Judäa, insbesondere Jerusalem) schildert Jesus wieder inmitten einer mitreisenden Volksmenge/ochloi, die er wie gewohnt lehrte.[2]

Auffällig ist, dass keine der Städte des Ethnarchen Antipas in Galiläa, Sepphoris und Tiberias als Ort der Verkündigung und des Wirkens Jesu erwähnt wird. Information darüber gelangte jedoch auch bis zum Landesherrn und bewog ihn zu versuchen, Jesus zu beseitigen, wie Pharisäer Jesus warnten, so wie er seinerzeit den Täufer eliminiert hatte (Lk 12,31). In Judäa, näherhin in Jerusalem konfrontieren die Synoptiker nach dem Einzug und der Tempelreinigung Jesus sozusagen mit allen tonangebenden Gruppierungen: Hohepriester, Schriftgelehrte, Älteste (Vollmachtsfrage: Mk 11,27 ff.), Pharisäer (Steuerfrage: Mk 12,13 ff.), Saduzäer (Auferstehungsfrage: 12,18 ff.), Schriftgelehrte (Davidsnachfolge: 12,35 ff.).

Der Auferstandene gibt den Jüngern entsprechend seiner nunmehr universalen Vollmacht im Himmel und auf Erden den Auftrag, alle Völker zu Jüngern zu machen (Mt 28,19: alle Völker; Mk 16,15: die ganze Schöpfung; Lk 24,47: alle Völker).

2. Öffentlichkeit bzw. Verborgenheit im Johannesevangelium

Zwar stellt die Überlieferung das Johannesevangelium mit dem Titel euangelion als Erzählung von Jesu Weg und Wirken zur gleichen Gattung wie die Synoptiker. Doch bei ihm finden sich weder Verbum noch Substantiv: euangelizesthai oder euangelion. Sein Wort für Jesu Predigen ist neben «sprechen, reden/lalein» das Wort «Zeugnis geben/martyrein». Der entsprechende Titel seines Evangeliums müsste eigentlich «Zeugnis/martyria» lauten.[3]

Es ist immer und überall Zeugnis für oder von Jesus Christus, von Jesus als dem Christus. Für ihn gibt der Täufer Zeugnis, vgl. das «Buch der Zeugnisse» (Joh 1,19–51). Für ihn gibt der Vater Zeugnis, der Geist (15,26), Jesus selbst durch die Werke, die der Vater ihm gegeben hat

---

[2] Vgl. im Weiteren: 10,46: eine beträchtliche Volksmenge; 11,8: viele; 11,18: die Hohenpriester und Schriftgelehrten, das ganze Volk; 12,12: die Volksmenge.

[3] Vgl. martyrein: Joh 33 Mal, Mt 1 Mal, Mk fehlt, Lk 1 Mal, Apg 11 Mal; martyria: Joh 14 Mal, Mt 3 Mal, Mk 1 Mal, Apg 1 Mal. Vgl. Johannes Beutler, martyria und folgende Grundbegriffe in den Fussnoten, in EWNT II, 97–174, Stuttgart 1980.

(5,36), das Volk, die Jünger. Es ergibt sich eine Art Grobeinteilung des Werkes unter dem Gesichtspunkt des Zeugnisses:

- I. Zeugnis des Täufers, das eine Kettenreaktion von Zeugnissen auslöst (1,19–51).
- II. Zeugnis des Vaters durch die Werke und Zeichen, die er Jesus gab (2,1–12,50).
- III. Zeugnis des Geistes (15,26; Abschiedsreden insgesamt).

Zeugnis haben Zeugen in einem Gericht zu geben,[4] wo sich die Parteien gegenüberstehen, wo es darum geht, wer recht hat. Das sind denn auch der Rahmen und die Situation des Johannesevangeliums. Die Wurzel der ganzen Vorstellung ist ebenfalls Deuterojesaia. Dort findet sich die Vorstellung von einem Prozess. Dort ging es darum, ob der Gott Israels wirklich Gott, Lenker der Geschichte ist oder die Götter Babels: «Ihr sollt mir Zeugen sein und ich bin Zeuge, spricht der Herr, und der Knecht, den ich erwählt habe, damit ihr erkennet, glaubet und verstehet, dass ich bin/oti egô eimi; vor mir ist kein anderer gebildet und nach mir wird kein anderer sein» (Jes 43,10).

Ein Prozess spielt sich vor einem Forum ab. Das Forum des von Johannes dargestellten Prozesses ist der Kosmos, die Welt, die ökumenische Öffentlichkeit.[5] Unter der Decke konkreter Vorgänge, Wege und Orte vollzieht sich dieser kosmische Prozess. Bei diesem Prozess geht es darum: Wer hat recht? Es geht um die Wahrheit/alêtheia.[6] Diese Wahrheit ist nicht einfach Information. Sie ist nicht allein die formale Übereinstimmung der Aussage mit dem Sachverhalt, sondern die Sache selbst, mit der die Aussage, mit der die Botschaft übereinstimmt. Sie ist Wahrheit in Person (Joh 14,6). Sie ist die Wahrheit Gottes selbst, die in Jesus Christus offenbar geworden ist.

Der Prozess vollzieht sich durch den aus dem Bereich Gottes herabgestiegenen und wieder aufsteigenden Gesandten Gottes, Jesus. Er ist der präexistente Zeuge bzw. Offenbarer Gottes des Vaters. Dies zeigt sich auf

---

[4] Zeugnis: Joh 11 Mal, Mt 12 Mal, Mk fehlt, Lk 4 Mal; Apg 1 Mal; richten: Joh 19 Mal; Mt 6 Mal; Mk fehlt, Lk 6 Mal; Apg 21 Mal.
[5] kosmos: Joh 78 Mal, Mt 8 Mal, Mk 3 Mal, Lk 3 Mal, Apg fehlt.
[6] alêtheia: Joh 25 Mal, Mt 1 Mal, Mk 3 Mal, Lk 3 Mal; alêthês: Joh 14 Mal, Mt 1 Mal, Mk 1 Mal, Lk fehlt, Apg 4 Mal.

dem Höhepunkt des Prozesses in der Szene vor Pilatus. Es geht zuletzt um Jesus als den Gottgesandten oder den Kaiser als Exponenten des Kosmos (Joh 19,3.12). «Dazu bin ich geboren und dazu bin ich in die Welt gekommen, damit ich Zeugnis gebe für die Wahrheit. Es sagte zu ihm Pilatus: Was ist Wahrheit?» (Joh 18,37 f.).

Rückblick Jesu
Nach den Synoptikern hat Jesus bei seiner Gefangennahme das Verhaftungskommando – bei Mt 26,55 ochloi/die Menge – rückblickend auf sein öffentliches Wirken auf das unverhältnismässige Aufgebot hingewiesen. «Wie gegen einen Räuber seid ihr ausgezogen mit Schwertern und Knüppeln, mich zu verhaften, der täglich mit euch war im Tempel lehrend» (vgl. Mk 14,49; Mt 26,55; Lk 22,53).

Bei Johannes fehlt dieser Vorwurf in seiner Ausgestaltung der Verhaftung Jesu. Er findet sich jedoch als Rückblick auf das gesamte Wirken Jesu unter dem Gesichtspunkt der Öffentlichkeit nach der Gefangennahme beim Vorverhör durch den Schwiegervater des Kaiaphas, bei Hannas. Dieser wollte Jesus über seine Jünger und über seine Lehre befragen. Jesus antwortete ihm: «Ich habe öffentlich/parrhêsia zur Welt/tô kosmô geredet. Ich habe jedes Mal in der Synagoge gelehrt und im Tempel, wo alle Juden zusammenkommen, und nichts habe ich im Verborgenen/en kryptô geredet. Was frägst du mich? Frage die, die gehört haben, was ich zu ihnen redete; sie wissen, was ich gesagt habe» (Joh 18,20 f.).

Die Antwort Jesu ist johanneisch formuliert. Parrhêsia/öffentlich im Dativ ohne Präposition ist johanneisches Vorzugswort (9 Mal). Adressat ist der Kosmos, die Menschenwelt. Das Ich Jesu ist betont, anaphorisch am Anfang der ersten Sätze und ans Ende des letzten gesetzt.

Reden/lalein ist das Reden Jesu als Offenbarer Gottes. Die Aussage hat das ganze Offenbarungsgeschehen im Blick. Die Menschenwelt schlechthin ist ihr Adressat und ihr Publikum. Vgl. Joh 8,26: «Was ich von ihm (dem Vater) gehört habe, rede ich zur Welt.» Konkret geschah es an den jüdischen öffentlichen Versammlungsorten, in der Synagoge und im Tempel. Die Aussage beendet der kategorische Ausschluss, etwas im Verborgenen geredet zu haben.

Verborgenheit oder Öffentlichkeit – Joh 7,1–12
Die Frage, ob öffentlichen Auftritt oder nicht, wird in Kapitel 7 des Johannesevangeliums besprochen, zur Zeit des Laubhüttenfestes in Jerusalem. Es beginnt mit einer Art Vorspiel. Jesus weilt noch in Galiläa. Dorthin hatte er sich zurückgezogen, da ihn die Juden in Jerusalem zu töten suchten (Joh 5,18). Sollte er trotzdem zum Fest nach Jerusalem gehen? Sollte er dort in der Öffentlichkeit auftreten? Seine Brüder drängten ihn dazu, aus dem abgelegenen Galiläa in das religiöse Zentrum der Judenschaft nach Jerusalem zu gehen:

Aufforderung der Brüder
> *Vers 3*
> *«Geh weg von hier und geh nach Judäa,*
> *damit deine Jünger die Werke sehen, die du tust.»*

Begründung
> *Vers 4*
> *«Denn niemand tut etwas im Verborgenen/en kryptô*
> *und will selbst in der Öffentlichkeit sein/en parrêsia.*
> *Wenn du dies tust, offenbare dich der Welt/phanérôson seauton tô kosmô!»*

Als Begründung, nach Jerusalem umzusiedeln und dort öffentlich Wunder zu wirken, weisen die Brüder auf eine Selbstverständlichkeit. Der Evangelist erklärt dazu Joh 7,5: «Denn auch seine Jünger glaubten nicht an ihn.»

Zuvor hatte der Evangelist auf die Zeichen/sêmeia hingewiesen, die die zahlreiche Menge/ochlos polys, die Jesus gefolgt war, sah, die er an Kranken tat. Anschliessend berichtete er von der Speisung der 5000. Es geschah nicht im Verborgenen, sondern in grosser Öffentlichkeit, sodass Jesus befürchten musste, dass man ihn mit Gewalt zum König machen wollte. Solchem Ansinnen musste er sich entziehen. Doch galiläische Öffentlichkeit scheint den Brüdern von geringerer Bedeutung als jene in Jerusalem.

Antwort Jesu:

Vers 6

> «Meine Zeit ist noch nicht da/o kairos o emos oupô parestin.
> Aber eure Zeit jederzeit bereit.»

Vers 7

> «Euch kann die Welt nicht hassen;
> Mich aber hasst sie;
> Denn ich bezeuge über sie,
> dass ihre Werke böse/ponêra sind.»

Vers 8

> «Ihr, geht hinauf zum Fest,
> ich aber gehe nicht hinauf zu diesem Fest,
> weil meine Zeit noch nicht erfüllt ist/
> hoti ho emou kairos oupô peplêrôtai.»

Zweimal erklärt Jesus, seine Zeit sei noch nicht da bzw. noch nicht erfüllt. Er steht zwar wie jeder Mensch im Fluss der Zeit. Doch für ihn gibt es in der Zeitenfolge qualifizierte Zeit, einen entscheidenden Zeitpunkt. Noch ist er nicht da, die Zeit noch nicht voll. Davon war schon im Zusammenhang mit dem ersten Zeichen die Rede. Zu seiner Mutter, die ihn auf das Ausgehen des Weines bei der Hochzeit zu Kana aufmerksam machte – implizit eine Bitte um Abhilfe –, antwortete Jesus schroff: «Frau, was ist mir und dir? Meine Stunde ist noch nicht gekommen/oupô hêkei hê hôra mou» (Joh 2,4). Kairos und Stunde bezeichnen dasselbe. Seine Stunde ist die vom Vater bestimmte Stunde, der vom Vater festgesetzte Zeitpunkt seines Todes und seiner Auferstehung und Erhöhung und Verherrlichung. Dass hier nicht Stunde/hôra gebraucht wird, hat seinen Grund darin, dass auch vom Zeitpunkt/kairos der Brüder die Rede ist. Jetzt schon nach Jerusalem zu gehen, wäre für Jesus eigenmächtiges Vorgreifen gegen Gottes Plan und Willen. Es könnte nur Gehen zur eigenmächtigen Selbstdarstellung, zur Selbstdemonstration sein, sich selbst Gott gleich machen, wie Jesus nach der Heilung des Gelähmten in Bethzatha vorgeworfen wird (Joh 5,18). Es wäre Ehre/doxa von Menschen suchen und annehmen, nicht von Gott allein. Solches Verhalten Jesu wäre «böse», ganz im Sinn der Welt. Und er wäre ihr Komplize. Jesus sucht hingegen nicht Ehre, Anerkennung von Seiten der Menschen. Solche Ehrung nimmt er nicht an (Joh 5,41.44). So tun seine Gegner. Sie nehmen Ehrungen voneinander an, suchen aber nicht die Ehre und Anerkennung von Seiten des einen Gottes. Diesen Vorwurf erhebt Jesus rückblickend auf sein Wirken gegen viele Führenden/archontes, die zwar an ihn glauben, sich aber nicht zu ihm bekennen, um nicht aus der Synagoge ausgeschlossen zu werden: «Sie liebten die Ehre/doxa von Seiten der Menschen mehr als die Ehre Gottes» (Joh 12,43).

Jesus denunziert die Bosheit seiner Gegner. Damit handelt er sich ihren Hass ein, den Hass der Welt. Für seine Brüder gilt dies nicht. Als nicht an Jesus Glaubende gehören sie zur Welt, zum Kosmos. Über ihnen waltet nicht Gottes Plan wie über Jesus.

Jesu Gang nach Jerusalem zur Mitte des Festes
  Joh 7,9f.
> *«Nachdem er dies gesagt hatte, blieb er selber in Galiläa.*
> *Als aber seine Brüder zum Fest hinaufgegangen waren,*
> *da ging auch er hinauf,*
> *nicht öffentlich/phanerôs, sondern im Verborgenen/en kryptô.»*

Überraschenderweise geht nun Jesus doch nach Jerusalem um die Mitte des Festes. Freilich nicht öffentlich, wie seine Brüder verlangt hatten, sondern im Verborgenen. Auch wenn es hier nicht ausdrücklich gesagt wird, ging Jesus zum Fest nach Jerusalem auf das Zeigen des Vaters (Joh 5,20) hin:

> *«Amen, amen ich sage euch: der Sohn kann aus sich selbst nichts tun, wenn er nicht den Vater etwas tun sieht (Joh 5,19). Ich kann nichts aus mir selber tun. Wie ich höre, richte ich … Ich suche nicht meinen Willen, sondern den Willen dessen, der mich gesandt hat» (Joh 5,30).*

Seine Stunde ist freilich noch nicht da. Darum kann ihm auch noch nichts angetan werden (Joh 7,30.44).

Meinungen über Jesus
Jesu nichtöffentliche, verborgene Gegenwart veranlasste grosses Geraune/gongysmos, grosse Diskussion unter der Menge über ihn. Die einen sagten: Er ist ein Guter. Andere sagten: Nein, er verführt das Volk (Joh 7,12). Diese übernahmen die Beurteilung Jesu durch die «Juden», d.h. konkret

die Meinung der Mehrheit des Synedriums. Es war keine Diskussion der Öffentlichkeit mit dem Ziel eines Konsenses möglich: Niemand redet offen/parrhêsia über ihn wegen der Furcht vor den «Juden» (Joh 7,13).

Jesus stellt sich öffentlicher Auseinandersetzung
Mit seinem öffentlichen Auftreten im Tempel zur Mitte des Laubhüttenfestes stellt sich Jesus sozusagen der Öffentlichkeit: «siehe, er redet offen/parrhêsia» (Joh 7,25 f.). Es folgt die Verhandlung über ihn selbst, über seine Lehre, sein Woher; ist er der Christus?

Seine Lehre: Sie ist nicht von ihm, sondern von dem, der ihn gesandt hat, aus Gott (Joh 7,16 f.).

Sein Woher/pothen estin: Er kam nicht von sich aus, sondern von dem, der ihn gesandt hat (Joh 7,28).

Das Ergebnis ist offen, geteilt/schisma (Joh 7,43). So in der nicht regierenden Öffentlichkeit. Seitens der Mehrheit der Führenden/archontes (Hohepriester, Pharisäer, Synedristen; Joh 7,45–50) ist sie negativ.

Das Verhör des geheilten Blindgeborenen (Joh 9,13 ff.) zeigt einen Mann aus dem Volk, der durch seine Argumentation den Pharisäern die Stirn bietet, sodass sie nicht mehr sachlich antworten können, sondern nur mit Hinauswurf aus der Synagoge: «Von Ewigkeit her wurde nicht gehört, dass einer Augen eines Blindgeborenen geöffnet hat; wenn dieser nicht von Gott wäre, könnte er nichts tun» (Joh 9,32 f.).

Rückblickend auf das ganze öffentliche Wirken Jesu muss der Evangelist feststellen: «Zwar glaubten viele der Führenden an Jesus. Doch wegen der Pharisäer bekannten sie (sich) nicht (zu ihm), damit sie nicht aus der Synagoge ausgeschlossen würden. Denn sie liebten die Ehre/doxa der Menschen mehr als die Ehre Gottes» (12,42 f.).

Nach dem Einzug in Jerusalem und den dortigen Auseinandersetzungen heisst es: «Jesus ging weg und verbarg sich vor ihnen» (12,36). Den Unglauben, trotz so vieler Zeichen, vermag der Evangelist schliesslich nur durch die Prophetie des Jesaia von Gottes verdunkelndem Wirken zu erklären (Joh 9,39; Jes 6,10), wie schon die Synoptiker (Mk 4,13; Mt 13,15) und Paulus (Apg 28,26 f.).

3. Kêryssein und martyrein?

Man hat kêryssein und martyrein einander gegenübergestellt und als Ausdruck zweier unterschiedlicher Weisen der Mitteilung des Glaubens bezeichnet: Proklamation, Wortverkündigung einerseits, Erfahrungs- und Lebenszeugnis andererseits. Man hat sie als verschiedene Phasen der Weitergabe des Glaubens beurteilt: Wortverkündigung, Proklamation in den Anfängen, Erfahrungs- und Lebenszeugnis angesichts des Unglaubens später.[7] Die erste Form heute wiederbeleben zu wollen, wäre ein Irrweg. Der gegenwärtigen Zeit gemäss wäre die zweite. Bei allen Unterschieden bedeutet martyrein, martyria ebenso direkte Wortverkündigung. Auch das Zeugnis geschieht durch Rede/lalein. Umgekehrt gehört zur Wortverkündigung als Proklamation ebenso das Lebenszeugnis.

Abschluss

Als Frohe Botschaft des einen Gottes ergeht das Evangelium an den einzelnen Menschen und an die ganze Menschenwelt. Es richtet sich ohne Einschränkung an den privaten und an den öffentlichen Raum.

Die Verkündigung muss gedeckt werden durch das private und das öffentliche Lebenszeugnis der Boten und der Glaubensgemeinschaft, um glaubwürdig zu sein. Wenn auch durch das Zeugnis immer mehr Menschen Heilserfahrungen machen können sollen, sodass aus immer mehr beglückten lebendigen Menschen Danksagung zur Ehre Gottes aufsteigt (vgl. 2 Kor 4,15), darf es allein Gottes Wohlgefallen, Gottes Ehre und Herrlichkeit (doxa) zum Motiv haben, nicht Menschenehre und Menschengefallen.

Der johanneische Vorwurf an die religiösen und politischen Repräsentanten, Menschenehre zu suchen, nicht Gottes Ehre, muss bei allen kirchlichen Repräsentanten und Repräsentationen zur Prüfung herausfordern: Dienen sie der Darstellung der Botschaft oder der Selbstdarstellung?

---

[7] Jean-Pierre Jossua, Zeugnis, in: Peter Eicher (Hg.), *Neues Handbuch theologischer Grundbegriffe 4*, München, Kösel, 1991, S. 332–342.

Georg Schelbert SMB, *1922 , em. Professor für Bibelwissenschaft. Studium der Theologie am Missionsseminar der Schweizerischen Missionsgesellschaft Bethlehem (SMB) und an der Universität Gregoriana, der Bibelwissenschaft am PIB in Rom, des aram. Targum bei Prof. P. Kahle in Oxford. Lehrtätigkeit für Altes und Neues Testament am Missionsseminar der SMB, Einführung in die Theologie des Neuen Testaments, Milieu biblique, Littérature intertestamentaire, aramäische Sprache an der Theologischen Fakultät der Universität Freiburg (CH), Neues Testament am Katechetischen Institut Luzern. Emeritiert 1992. Besondere Erwähnung verdient sein Werk: *«Abba Vater». Der literarische Befund vom Altaramäischen bis zu den späten Midrasch- und Haggada-Werken in Auseinandersetzung mit den Thesen von Joachim Jeremias,* NTOA 81, Göttingen 2011.

Missionshaus Bethlehem, Bethlehemweg 10, CH-6405 Immensee, Schweiz
gschelbert@gmx.ch

Kirche in der Öffentlichkeit
Ein Beispiel aus Indonesien
Olaf Schumann

Summary

The focus of this article is an internal conflict that took place in the 1990s in the Church of the Toba-Batak in North Sumatra, one of the major churches in Indonesia. Intervention by government security forces on behalf of one of the conflicting parties prevented a reconciliation and almost led to a split in the church. The author traces the causes that led to this scandal and tries to analyse some relevant political-social developments during the era of General Suharto's rule which mark the historical background of the increasing crisis in the relationship between this church, some of its leaders, and the government. Special attention is given to the roles some of the decisive personalities played in this conflict at a national level before it broke out in a regional one. Finally, as a consequence of these and similar experiences, the Toba-Batak church and others are challenged to reconsider their attitudes towards Adat (tradition) as the basic guideline for their social attitudes and how far they should adapt themselves, living in a plural society, to the rules of a civil society. This conflict showed that when guided by the norms of Adat, the church was too weak to defend its integrity against the aggressive power of the State.

Religion im «religiösen» Staat

Als ich um das Jahr 2000 an der Theologischen Hochschule der Christlich-Protestantischen Batak-Kirche[1] in Pematang Siantar, Nord-Sumatra (siehe Indonesien-Karte, Seite 106), einen Intensivkurs über das Verhältnis der Kirche zu ihrer gesellschaftlichen Umwelt, insbesondere der islamisch geprägten, abhielt, kam auch das Thema «Kirche und Zivilgesellschaft» zur Sprache. Angesichts der vom damaligen Staatspräsidenten, General Suharto (1921–2008, reg. 1967–1998), geprägten totalitären Ten-

---

[1] *Huria Kristen Batak Protestan*, HKBP. Traditionelles Zentrum dieser vor allem von den Toba-Batak gegründeten Kirche ist die Landschaft (Nord-)Tapanuli im Süden und Südosten des Toba-Sees in Nord-Sumatra. Sie hat derzeit etwa 3,6 Mio. Mitglieder und gilt als die grösste lutherische Kirche in Asien.

denzen der Staatsführung, die alle Bereiche des zivilen Lebens mehr und mehr einschnürte, hatte sich unter Intellektuellen, Theologen und Wissenschaftlern eine Debatte um Sinn und Bedeutung einer Zivilgesellschaft im modernen Staat – und als solchen wollte man auch Indonesien betrachten können – entfaltet, die allerdings von der Regierung zunehmend als subversiv beargwöhnt wurde und sich deshalb unter strikter Aufsicht der Sicherheitsbehörden vollzog. Es waren vor allem muslimische Intellektuelle und Theologen, die diese Debatte vorantrieben, und entsprechend ihren unterschiedlichen innerislamischen Positionen zum Verhältnis von «Religion und Staat» war auch das Spektrum der vorgetragenen Meinungen weit gestreut und bewegte sich von Orientierungen an der «Stadt des Propheten»[2] über die von islamischen Philosophen der klassischen Zeit weitergeführten Diskurse über die «vorzügliche, gesittete Stadt»[3], die sich insbesondere an Platons Ausführungen in den *Nomoi* und der *Politeia* zur *polis* orientierten, bis hin zu innerislamischen Auseinandersetzungen mit modernen Entwürfen über die Rolle der Religion im säkularen Staat bzw. in der zivilen Gesellschaft.

Eines der Eckdaten, die dem speziell indonesischen Charakter dieser Debatten um die Zivilgesellschaft den Rahmen setzten, war das einerseits auch sonst in der islamischen Welt weitverbreitete, gleichwohl keineswegs auf Muhammad zurückgehende, sondern erst viel später von Herrschern und im Interesse des Erhalts ihrer jeweiligen Dynastie gepräg-

---

[2] *Madīnat an-nabī,* das von Muhammad und den Häuptern der damals in Yathrib (jetzt: Medina) lebenden arabischen Stämme vertraglich vereinbarte Gemeinwesen, oft als *Blueprint* für einen «islamischen Staat» deklariert.

[3] *Al-madīna al-fādila,* deren «kalif» oder Oberhaupt nach dem Ende der prophetischen Ära (mit Muhammads Tod 632 n.Chr.) aus dem Kreise der Weisen zu wählen gewesen wäre. Propheten und Philosophen waren nach Meinung dieser islamischen Philosophen in ähnlicher Weise vom göttlichen Geiste inspiriert und geleitet und deswegen befähigt, ein auf Gerechtigkeit und Sittlichkeit gründendes Gemeinwesen zu führen. Bei Versagen müssten sie abgewählt werden können. Damit wandten sie sich gegen das zur Erbdynastie verkommene Kalifat ihrer Zeit, wurden von den Kalifen und anderen Fürsten, unterstützt von deren «Hoftheologen», der Ketzerei bezichtigt und verloren in der Folgezeit ihren Einfluss auf die intellektuelle Weiterentwicklung des Islam im Mittelalter.

te Diktum, dass der Islam sowohl Religion als auch Staat sei.[4] Andererseits muss sich jede in Indonesien um das Verhältnis von Religion und Staat geführte Debatte an die Vorgaben der in der Verfassung verankerten Staatsphilosophie «Pancasila» (Fünf Prinzipien)[5] zu diesem Thema halten. Die Pancasila verpflichtet den Staat in ihrem ersten Prinzip, eine «all-eine göttliche Herrschaft»[6] anzuerkennen, wobei in den dazugehörenden Interpretationen stets betont wurde, dass die Erklärung dessen, was unter

[4] *Al-Islâm dîn wa-daula,* «Islam ist Religion und ‹Staat›»; doch ist bereits die Übersetzung von *daula,* im Türkischen *devlet,* mit «Staat», im Indonesischen mit *«negara»,* irreführend, denn *daula* bedeutet «Dynastie», im Indonesischen *«wangsa».* Dieses Diktum findet sich weder im Koran noch in der prophetischen Sunna.

[5] Die Fünf Prinzipien sind die Grundlage des Staates, keine von ihnen macht eine theologische Aussage: 1) Anerkennung einer all-einen göttlichen Herrschaft *(ketuhanan yang maha esa);* 2) gerechte und zivile Humanität *(perikemanusiaan yang adil dan beradab,* manchmal als «Internationalismus» oder «Antikolonialismus» interpretiert); 3) die nationale Einheit Indonesiens *(persatuan Indonesia,* «Nationalismus»); 4) Demokratie durch in Weisheit geführte Verhandlungen und Konsens *(kerakyatan yang dipimpin oleh hikmat kebijaksanaan dalam permusyawaratan/perwakilan);* 5) soziale Gerechtigkeit für das ganze indonesische Volk *(keadilan sosial buat seluruh rakyat Indonesia).*

[6] *Ketuhanan yang maha esa.* Das Wort *«ketuhanan»* ist ein Abstraktum ([göttliche] Herrschaft), abgeleitet von *Tuhan,* der (göttliche) Herr. Es mit «Gott» oder «Allah» zu übersetzen und damit zu personalisieren, ist irreführend und verfehlt seinen Sinn, denn der Staat selbst hat weder eine eigene Theologie noch eine Liturgie. Bei bestimmten Anlässen kann er sich eine solche bei einer der anerkannten Religionen «ausleihen». Vom Staat anerkannte Religionen sind der Islam, der Protestantismus, der Katholizismus, der Hinduismus und der Buddhismus. Unter der Präsidentschaft von Abdurrahman Wahid (1999–2001) kam der Konfuzianismus dazu. Die Behandlung von Protestantismus und Katholizismus als verschiedene Religionen geht auf die Anfänge der Missionsgeschichte im südostasiatischen Archipel zurück, als, entsprechend dem in Europa damals üblichen Sprachgebrauch, beide als unterschiedliche *religiones* eingeführt wurden. – Zur Pancasila vgl. u. a. Eka Darmaputra, *Pancasila and the Search for Identity and Modernity in Indonesian Society,* Leiden, Brill, 1988; Ingo Wandelt, *Der Weg zum Pancasila-Menschen. Die Pancasila-Lehre unter dem P-4 Beschluss des Jahres 1978,* Frankfurt/Main, P. Lang Verlag, 1989; Olaf Schumann, Herausgefordert durch die Pancasila. Die Religionen in Indonesien, in: Udo Tworuschka (Hg.), *Gottes ist der Orient – Gottes ist der Okzident.* Festschrift für A. Falaturi, Köln-Wien, Böhlau 1991, 322–343, abgedr. in: Olaf Schumann, *Selbstverständnis und Fremdwahrnehmung,* hg. von Klaus Hock, Münster, LIT 1999, 75–99 (Rostocker Theologische Studien, 2); Dieter Becker, *Die Kirchen und der Pancasila-Staat. Indonesische Christen zwischen Konsens und Konflikt,* Erlangen, Verlag der Ev.-Luth. Mission, 1996 (Missionswissenschaftliche Forschungen, NF Bd. 1).

«*ketuhanan*» (göttliche Herrschaft) zu verstehen sei, den verschiedenen Religionsgemeinschaften selbst überlassen werden müsse. Es handelt sich um ein politisches Prinzip, nicht um eine theologische Aussage; *ketuhanan* ist nicht *Tuhan* (der «göttliche» Herr). Der Staat erkennt das Prinzip an und ist damit verpflichtet, den Religionsgemeinschaften den Freiraum zu garantieren, in dem sie ihr religiöses Bekenntnis formulieren und ihren religiösen Verpflichtungen – sowohl im rituellen/gottesdienstlichen als auch im sozialen Bereich – nachkommen können. Damit wird ausdrücklich die öffentliche Dimension religiösen Lebens anerkannt und unter den Schutz des Staates gestellt. Allerdings hat er auch hier, ähnlich wie in früheren christlichen Definitionen über das Verhältnis von Kirchen und Staat, das Recht, als Ordnungsmacht einzugreifen, wenn innerhalb einer religiösen Gemeinschaft oder zwischen verschiedenen von ihnen Gegensätze auftreten, die den gesellschaftlichen Frieden, die «öffentliche Ordnung», stören. Eingriffe in die inneren weltanschaulichen Angelegenheiten einer Religionsgemeinschaft oder auch in ihr dogmatisches Selbstverständnis sind dem Staat durch den Verfassungstext untersagt.

Die Pancasila als Grundlage der Verfassung wurde als Alternative zu der in der Gründungsphase der *Republik Indonesia* von einigen muslimischen Kreisen geforderten Errichtung des unabhängigen Indonesien als

«Islam-Staat», dessen ideologisches Fundament die islamische *sharî'a*[7] sein müsse, angenommen. Kein «Islam-Staat», aber auch kein «säkularer Staat» wurde Indonesien, sondern ein «religiöser Staat». Damit war der Weg für alle Indonesier, unabhängig von ihrer ethnischen oder religiösen Zugehörigkeit, offen, als gleichberechtigte Staatsbürger anerkannt zu werden. Damit waren aber auch alle zur Verteidigung ihrer staatsbürgerlichen Rechte und zur Wahrnehmung staatsbürgerlicher Aufgaben angehalten.

[7] *Sharî'a* (*šarî'a*), die islamische Pflichtenlehre, oft ungenau als «islamisches Recht» übersetzt. Der Begriff kommt im Qur'an nur ein einziges Mal vor (QS 45,18: فَاتَّبِعْهَا الأَمْرِ مِنَ شَرِيعَةٍ عَلَى جَعَلْنَاكَ ثُمَّ, danach machten wir Dir einen Weg und befahlen, ihn zu befolgen); auch das nahe verwandte Wort *shir'a* erscheint nur einmal in QS 5,45 im Sinne von «Ordnung», «Brauchtum» (nach R. Paret), zusammen mit dem Wort «Weg» *(minhâj)*, während andere, von der Wortwurzel *š r'* abgeleitete Wörter insgesamt noch dreimal vorkommen (QS 42,21; 42,13; 7,163), als Verb «erklären». Aus diesem spärlichen Befund lässt sich ableiten, dass nahezu alle späteren Erklärungen dessen, was *Sharî'a* sein soll und wie sie sich vom *Fiqh*, der Rechtwissenschaft, unterscheidet, Ergebnisse von Gelehrtendisputationen sind. Zu Recht betonten diese, dass die Quelle dessen, was als *Sharî'a* anerkannt wird, der Qur'an, also die Offenbarung, ist. Doch gerade als Quelle ist er offen für unterschiedliche Interpretationen. Es gibt also keinen einheitlichen Kodex dessen, was allgemein als *Sharî'a* anerkannt wird. Als «Pflichtenlehre» ist sie eher an den ethischen und sittlichen Grundlagen der staatlichen und gesellschaftlichen Ordnungen interessiert, die kontextuell durchaus unterschiedliche Akzente setzen. Dazu kann es ebenfalls detaillierte Vorschriften geben, etwa im Blick auf religiöse Riten oder das Familienrecht, die jedoch keinen automatischen Anspruch auf Allgemeingültigkeit haben. «Offenbart» und damit allgemein verbindlich ist nur das ewige Wort Gottes, also der Qur'an, nicht jedoch die aus ihm abgeleiteten, von den Gelehrten, also Menschen, formulierten Richtlinien oder «Wegweisungen». Dieses Grundverständnis wurde jedoch in der Geschichte des Islam wiederholt von Herrschern und ihrer Klientel («Palastgelehrten») in Frage gestellt, die ihrer eigenen Gesetzgebung den Nimbus göttlicher Autorität geben wollten, indem sie sie mit dem Hinweis auf die *Sharî'a* als «offenbartem Gottesrecht», das ebenfalls Grundlage des eigenen Herrscherrechts sein soll, begründeten. Auch die Redensart, der Islam sei «Religion und Staat» (siehe Anm. 4), hat hierin ihren Ursprung. Weitere Literatur: Artikel «Sharî'a», in: *Encyclopaedia of Islam*, 2. Auflage, vol. 9, Leiden, Brill 1997; Olaf Schumann, Hukum Syari'a dan Pemisahan Agama dengan Negara (Shari'a-Recht und die Trennung von Religion und Staat), in: J. Mardimin (Hg.), *Mempercakapkan Relasi Agama & Negara. Menata Ulang Hubungan Agama dan Negara di Indonesia* (Gespräch über die Beziehungen zwischen Religion & Staat. Neubestimmung des Verhältnisses von Religion und Staat in Indonesien). Yogyakarta, Sinode GKJTU 2011, S. 76–106.

An diesem Verständnis entzündete sich jedoch der Konflikt zwischen der Gesellschaft und der Staatsmacht, insbesondere unter der Regierung Suharto, die die zivilen Rechte zunehmend beschnitt, den Staat in ein zentral gesteuertes Wirtschaftsimperium ummodellierte, die Staatsbürger als «Arbeitskräfte» *(tenaga kerja)* betrachtete und die gut ausgebildeten unter ihnen aufforderte, ihr Wissen und ihre Erfahrungen als «Technokraten» der Regierung zur Verfügung zu stellen, sich aber nicht in Richtungsdebatten über Weg und Ziel des staatlichen und wirtschaftlichen Aufbaus einzumischen. Dafür gab es bestimmte Institutionen wie *Bappenas*[8], die staatliche Planungsbehörde, oder *CSIS*[9], das von Suhartos persönlichem

---

[8] *Badan Perencanaan Pembangunan Nasional* (Behörde für die Planung des Nationalen Aufbaus).

[9] *Center for Strategic and International Studies,* ein Think-Tank, der entscheidenden Einfluss auf Suhartos politische, ideologische und wirtschaftliche Entwicklungspläne bis in die späten 1980er-Jahre ausüben sollte. Neben dem – nun allerdings verbotenen – Kommunismus galten ihm als ideologische Gegner vor allem der politische Islam und das Konzept der «liberalen Demokratie», selbst vertrat es die «Pancasila-Demokratie». Unterstützung erhielt es vor allem aus den USA. Damit stand es dem Militär nahe, und nicht wenige hohe Offiziere waren in ihm aktiv, desgleichen katholische Technokraten und Militärs. Aus diesem Grunde wurde es von islamischen Politikern gern als verkappter «christlicher» Stützpunkt angesehen und kritisiert. Vgl. Mujiburrahman, *Feeling Threatened. Muslim-Christian Relations in Indonesia's New Order,* Leiden, Amsterdam Univ. Press 2006, 139 ff., 216 ff. – Die der Pancasila-Demokratie innewohnenden Tendenzen zu einer totalitären oder «integrationalistischen», neuhegelianischen Regierungsform hat Marsillam Simanjuntak untersucht: *Pandangan Negara Integralistik,* Jakarta, Grafiti Pers, 1994. Dort wird auch auf die Gründe für das tief verwurzelte Harmoniebedürfnis zwischen dem Volk und der Herrschaft verwiesen. Die von Adat (siehe Anm. 9) und Neuhegelianismus geprägten Gemeinschafts- und Machtstrukturen sind nahe verwandt und wurden deshalb vom späteren Sukarno (1901–1970), von Suharto (1921–2008) und anderen von der Adat geprägten Politikern und gesellschaftlichen Führern einschliesslich Kirchenpräsidenten als die indonesischer Mentalität angemessene Regierungsform propagiert, vgl. O. Schumann, Zur politischen Konvivenz. Die Debatte um das Verhältnis von Staat und Gesellchaft in Indonesien, in: D. Becker (Hg.), *Mit dem Fremden leben.* Teil 1: Religion – Religionen (Festschrift Theo Sundermeier). Erlangen, Verlag der Evang.-Luth. Mission, 2000, 193–210. – Ob dieser Gegensatz «Pancasila-Demokratie *versus* liberale bzw. zivilgesellschaftliche Demokratie» stimmt, hätte nach dem Ende der Suharto-Diktatur untersucht werden müssen. Das machtpolitische Durcheinander in der Staatsführung und sein Abklatsch in der Gesellschaft haben einen solchen Klärungsprozess bisher verhindert.

Referenten Ali Murtopo 1971 gegründet wurde. Seine Mitglieder waren insbesondere in den USA (Kalifornien) ausgebildete Fachkräfte, die zumeist in weltanschaulicher Hinsicht dem auch von Suharto gepflegten «javanischen Mystizismus» (kebatinan) nahestanden und ihr technisches, ökonomisches, aber auch militärtechnisches Know-how der staatlichen Führung zur Verfügung stellten. Einige empfahlen sich zusätzlich dadurch, dass sie Leitungspositionen in irgendeinem Geheimdienst innehatten und damit der Durchsetzung des innenpolitischen Leitmotivs, «Sicherheit und Ordnung» (keamanan dan ketertiban) – um Störungen des Aufbauprogramms der Regierung zu verhindern –, auf verschiedene Weise dienen konnten. Darin wurden sie von den «christlichen» Nationen im Westen und ihren Entwicklungshilfeprogrammatikern unterstützt; damals herrschte noch der «Kalte Krieg» und alles, was sich als «antikommunistisch» ausgab – und das tat die Suharto-Regierung seit ihrer Inauguration –, galt als «gut». Eine andere Gruppe, die im CSIS sehr einflussreich wurde, waren katholische «Technokraten».

Vom «religiösen» Staat zum Machtstaat

Unter anderen Faktoren war es die zunehmende Missachtung der staatsbürgerlichen, zivilen Rechte, die schliesslich in Indonesien die Debatte um die Zivilgesellschaft angeregt hat. Sie hätte eigentlich alle gesellschaftlichen Gruppen, vor allem jedoch diejenigen, denen man ein ziviles Bewusstsein zumuten konnte, zur Beteiligung ermuntern müssen. Es waren jedoch vor allem muslimische Theologen und Intellektuelle, die sie vorantrieben. Doch auch katholische Akademiker, zumeist aus Zentral-Java oder den Kleinen Sunda-Inseln stammend, waren verhältnismässig zahlreich vertreten, während sich auf protestantischer Seite bemerkenswerterweise nur wenige in dieser Frage engagierten.

Diese Beobachtung hatte mich veranlasst, in dem eingangs erwähnten Kurs das Gespräch auf das Thema Zivilgesellschaft und die Rolle der Religion(en) in ihr zu bringen. Das Phänomen der weitgehenden Absenz protestantischer Beteiligung an dieser Debatte veranlasste mich zu der Frage, ob die am Kurs Teilnehmenden dafür einen Grund benennen könnten. Zunächst herrschte etwas betretenes Schweigen. Dann meldete sich ein stämmiger batakscher Student und meinte: «Die Zivilgesellschaft in Tapanuli ist die HKBP. Da brauchen wir keine Debatte darüber, was eine Zivilgesellschaft sein könnte.»

Das war eine klare Antwort. Aber was schwang da alles mit? Zum einen, dass die HKBP in ihrem Stammgebiet die Mehrzahl der Bevölkerung umfasst und damit sich mit dem Anspruch selbst Mut macht, nicht nur die führende religiöse, sondern auch die führende gesellschaftliche Gruppe zu sein und dort die soziale Entwicklung zu bestimmen, ähnlich wie es einige muslimische Gruppen dort tun, wo sie die Majorität der Bevölkerung bilden. Dass dieser Hinweis auf primordiale Majoritäten diametral der Philosophie der Pancasila widerspricht, wird dabei grosszügig übersehen, obwohl man sich sonst gern auf sie beruft, insbesondere, um überhaupt das Recht auf soziale und damit öffentliche Aktivitäten im mehrheitlich von Muslimen bewohnten Staat zu begründen. Eine zivile Gesellschaft kann eigentlich nur eine plurale sein, in der sich die Mitglieder gegenseitig und unabhängig von der Grösse ihrer jeweiligen Gruppe als rechtlich gleichgestellte Staatsbürger anerkennen. Hier also irrte sich jener Student, wenn er meinte, die HKBP vertrete, zumindest in Nord-Tapanuli, die gesamte (zivile) Gesellschaft. Die anderen sind auch da und gehören mit dazu.

Die Kirche als Hüterin gesellschaftlicher Zivilität?

In der damals aktuellen Situation der HKBP stand noch ein anderes Argument im Raum, das insbesondere bei den anderen Teilnehmern/Teilnehmerinnen einige Beklemmung hervorrief. Die Zivilgesellschaft beansprucht nicht nur die Einhaltung ziviler Rechte und den Respekt vor ihnen seitens der Inhaber der staatlichen Macht, sondern sie verpflichtet ihre Mitglieder auch zu zivilem Handeln insbesondere inmitten sozialer Konflikte. Seit dem Jahr 1998 war die HKBP gerade dabei, ihren damals letzten grossen inneren Konflikt zu überwinden, der in den vergangenen Jahren – seit 1992 – nicht nur zu heftigen und teilweise blutigen Zusammenstössen zwischen verschiedenen Fraktionen mit einigen Todesopfern innerhalb der Kirche geführt hatte, sondern die Kirche an den Rand der Spaltung brachte. An diese und andere Vorkommnisse aus der neueren

Geschichte der HKBP erinnernd, fragte ich dann zurück, ob die HKBP wirklich so uneingeschränkt ein Vorbild für eine zivile Gesellschaft biete.

Die daraufhin gegebenen Antworten machten deutlich, dass das Entsetzen über die Vorkommnisse tief ging und die Zeiten theologischer Selbstzufriedenheit und die Adat[10] unhinterfragt rezipierender Romantik zumindest bei einem Teil der jüngeren Theologinnen und Theologen in Frage gestellt werden. Bei der führenden Rolle der HKBP in Nord-Tapanuli möge es zwar bleiben, doch bedarf ihr Umgang mit internen Krisen, der schliesslich auch ihr Erscheinungsbild, das sich der Öffentlichkeit zeigt, prägt, einer gründlichen theologischen und sozialethischen Revision.

Die internen Spannungen und Auseinandersetzungen innerhalb der HKBP hat Dieter Becker ausführlich behandelt[11]; das dort Gesagte braucht nicht wiederholt zu werden. Nicht weniger bedeutungsvoll sind die politischen und gesellschaftlichen Umstände und Hintergründe, die diesen im Wesentlichen innerkirchlichen Konflikt zu einer Angelegenheit werden liessen, die nicht nur in der Öffentlichkeit weite Beachtung fand, sondern in der sich auch charakteristische Aspekte der sozio-politischen Beschaffenheit der indonesischen Gesellschaft und ihres Staates sowie der Kirchen widerspiegelten.

Schon die Grösse dieser Kirche und die gesellschaftliche Rolle ihrer Mitglieder nicht nur im Norden Sumatras, sondern auch in anderen Gegenden Indonesiens, wo Batakter als Staatsdiener oder Soldaten dienen oder in der Wirtschaft, im Bildungs- und im Bankwesen bedeutende Posten ausfüllen, verbietet es, sie als quantité négligeable in der Gesellschaft und im Staate zu betrachten. Wo immer möglich gründen sie ihre eigenen Kirchgemeinden, in denen Bataksch die Umgangssprache und zumeist

---

[10] *Adat:* die religiöse, kulturelle und rechtliche Tradition eines Volksstammes, vom arabischen *'âda*, Brauchtum, «das, was sich ständig wiederholt». Sie wird als Setzung der Ahnen verstanden, ist damit von ihrer Konzeption her konservativ und exklusiv gegenüber Aussenstehenden.

[11] Dieter Becker, Eine Kirche in der Krise. Leitungskonflikte in Nordsumatra im Jahre 1993, in: ders., *Besseres als Gewalt. Interkulturelle Studien aus Religion, Kirche und Gesellschaft,* hg. von Moritz Fischer, Frankfurt/M, Lembeck, 2010, 131–151; ders., Streiten ohne Ende? Die Batak-Kirche zwischen 1988 und 1998, in: *Besseres als Gewalt,* a.a.O., 153–183.

auch die Predigtsprache ist. Damit sind sie nach aussen hin weitgehend abgeschlossen. An lokalen oder regionalen ökumenischen Gremien sind sie zwar beteiligt, spielen aber gerne eine Sonderrolle. Dennoch nehmen nicht wenige ihrer Glieder im protestantisch-ökumenischen Spektrum bedeutende Posten ein.

Wer Erfolg und auch ausserhalb der eigenen Gemeinschaft sich einen Namen erworben hat, dem gilt Respekt. Da aber seine oder ihre Erfahrungen in fremder Umgebung sich nicht immer problemlos der eigenen Gemeinschaft und vor allem jenen, denen im Wesentlichen nur die eigene Gemeinschaft vertraut ist, vermitteln lassen, kommt es bei ihrer Rückkehr, falls sie leitende Posten übernehmen, leicht zu Spannungen, insbesondere wenn es um Grundsatzfragen über die künftige Gestaltung der Kirche, ihr Selbstverständnis und ihre gesellschaftliche Rolle geht. Die Verhaltensmuster und das ethische und moralische Wertesystem sind von der Adat geprägt, der sich auch das Evangelium weitgehend «inkulturiert», d.h. angepasst hat, und diesen Zustand gälte es um der eigenen Identität willen zu erhalten.[12] Die Adat ist, ihrer eigenen Konzeption entsprechend, rückwärts gewandt, sie bezieht sich auf die Ahnen, und deren Vermächtnis gilt es zu bewahren. Korrekterweise muss allerdings auch gesagt werden, dass in der Praxis, und damit im Gegensatz zur Theorie, Adat eine erhebliche Dynamik entfalten und durchaus Fähigkeiten entwickeln kann, sich ändernden gesellschaftlichen und politischen Gegebenheiten anzupassen. Diese Dynamik findet vornehmlich in der Mythenbil-

---

[12] Diesem Problemfeld hatte sich Lothar Schreiner in seiner Habilitationsschrift gewidmet: *Adat und Evangelium. Zur Bedeutung der altvölkischen Lebensordnungen für Kirche und Mission unter den Batak in Nordsumatra*, Gütersloh, Mohn, 1972. Obwohl diese Arbeit auch in einer indonesischen Übersetzung erschien *(Telah kudengar dari Ayahku. Perjumpaan Adat dengan Iman Kristen di Tanah Batak*, Jakarta, BPK [Badan Penerbit Kristen, Christl. Verlagshaus] 1978) ist von ihren theologischen Herausforderungen an die Adatgemeinschaft der HKBP noch wenig theologisch rezipiert worden, wie etliche der Beiträge in einer Schreiner zu seinem 75. Geburtstag gewidmeten Festschrift zeigen *(Injil Dan Tata Hidup/The Gospel and Life Order/Evangelium und Lebensordnung*, hg. von Adelbert A. Sitompul und Karl H. Federschmidt, Pematang Siantar, STT HKBP [Theol. Hochschule der HKBP]/Jakarta, PT. Rapi Budi Mulia/Waltrop, Hartmut Spenner, 2001).

dung[13] ihren Ausdruck, die aber trotzdem dem Grundsatz verhaftet bleibt, dass die Adat ihren Ursprung bei den Ahnen hat und ihnen gegenüber verpflichtet bleibt. Allerdings sehen dies nicht wenige Bataker, die ihre Lebenserfahrungen inzwischen ausserhalb der batakschen Gemeinschaft gemacht haben, oft anders, und vertreten es auch nach ihrer Rückkehr. Damit werden Richtungsfragen schnell personalisiert, und nicht der Sachgehalt eines Arguments, sondern die Person, die es vertritt, entscheiden über richtig oder falsch, über Annahme oder Ablehnung.

Personen im Konflikt

Kristallisationsfiguren der 1992 offen ausgebrochenen Krise waren einerseits der damalige Ephorus (Bischof) der HKBP, Dr. Soritua A. E. Nababan, dessen Wieder- oder Abwahl auf einer im November 1992 turnusgemäss einberufenen Synode zur Entscheidung anstand. Als Widersacher profilierte sich Dr. Sountilon N. Siahaan, Leiter des Kirchendistrikts *(Resort)* der HKBP in Bandung, West-Java. Der Konflikt brach aus, als es der Synode nicht gelang, innerhalb der von der Regierung genehmigten Zeit den Wahlvorgang abzuschliessen. Die Ursache dafür waren tumultuarische Auseinandersetzungen, die von einem Teil der Synodalen unter der Leitung von Dr. S. Siahaan hervorgerufen worden waren und die Wiederwahl von Dr. S. A. E. Nababan um jeden Preis verhindern wollten. Darin wurden sie von dem anwesenden Militär unterstützt. Kurz vor Ablauf der von der Regierung genehmigten Zeit für die Synode unterbrach Nababan als Ephorus die Sitzung bis zu dem Zeitpunkt, zu dem eine neue Genehmigung vorliege und die Wahl ordnungsgemäss ablaufen könne. Darauf verliess er den Sitzungsort. Anschliessend erklärte der Kommandeur von *Bakostanasda*[14] Dr. Nababan für abgesetzt und bestimmte Dr. Siahaan als *caretaker*-Ephorus, der noch für den Dezember eine neue Wahlsynode einberufen sollte. So ge-

---

[13] Mythen sind keine Märchen, sondern in die Urzeit projizierte Ereignisse, deren Erzählung den damaligen Vorgang wiederholt und für die Gegenwart relevant bzw. «wahr» macht.

[14] *Bakostanasda: Badan Kordinasi Stabilitas Nasional dan Daerah.* Staatliche, für die nationale und regionale Sicherheit zuständige Behörde. Sie unterstand direkt dem Befehl des Präsidenten. Regionaler Kommandeur in Nord-Sumatra war damals General Pramono.

schah es, nur wurden die meisten der Anhänger Dr. Nababans nicht eingeladen. Der in der Folgezeit unter Aufsicht des Militärs eingesetzten Kirchenleitung mit Dr. Siahaan als Generalsekretär wurde von einem grossen Teil der Kirchenglieder und Pastorenschaft die Anerkennung verweigert, doch bestanden die Regierung und das Militär darauf, dass nur diese Gruppe als legitime Kirchenleitung zu akzeptieren sei. Unter Hinweis auf den Namen des Hotels in Medan, in dem die inaugurierende Sitzung der vom Militär geschaffenen Kirchenleitung stattfand, wurde sie als «Tiara»-Kirche bezeichnet, während sich der «verfassungstreue» Flügel den Spruch aus Offb 2,10c zum Wahlspruch nahm: Seid getreu bis in den Tod.

Einen solchen Vorfall, nämlich das Eingreifen des staatlichen Machtapparates in die organisatorischen Angelegenheiten einer Religionsgemeinschaft, hatte es bis dahin in Indonesien noch nicht gegeben. Somit setzte sich schnell als allgemeiner Eindruck durch, dass die Religionsfreiheit gefährdet sei und dieser Vorfall als Präzedenzfall für künftige Aktionen seitens des Staates dienen könnte.

Zwei Argumente dienten zur Rechtfertigung für das Einschreiten des militärischen Sicherheitsapparats. Zum einen hatten einige Gegner des Ephorus Nababan bereits vorher Kontakt mit dem Sicherheitsapparat aufgenommen und offensichtlich das Szenario einschliesslich der Vereitelung der Wahl (gefürchtet wurde wohl eine Wiederwahl Dr. Nababans) und die Einsetzung des *caretaker*-Ephorus vorbereitet. Damit konnten die Regierungsstellen festhalten, dass ihr Eingreifen nicht auf Grund eigenmächtiger Beschlüsse, sondern auf Bitten kirchlicher Kreise selbst hin geschah. Über die Plausibilität dieses Arguments mag gestritten werden. Wenn der Staat durch seine Machtorgane hier als Ordnungshüter hätte auftreten wollen, dann hätte er zumindest von Vertretern beider Seiten dazu aufgefordert werden müssen. Das war nicht der Fall, stattdessen unterstützte er nur die eine Seite zum Schaden der anderen Seite. Er war also parteiisch.

Dies führt zum zweiten Argument. In jedem zivilisierten Staat, und damit auch in Indonesien, hat der Staat auf Grund des Grundgesetzes (Verfassung) das Recht zum Eingreifen, wo die öffentliche Ordnung gefährdet ist. Das war im Umfeld der genannten Synode zweifellos der Fall, und insofern hätte es auch keiner Einladung der einen oder anderen Seite zum Eingreifen bedurft, um ein solches zu rechtfertigen. Dieses Recht des Staates ist aber an Bedingungen gebunden, vor allem die, dass sich der Staat beiden Parteien gegenüber absolut neutral verhält, denn nur so ist er als Ordnungshüter glaubwürdig, akzeptabel und effektiv. Das war, wie gesehen, nicht der Fall. Damit hat sich der Staat bzw. haben sich die staatlichen Organe selbst der Legitimation ihres Eingreifens beraubt. Wo jedoch die Ausübung der Macht ohne Legitimation und in Verfolgung parteilicher Interessen geschieht, folgt daraus die zügellose Gewalt. Diese bestimmte dann den Alltag der HKBP in den kommenden Jahren.

Somit stellt sich nun die Frage, aus welchen Gründen der indonesische Staat einerseits die Wiederwahl Dr. Nababans auf jeden Fall verhindern wollte und andererseits an einer Machtposition Dr. Siahaans innerhalb der Leitung der HKBP interessiert war. Die Gegnerschaft der Regierung zu Nababan lässt sich jedenfalls nicht vorwiegend mit einer grundsätzlich oppositionellen Haltung gegenüber der Regierung während seiner Zeit als Ephorus erklären, obwohl er damit duchaus im Trend der Zeit gelegen hätte. Vielmehr prägte er dem Kirchenvolk fünf Leitlinien ein: 1. Respektiert die Regierung. 2. Folgt den Gesetzen und den hilfreichen Verordnungen. 3. Bezahlt regelmässig eure Steuern. 4. Helft Ruhe und Ordnung aufrechtzuerhalten. 5. Schliesst die Regierung in euer Fürbittengebet ein. Die massive Gegnerschaft der Regierung – und vor allem die des Präsidenten – muss also (auch) andere Gründe gehabt haben. Diese Frage kann nur vor dem Hintergrund länger zurückliegender Spannungen und der sich seit dem Ende der 1980er-Jahre abzeichnenden ideologischen Kursänderung und dem damit veränderten Regierungsstil Suhartos beantwortet werden. Das zu analysieren würde diesen Beitrag sprengen. Ich beschränke mich auf die für die HKBP-Krise wichtigen Aspekte und konzentriere mich auf die Rollen der Kontrahenten, insbesondere also die von Dr. Nababan und Dr. Siahaan, und beginne mit Letzterem, wobei ein kurzer Ausflug in die unmittelbare Zeitgeschichte unvermeidlich ist.

Suharto und die Religion
Der Ausbau und die Sicherung seines Wirtschaftsimperiums, das er auch in Bereichen staatlichen Eigentums korruptiv und zielstrebig verfolgte, und

74

die stets massiver werdende monopolisierende Machtpolitik hatten gegen Ende der 1980er-Jahre zu einer Entfremdung zwischen Präsident Suharto und den ihn bis dahin stützenden Militärs sowie den mit ihnen kooperierenden Think-Tanks der Wirtschaftsstrategen geführt. Ihre weltanschauliche Orientierung fanden die meisten von ihnen, mehr oder weniger und auch dann, wenn sie als Muslime registriert waren, in der javanischen Mystik, und von daher waren sie strikt gegen jegliche Ambitionen muslimischer Politiker, die in der *Republik Indonesia* einen stärkeren Einfluss der islamischen Shari'a[15] verfolgten. Intellektuelle, die diesen Ambitionen nahestanden oder einen solchen Eindruck erweckten, wurden marginalisiert. Deshalb begannen diese, seit Mitte der 1980er-Jahre über die Gründung einer eigenen Interessenvertretung nachzudenken, nämlich über einen «Verband muslimischer Intellektueller in Indonesien» (ICMI)[16].

Die Gründung des ICMI war seitens seiner Initiatoren wiederholt versucht, aber stets von der Regierung und besonders den Sicherheitsorganen untersagt worden. Die alte Aversion gegen alles, was sich nicht deutlich gegen die Vorstellung eines «Islam-Staates» abgrenzte, gab auch hier den Ausschlag für diese Haltung.[17] Die Entfremdung zu Militär und Think-Tanks (CSIS) veranlasste Suharto gegen Ende der 1980er-Jahre jedoch zu einer ideologischen Umorientierung, indem er versuchte, die bisher marginalisierten muslimischen Intellektuellen an sich zu binden. Auch im ICMI würde sich eine Reihe gut ausgebildeter Fachleute auf allen für die wirtschaftliche Entwicklung nötigen Fachgebieten finden lassen, auf deren Unterstützung sich Suharto verlassen könnte, insofern er ihnen attraktive Beschäftigung anbiete, die ihnen bisher wegen ihrer religiös-ideologischen Orientierung versagt worden war. Um nicht wieder eine Ablehnung des Gesuchs um Zulassung zu riskieren, entschlossen sich die

---

[15] *Shari'a:* siehe Anmerkung 7.

[16] *Ikatan Cendekiawan Muslimin Indonesia* (Verband muslimischer Inellektueller in Indonesien), abgekürzt ICMI. Vgl. Douglas E. Ramage, *Politics in Indonesia. Democracy, Islam and the Ideology of Tolerance,* London & New York, Routledge, 1997 (paperback), 75 ff.; Olaf Schumann, Zur politischen Dimension von Konvivenz. Die Debatte um das Verhältnis von Staat und Gesellschaft in Indonesien, a. a. O., bes. 203 ff.

[17] D. E. Ramage, *Politics in Indonesia, op. cit.,* 122 ff.

Veranstalter der für Dezember 1990 vorgesehenen Gründungsversammlung, Dr. B.J. Habibie als Redner einzuladen. Dr. B.J. Habibie war Minister für Forschung und Technologie und ein alter Vertrauter der Familie Suharto. Sein Ingenieurstudium hatte er in Deutschland absolviert und sich anschliessend bei MBB (Messerschmitt-Bölkow-Blohm – Rüstungskonzern) in Bayern umfassende Kenntnisse auf wehr- und flugtechnischem Gebiet erworben. Diese konnte er in Bandung u.a. durch Gründung einer eigenen Flugzeugfabrik und in Serpong bei Jakarta durch die Errichtung eines weitgefächerten technischen Instituts in die Praxis umsetzen. Weitgehende Unterstützung erhielt er aus Deutschland. – Nachdem ihm das Anliegen vorgetragen worden war, auf der geplanten Gründungsversammlung in Malang als Redner aufzutreten, beriet Habibie sich mit dem Präsidenten und bat um dessen Zustimmung. Diese erhielt er unter der Bedingung, dass dafür zu sorgen sei, dass Habibie auf dem Kongress als Vorsitzender der neuen Organisation gewählt werde.

So geschah es. Allerdings weigerten sich nach diesem Lauf der Dinge einige der führenden Intellektuellen, dem ICMI beizutreten. Sie befürchteten u.a., dass der ICMI unter diesen Voraussetzungen die Erwartungen der muslimischen Intellektuellen nicht erfüllen könne, sondern zu einem von Suharto genutzten Instrument für seine Politik missbraucht werden könnte.[18] In Erwartung, dass das im ICMI sich ansammelnde intellektuelle, wissenschaftliche und technologische Potenzial, gestärkt durch eine – allerdings von Dr. Habibie als Vorsitzendem zu überwachende und zu dirigierende – massive ideologische Orientierung, sich alsbald zu einem zu beachtenden Machtfaktor entwickeln werde, erhielt es vom Staat erhebliche Subventionen. Allerdings waren, um offene Konflikte mit dem Militär zu vermeiden, strikt die ideologischen Sprachregeln einzuhalten. Das galt insbesondere auch für das 1985 verabschiedete Gesetz, nach dem alle gesellschaftlichen Organisationen in ihren öffentlichen, nationalen und gesellschaftlichen Tätigkeiten die Pancasila als einzige Grundlage (*satu-satunya asas*) anzuerkennen hatten. Gemeint war damit zwar nicht die Pancasila

---

[18] Muhammad Abrar, *ICMI dan Harapan Umat (ICMI und die Hoffnung der islamischen Gemeinschaft)*, Jakarta, Grafiti Pers 1991.

von 1945, sondern ihre im *Leitfaden zur Belebung und Ausführung der Pancasila (Pedoman Penghayatan dan Pengamalan Pancasila,* meist abgek. P-4) von der Regierung festgelegte Interpretation, die 1978 vom Volkskongress in Gesetzesrang erhoben worden war.[19] Diese Interpretation der Pancasila wurde dann die Grundlage des Gesetzes von 1985. Unter diesem Schirm gelang es jedoch politisch orientierten Mitgliedern des ICMI, sowohl die Gesetzgebung als auch die gesellschaftliche Entwicklung mit islamistischen Zielvorstellungen zu durchsetzen. Damit konnten sie ausserdem in einigen Spezialeinheiten des Militärs, die Suharto nahestanden, eine starke Gruppe von Sympathisanten sammeln, die Suharto bei Sonderaufgaben zur Verfügung standen und nach Suhartos Abgang 1998 insbesondere in Ost-Indonesien in den dort um etwa 2000 ausbrechenden regionalen Konflikten die islamistischen Kämpfer unterstützten.

Reaktionen auf Suhartos Kursänderung

Diese unter der Pancasila-Rhetorik verborgene Strategie veranlasste moderate Muslime wie Abdurrahman Wahid, den Leiter der grössten islamischen Organisation in Indonesien, der traditionsorientierten «Nahdlatul Ulama» (NU), jegliche Mitarbeit im ICMI zu verweigern. Seitdem sich die NU unter seiner Leitung 1982 aus der aktiven Politik zurückgezogen und zu einer «sozialen Organisation» reformiert hatte, war es sein Ziel, den Islam in Indonesien zu entpolitisieren und ihn als soziale Kraft für die Besserung der sozialen Verhältnisse einzusetzen und die islamische Gemeinschaft für zivilgesellschaftliche Verhaltensweisen zu öffnen. Durch die massive Ausnutzung des ICMI seitens der Regierung Suharto für deren politische Ziele befürchtete er, dass der ICMI in die Rolle der alten, offiziell geächteten islamischen Partei «Masyumi»[20] hineinwachsen könnte.[21] Als

---

[19] Vgl. dazu die in Anm. 5 genannten Arbeiten von I. Wandelt und O. Schumann.

[20] *Masyumi: Majelis Syuro Muslimin Indonesia,* «Rat der Muslime Indonesiens». Ursprünglich von den Japanern 1943 gegründete islamische Dachorganisation, nach Kriegsende im November 1945 neu gegründet als «Islamische Einheitspartei». 1947 Austritt der «Partai Serikat Islam», 1952 Austritt der NU. Erstrebte die Errichtung eines «Islam-Staates». 1960 von Sukarno verboten.

[21] Adam Schwarz, *A Nation in Waiting. Indonesia in the 1990s,* St. Leonards (Australien), Allen & Unwin 1994, 187.

Antwort auf den ICMI, aber auch auf andere von der Regierung bzw. militärischen Sondereinheiten Ende 1990 gesteuerte Gewaltaktionen seitens radikaler islamischer Gruppen gründete er, zusammen mit Freunden aus unterschiedlichen gesellschaftlichen und religiösen Lagern, im März 1991 das «Forum Demokrasi», ein Diskussionsforum, in dem die ursprünglich 45 Teilnehmenden fast wie in einem nichtgewählten Scheinparlament über die anstehenden Fragen der aktuellen Politik in demokratischer Weise diskutierten.[22] Dieser Schritt trug ihm den langanhaltenden Zorn Suhartos, aber auch den des Militärs ein. Suharto verübelte ihm vor allem die Gegnerschaft zum ICMI, denn als muslimischer Intellektueller müsse er doch ein besonderes Interesse an dieser Organisation haben. Bitter war für Suharto insbesondere, dass es ihm durch Wahids Fernbleiben nicht möglich war, Sympathien aus dessen grosser Anhängerschaft unter den Muslimen auf sich zu ziehen. Während beim Militär und beim CSIS Wahids Haltung gegenüber dem ICMI begrüsst wurde, waren sie sich mit Suharto einig in ihrer Kritik an Wahids Eintreten für die Stärkung zivilgesellschaftlicher Verhältnisse, wie sie den Gründungsvätern und -müttern der Republik 1945 vorgeschwebt hatten, indem sie sich nicht nur am ersten Prinzip der Pancasila orientierten, sondern alle fünf Prinzipien in einem engen Beziehungsgeflecht einander zugeordnet sahen. Ihnen fühlte sich Wahid als Sohn eines alten Mitkämpfers von Sukarno, Wahid Hasyim, besonders verpflichtet. Solche «westlichen» Konzepte, die auf eine «liberale Demokratie» hinausliefen, galten schon für Sukarno, besonders jedoch nun für Suharto und das Militär als unvereinbar mit der von der Suharto-Regierung propagierten Pancasila-Demokratie. Diese antidemokratische, den integralen Staat favorisierende Koalition zwischen Militär und Präsident (gleichgültig um welchen es sich handelt) hatte bereits die Konstituante gelähmt. Unterstützt durch das «Grundgesetz» von 1945, favorisierte die Pancasila-Demokratie eine stramm geführte Präsidialdemokratie, in der das gewählte Parlament, ähnlich wie der allerdings nicht gewählte «Volksraad» während der Kolonialzeit, lediglich eine beratende Funktion hatte. Alarmierend für Präsident und Militär war die sich seit den späten 1970er-Jahren ausbrei-

---

[22] Douglas E. Ramage, *op. cit.*, 157 ff.; Adam Schwarz, *op. cit.*, 190 ff.

tende Sympathie der Intellektuellen nahezu aller religiöser Richtungen und der Studierenden für die «Theologie der Befreiung». Sie fand ihren Widerhall auch in Programmen im Bereich einer zivilgesellschaftlich orientierten Bewusstseinsbildung, die von NGOs[23], oft in Zusammenarbeit mit religiös geprägten regionalen Organisationen, durchgeführt wurden. Hier waren vor allem die NU und die katholische Kirche besonders aktiv.

Zivilrechtliche Ansprüche allerdings waren das Letzte, was die Staatsführung hätte brauchen können. So wurde die «Theologie der Befreiung», und das war ja nicht schwer, als marxistisch inspiriert und subersiv eingestuft, und die Beschuldigung, mit ihr zu sympathisieren, konnte für die beschuldigte Person gravierende Folgen haben. An diesem Punkte, nämlich der Durchsetzung demokratischer Prinzipien, sollte sich später während der Präsidentschaft von Abdurrahman Wahid der Machtkampf zwischen ihm, dem damals zum ersten Male frei gewählten Präsidenten, und dem Militär entzünden, den das Militär dank der Unterstützung durch die US-amerikanische Diplomatie gewann. Von seinem islamisch geprägten sozialethischen Ansatz her, aber auch auf Grund der weitverbreiteten Armut der vorwiegend dörflichen Anhängerschaft der NU hatte er sich intensiv an den Diskussionen mit anderen Sympathisanten der «Theologie der Befreiung» beteiligt.

Zunächst jedoch, seit Beginn der 1990er-Jahre, wurden als Antwort auf A. Wahids Unbotmässigkeit in der Folgezeit auf Java, besonders in Ost-Java, der Hochburg der NU und damit der Anhängerschaft A. Wahids, zahlreiche vandalistische Aktionen mit Todesopfern gegen Christen und Chinesen inszeniert, die der muslimischen Nachbarschaft, zumeist also NU-Sympathisanten oder Mitgliedern, angelastet wurden, obwohl der An- und Abtransport der Akteure auf Militärwagen vor den Augen der Öffentlichkeit geschah. Damit sollte der Nimbus A. Wahids, als Vorkämpfer für interreligiöse Kooperation und *convivencia* einzutreten, mit dem Hinweis zerstört werden, dass ihm «offensichtlich» dieses Programm nicht einmal in der eigenen Gefolgschaft gelänge. Viele Indonesier und vor allem Ausländer glaubten diese offizielle Version der Ausschreitungen.

---

[23] *Non-governmental organizations.*

Auch Dr. B. J. Habibie propagierte eine – wenn auch eigentümliche – Art von Demokratie, nämlich eine «proportionale» Demokratie, die er mit der von Suharto propagierten Pancasila-Demokratie identifizierte.[24] Ihr zufolge sollten alle staatlichen Behörden und Institutionen, aber auch das Parlament entsprechend dem Religionsproporz, der anhand von Volkszählungen festgestellt werden sollte, besetzt werden. Und die Parteien wurden angehalten, mit Hilfe des ICMI ihre Wahlkandidaten entsprechend dem Proporz aufzustellen. Dieses Prozedere kam nicht den Muslimen allgemein, sondern insbesondere den regierungstreuen zugute.

Mit Hilfe des ICMI, der innerhalb kurzer Zeit Zweigstellen in verschiedenen Zentren der Republik gründen konnte, gelang es Habibie, einen Kontrollapparat aufzubauen, der insbesondere die politischen, aber auch die gesellschaftlichen Organisationen hinsichtlich ihrer Pancasila-Treue «beriet» und beeinflusste und sie, etwa bei der bereits genannten Vorbereitung auf die Parlamentswahlen von 1992, vor allem zur Einhaltung des Religionsproporzes bei der Besetzung von Dienststellen anhielt. Nichtmuslimische Fachleute verloren auf diese Weise ihre Arbeitsplätze und wurden durch ICMI-treue Dilettanten ersetzt. In bis dahin während der Suharto-Ära noch nicht gekanntem Ausmasse waren diese Wahlen im Vorfeld, angefangen mit der vorher bereits durchgeführten Aussortierung von der Regierung nicht genehmen Kandidaten und Kandidatinnen, durch Eingriffe der Regierung manipuliert worden. Dem Eindruck, dass diese Wahl verhältnismässig ruhig und geordnet verlief[25], waren also erhebliche Vorarbeiten vorangegangen. Deshalb konnten sich dann am Wahltag die Wähler relativ ungetrübt auf die übriggebliebenen Kandidaten konzentrieren.

Entscheidend für die Regierungsorgane, in die innere Verfasstheit der HKBP einzudringen, war offensichtlich die Bekanntschaft von Dr. B. J. Habibie und Dr. S. N. Siahaan. Seit ihren gemeinsamen Studienzeiten in Deutschland waren beide miteinander gut bekannt; manche meinten, sie

[24] D. E. Ramage, *op. cit.*, 98 ff.
[25] D. Becker, *op. cit.*, 133, Anm. 7. Dabei ist es allerdings erstaunlich, dass sich die erwähnten Beobachter offensichtlich keine Mühe gemacht hatten, die Hintergründe dafür zu erkunden, warum diese Wahlen so «ruhig» verliefen; zumindest findet sich bei Becker kein Hinweis darauf.

seien befreundet. Auf jeden Fall klärt diese Bekanntschaft nicht nur die Frage, wieso die in Aktion tretenden Regierungs- und Machtorgane recht gut über die internen Verhältnisse in der HKBP unterrichtet waren, sondern sie macht auch deutlich, in welchem politischen Rahmen und mit welchem politischen Ziel der Eingriff der Regierung in die Angelegenheiten der HKBP zu verstehen ist. Es galt, eine widerspenstige Organisation zu disziplinieren und in ihre Führung einen Personenkreis zu befördern, der verlässlich und möglichst vertraut ist. Ähnliche Erfahrungen machten damals auch die NU unter A. Wahid und sogar eine politische Partei, die von der Tochter des ersten Präsidenten der Republik, Megawati Sukarnoputri, geleitete «Partai Demokrasi Indonesia», deren Wiederwahl als Parteivorsitzende auf einem Kongress in Medan verhindert wurde; die Folge war eine Spaltung der Partei. In der NU gelang es, auf deren Wahlkongress eine formale Spaltung zu verhindern und sich, zur Enttäuschung der Regierung, aber im Interesse ihrer Organisation, in letzter Minute auf einen Kompromiss zu einigen.

Die Disziplinierung politischer Gegner

Eine solche Lösung gelang der HKBP nicht. Habibies Auftrag, rebellische Organisationen zu disziplinieren und die Verantwortlichen zu entmachten, führte in diesem Falle zum Erfolg. Eine Verlängerung der Amtszeit von Dr. Nababan als Ephorus wurde erfolgreich, wenn auch verfassungswidrig, verhindert. Die folgenden Spannungen in dieser Organisation, also der HKBP, schwächte sie zusätzlich. Die Identität der für die verschärfende Agitation verantwortlichen, von aussen kommenden Elemente, in deren Kalkül eine formale Spaltung der Kirche durchaus eingeplant war, ist nie eindeutig zu klären gewesen. Allerdings ist es ebenfalls eine offene Frage, wie tief die Bereitschaft zu einer Spaltung in beiden Gruppen innerhalb der HKBP selbst reichte. Besonnene kirchliche Persönlichkeiten auf beiden Seiten vermieden es, von einer Spaltung zu reden. Diese Zurückhaltung hat die sofort nach Suhartos Fall im Mai 1998 einsetzenden Bemühungen um Versöhnung erheblich erleichtert.

Bei der Vereitelung der Wiederwahl Nababans zu helfen, war offensichtlich Dr. Siahaan bereit. Er hatte in Hamburg im Fachgebiet «Altes

Testament» promoviert und vertrat theologisch eine Richtung, die das Evangelium nicht als grundsätzliche Kritik an der Adat verstand, sondern gewissermassen die Adat weiterführte, wodurch den Batakern ihr in der Adat wurzelndes Identitätsgefühl erhalten bleiben konnte. Diese Einstellung gegenüber dem kulturellen und weltanschaulichen Erbe war durchaus verwandt mit Suhartos Verwurzelung im *kebatinan*. Sie unterschied sich grundlegend von der theologischen Orientierung Nababans, der bei Günter Bornkamm in Heidelberg promoviert hatte und damit auch mit den Anliegen einer sozialkritischen Exegese des Evangeliums vertraut war. Was veranlasste nun die Regierung zu ihrer kompromisslosen Haltung gegenüber Nababan?

Die Christen als «positive, kreative, kritische und realistische» Partner der Regierung?

Nababan hatte sich auch nach seiner Rückkehr aus Deutschland Anfang der 1960er-Jahre, also noch in der Sukarno-Ära, als leitende Figur in der indonesischen christlichen Studentenbewegung als Exponent einer (damals) jüngeren progressiven und den sozialen wie nationalen Fragen offen und kritisch zugewandten Generation von Theologen hervorgetan. 1967 wurde er zum Generalsekretär des *Rates der Kirchen in Indonesien* (DGI) gewählt.[26] Auf Grund seines energischen Temperaments wurde der DGI rasch zu einer effektiven Organisation umgestaltet, deren Aktionsprogramme nicht nur auf wortreichen Sitzungen beschlossen, sondern hinterher auch in die Tat umgesetzt wurden. Das gefiel nicht allen und brachte ihm schon damals eine Reihe von Gegnern ein, zumeist stillen, doch auch einigen ausgesprochenen. Unterstützt wurde er u. a. vom damaligen Ehrenpräsidenten des DGI, Dr. Johannes Leimena, von Beruf Arzt und vor 1965 öfters Minister in Kabinetten von Präsident Sukarno sowie gelegentlich dessen Vertreter als amtierender Staatspräsident, wenn Sukarno auf Auslandsreisen war; auch unter den Vertretern des politischen Islam er-

---

[26] *Dewan Gereja-gereja di Indonesia* (DGI), seit 1984 «Gemeinschaft der Kirchen in Indonesien» (*Persekutuan Gereja-gereja di Indonesia*, PGI). Der DGI wurde 1950 von 28 damals selbständigen protestantischen indonesischen Kirchen gegründet. Inzwischen hat die PGI 84 protestantische Mitgliedskirchen.

freute er sich auf Grund seiner Unbestechlichkeit und Humanität hohen Ansehens.

Neben anderen Führungspersönlichkeiten im DGI war es vor allem einer von deren Vorsitzenden, General a. D. T. B. Simatupang, ebenfalls ein Bataker, der mit Nababan eng kooperierte. Er gehörte allerdings nicht der HKBP an, sondern der «Christlichen indonesischen Kirche in West-Jawa», einer Kirche mit vorwiegend ethnisch-chinesischem Hintergrund. Seine militärische Ausbildung begann noch unter den Niederländern, später, nach 1945, beteiligte er sich an den Guerillakämpfen gegen die Niederländer, wurde Stellvertreter des Nationalhelden General Sudirman. Nach der Anerkennung der Unabhängigkeit Indonesiens durch die ehemalige Kolonialmacht im Dezember 1949 ernannte ihn Präsident Sukarno 1950, mit 30 Jahren, zum ersten Chef des Generalstabs. Sein Ziel und das seiner damaligen Kollegen war es, das indonesische Militär als eine professionelle Streitmacht aufzubauen, die – zwar der Pancasila verpflichtet, denn im Militär dienten Mitglieder aller gesellschaftlichen Gruppen – keine eigene Politik betreibt und innerhalb der zivilen Struktur des Staates ihren Platz hat. Schon 1952 wurde er vom Präsidenten «kaltgestellt». Mit 39 Jahren wurde er wegen tiefgehender Meinungsverschiedenheiten mit Sukarno über die politische Rolle des Militärs pensioniert und ein Jahr später, 1960, zu einem der drei Präsidenten des DGI gewählt.[27] Auch er forderte ein grösseres Engagement der Kirchen in gesellschaftlichen Fragen. Seine intellektuelle Bildung erhielt er von drei deutschsprachigen «Karls» (die er in der Originalsprache las): Carl von Clausewitz, Karl Marx und Karl Barth. Bereits 1962 fand unter seiner Leitung die erste vom DGI veranstaltete *Konferenz über Kirche und Gesellschaft* statt – Vorbild für die 1966 vom Ökumenischen Rat der Kirchen (ÖRK) einberufene Konferenz gleichen Titels und erste in einer Reihe gleichnamiger Konferenzen, die vom DGI turnusmässig etwa alle fünf Jahre abgehalten wurden.

---

[27] Tahi Bonar Simatupang, *Gelebte Theologie in Indonesien. Zur gesellschaftlichen Verantwortung der Christen,* hg. von Olaf Schumann und Heinz-J. Fischer, Göttingen, Vandenhoeck & Ruprecht, 1992. In diesem Buch finden sich eine ausführliche Selbstbiografie sowie ein Geleitwort von S. A. E. Nababan.

Mit dem Sturz Sukarnos, eingeleitet im Oktober 1965 und vollzogen im März 1967 mit der Ernennung Suhartos zum neuen Präsidenten, veränderte sich das politische Klima, auch für die Kirchen. Das revolutionäre Pathos, auf der Grundlage der Pancasila als Weltanschauung die Indonesier zu einer solidarischen Nation zusammenzuführen, wich nun dem neuen Paradigma der «neuen Ordnung» unter General Suharto (seit 1967 Präsident), den Pancasila-Staat aufzubauen bzw. zu entwickeln. Diese Aufgabe wurde innerhalb der protestantischen Kirchen hauptsächlich von den mit sozialen Aufgaben betreuten Abteilungen des DGI übernommen und koordiniert und prägte ihre Programme einschliesslich die Themen der kommenden «Konferenzen für Kirche und Gesellschaft»: In verschiedenen Variationen wurden immer wieder sowohl die «Teilnahme (*partisipasi*) der Christen am Aufbau des Pancasila-Staates» als auch ihre vom Evangelium her gegebene Verpflichtung dazu (*tugas*) betont. Damit wollte die DGI-Leitung ihre Unterstützung und Solidarität mit der Regierung und ihren Programmen unterstreichen. Damals allerdings war noch kaum deutlich, dass Suharto für seine Aufbaupläne keine «Partner», sondern Technokraten brauchte, dass Partner insofern unbeliebt waren, weil sie sich auch Fragen der Aufbauziele und ihrer Methoden, insbesondere der in Indonesien stets virulenten Frage des Umgangs mit der Armut und den Armen (vgl. 5. Prinzip der Pancasila: soziale Gerechtigkeit für das ganze indonesische Volk), annehmen könnten, und in dieser Hinsicht duldete Suharto keine Meinung ausser seiner eigenen. Die gutgemeinte, aber wohl doch etwas zu naive Vorstellung einer «Partnerschaft» mit der Regierung wirkte eher anmassend. Allerdings drückt sie Simatupangs Verständnis dafür aus, unter welchen Umständen christliche Teilnahme am wirtschaftlichen und gesellschaftlichen Aufbau überhaupt sinnvoll ist. Eine gängige Formel, die auch später bei ihm immer wieder auftauchte und auch von anderen übernommen wurde, hatte er bereits 1962 in seiner Rede auf der damaligen Konferenz für Kiche und Gesellschaft geprägt: Im Lichte des Evangeliums von der Königsherrschaft Gottes hat die Kirche positiv, kreativ, kritisch und realistisch denkend ihren Beitrag zu leisten.[28]

[28] T. B. Simatupang, *op. cit.*, 22.

Mission und Diakonie als Ärgernis

Daneben wird im Nachhinein beim Betrachten dieser Erklärungen noch etwas anderes deutlich, woran Suharto möglicherweise damals schon Anstoss nahm. Im Anschluss an die politische Diktion, die von Indonesien als «Einheitsstaat» sprach, nämlich geeint durch die Pancasila (im Gegensatz zu allen föderativen Varianten), betonten die Kirchen, dass auch sie ihre Entwicklungsprogramme aus ihrer Vision von Indonesien als «einem Missionsfeld» im Rahmen der von der DGI-Verfassung angestrebten «einen Christlichen Kirche in Indonesien» konzipierten. Damit wollten sie vor allem der Eigenbrötelei der vielen Regionalkirchen entgegenwirken. Aus nichtchristlicher Perspektive konnte hinter dieser Version jedoch ein Generalplan zur «Christianisierung» Indonesiens vermutet werden, in den die Entwicklungsaktivitäten der Kirche(n) integriert werden sollten. Diese Thematik prägte die 7. Vollversammlung des DGI in Pematang Siantar 1971, und sie fand ihre Fortsetzung in den bald darauf einsetzenden Auseinandersetzungen um den Plan des Ökumenischen Rates der Kirchen, seine nächste Vollversammlung 1974 in Jakarta abzuhalten. Um den christlichen Gemeinden den ÖRK bekannt zu machen, verfasste T. B. Simatupang die kleine Broschüre *Von Edinburgh nach Jakarta,* in der er auf die «Geburtsstunde» der ökumenischen Bewegung auf der Weltmissionskonferenz in Edinburgh 1910 und die daran anschliessenden drei Bewegungen «Praktisches Christentum» *(Life and Work),* «Glaube und Kirchenverfassung» *(Faith and Order)* und die im «Internationalen Missionsrat» *(International Missionary Council,* IMC) zuammengefasste internationale Missionsbewegung, die Gründung des ÖRK 1948 in Amsterdam und den (verspäteten) Eintritt des IMC auf der Vollversammlung des ÖRK in New Delhi 1961 einging. Diese Schrift nahm der inzwischen auch durch andere Streitschriften bekannt gewordene Professor für islamisches Recht an der «Universitas Indonesia» (Jakarta), Dr. H. M. Rasjidi, zum Anlass, in einer Gegenschrift die islamische Gemeinschaft vor dem bevorstehenden Generalangriff auf ihre Integrität zu warnen. Während der daraufhin entstehenden zunehmend gewalttätigeren Konflikte, in deren Verlauf auch ein anglikanischer Priester auf dem Komplex der im Zentrum Jakartas gelegenen anglikanischen Kirche ermordet wurde, wurde deutlich, dass die geplante Vollversammlung nur unter umfassenden Sicherheitsmassnahmen werde stattfinden können. Nach Gesprächen, die Simatupang mit einigen führenden Muslimen und auch mit Präsident Suharto führte, wurde ihm klar, dass es besser sei, den ÖRK zur Verlegung der Vollversammlung an einen anderen Ort zu bitten[29]; sie fand schliesslich 1975 in Nairobi, Kenia, statt. Allerdings ist festzuhalten, dass während der ganzen Auseinandersetzungen Suharto stets seine Bereitschaft unterstrich, zur Sicherheit der Vollversammlung den staatlichen Sicherheitsapparat voll einzusetzen. Dafür wurde ihm seitens des DGI, aber auch seitens des ÖRK, gebührend gedankt, doch erschien den Kirchenvertretern eine kirchliche Versammlung unter Militärschutz doch etwas unangemessen.

Was das Thema «Mission» betraf, so betonte Suharto bei einer späteren Gelegenheit, bei der er auf das Gespräch mit Simatupang und die Affäre um die Vollversammlung des ÖRK zu sprechen kam, die bereits mehrfach seitens der Regierung vorgetragene und von den Muslimen – insofern sie sich dazu äusserten – unterstützte Meinung, dass unter Menschen, die bereits einer Religion folgen, keine religiöse Propaganda zur Abwerbung betrieben werden sollte. Dieses Anliegen war allerdings bereits auf der allerersten von der Regierung Suharto einberufenen «interreligiösen Zusammenkunft» 1967 angesprochen und von den Christen abgelehnt worden mit der Begründung, dass die öffentliche Erklärung des Glaubens zu den menschlichen Grundrechten gehöre und von niemandem eingeschränkt werden dürfe. Ausserdem verlange niemand von den Muslimen, dass sie ihre Da'wa[30] unter Christen einstellen. Somit galt diese Zusammenkunft als gescheitert, wofür die Christen, und vor allem Simatupang als einer ihrer Wortführer, die Verantwortung trügen. Als Folge davon wurde damals die islamische Da'wa intensiviert und von einem zentralen Organ koordiniert. Die Entscheidung, die Vollversammlung des ÖRK zu verlegen, entspannte zweifellos vorübergehend das Verhältnis

---

[29] Siehe Mujiburrahman, *op. cit.*, 65 f. (Anmerkung 8).

[30] *Da'wa* (arabisch): Ruf, Einladung, eine im Islam übliche Methode, durch Erziehung und Vermittlung von Bildung für den Islam zu werben und zu seiner Annahme «einzuladen», gelegentlich mit christlicher Mission verglichen.

zwischen Regierung einerseits und protestantischen Kirchen – und desgleichen zur katholischen Kirche – andererseits.

Doch blieb das Thema «*Mission und Da'wa*» in Indonesien auch weiterhin aktuell. Im Juni 1976 lud das Redaktionskomitee der vom ÖRK herausgegebenen *International Review of Mission (IRM)* zu einer Tagung über «*Mission and Da'wa*» nach Chambésy ein, an der aus Indonesien Prof. Dr. H. M. Rasjidi und Prof. Ihromi, Alttestamentler an der Theologischen Hochschule in Jakarta und Schwager T. B. Simatupangs, teilnahmen.[31] Rasjidis heftige Kritik an jeglicher Art von christlicher Diakonie als hinterhältiges Mittel zur Ausbreitung der christlichen Religion wurde von dem norwegischen lutherischen Bischof Rudvin als Aufruf zu innerer Einkehr aufgenommen, und damit unterstützte er die in der Schlusserklärung gemachte Forderung, jegliche Diakonie einzustellen oder, um ihre Ziele durchsichtig zu machen, die vom Ausland in die überseeischen Partnerkirchen geschleusten Finanzmittel durch staatliche Dienststellen – in Indonesien etwa durch das Religionsministerium – zu kanalisieren und damit einer gewissen staatlichen Aufsicht zu unterordnen. Auf den Text dieser Schlusserklärung wurde bereits in der Rede Bezug genommen, die Präsident Suharto eine Woche später auf der Vollversammlung des DGI in Salatiga, Mittel-Java, hielt. In ihr konnte man eine Kritik des Präsidenten an den DGI-Kirchen heraushören, die in ihrer Weigerung, ihre Hilfsgelder über regierungsamtliche Stellen fliessen zu lassen, und ihre Diakonie nach wie vor in eigener Regie betrieben und sie als Teil ihrer Mission verständen, in ihrem Missionsverständnis hinter den anderen Kirchen in der Ökumene zurückgeblieben seien. Nach Neuwahlen des Parlaments 1977 erliess der neue Religionsminister, auch ein pensionierter General und Vertrauter Suhartos, jedoch mit deutlichen Sympathien für islampolitische Ansichten, zwei ministerielle Erlasse, in denen Missionsaktivitäten, vor allem solchen in ökumenischer Zusammenarbeit mit internationalen Partnern, strikte Auflagen erteilt wurden und verordnet wurde, dass alle Hilfsgelder über Regierungsstellen fliessen müssten. Generell sei der Ein-

---

[31] Die auf dieser Tagung gehaltenen Vorträge, Diskussionsprotokolle und die Schlusserklärung finden sich in Nr. 260 (Okt. 1976) der *International Review of Mission*.

fluss des Auslandes so weit wie möglich einzustellen. Umgehend erklärten DGI und MAWI[32] ihren Protest und wiesen sie als unvereinbar mit dem unaufhebbaren und auch durch die Pancasila bestätigten Recht auf freie Religionsausübung zurück.[33]

Damit wurde deutlich, dass die Suharto-Regierung sich zunehmend dem Einfluss islamistischer Gruppen und deren antichristlicher Rhetorik öffnete. Sie mag befürchtet haben, dass sich im Gefolge der christlichen Missionspraxis das ohnehin labile Verhältnis zwischen Christen und Muslimen, die dort, wo nicht Adat-Bindungen (z. B. Familie) noch ein eingeschränktes Zusammenleben fördern, mehr nebeneinanderher als miteinander leben, weiter verschlechtern könnte. Diese Befürchtung mochte ihre Gründe haben, als Begründung für regierungsamtliche Massnahmen wie die Erlasse des Religionsministers oder andere taugte sie aber so lange nicht, als die ebenfalls zunehmend aggressive islamische Da'wa unter Christen und anderen Nichtmuslimen nicht mit gleicher Aufmerksamkeit und gleichen Konsequenzen verfolgt wurde.

Rückblickend legt sich die Vermutung nahe, dass bereits zu diesem Zeitpunkt (1976/1977) Suhartos Umorientierung hin zu einer freundlicheren Haltung gegenüber radikaleren Gruppen im Islam stattfand. Die Ablösung von Dr. A. Mukti Ali, Hochschullehrer am Staatlichen Islam-Institut in Yogyakarta und auch in dialogisch orientierten Kreisen des ÖRK als Partner gut bekannt (Tagung in Ajaltoun, Libanon, 1970), durch General Alamsyah Ratu Prawiranegara als Religionsminister 1977 könnte darauf hinweisen. Solahuddin bemerkt, dass die christenfeindliche Haltung in West-Java – anders allerdings in Sulawesi – eine Spezialität des politischen, ursprünglich also nicht des militanten, d. h. des dem Darul-

---

[32] *Majelis Agung Waligereja Indonesia* – MAWI, Oberstes Gremium der (katholischen) Kirchenprovinz Indonesien.

[33] Mujiburrahman, *op. cit.*, 78 ff, 81 ff. In seiner sachlichen Analyse geht der Verfasser auch auf die Reaktionen aus dem Lager der Muslime ein. Ihm scheint sicher zu sein, dass die Dekrete des neuen (seit 1977) amtierenden Religionsministers, Alamsyah Ratu Prawiranegara, als eine der Bemühungen Suhartos zu bewerten sei, eine Versöhnung mit den islamischen Gruppen zu erreichen, vgl. S. 89.

Islam zuneigenden Flügels im Islam war.[34] Diese Einschätzung lässt sich dadurch stützen, dass in der Konstituante, der 1955 gewählten und 1959 von Sukarno aufgelösten «Verfassunggebenden Versammlung», die Masyumi[35] zusammen mit der christl.-protestantischen «Parkindo», der «Partai Katolik» und der «Partai Sosialis» sich nachdrücklich dafür einsetzte, in der zu erstellenden Verfassung die «parlamentarische Demokratie» mit einem Mehrparteiensystem festzuschreiben[36] und damit die Position des Präsidenten zu schwächen, zum Ärger Sukarnos.[37] Erst nach ihrem Verbot 1960, vor allem jedoch nach dem Machtwechsel von 1965 und der Einsicht, dass mit einer Wiederzulassung auch unter Suharto nicht zu rechnen war, verstärkten ihre Ex-Mitglieder ihre antichristliche Propaganda, die dann in der Mitte der 1970er-Jahre ihren ersten Höhepunkt erreichte und von den radikalen Gruppen aufgenommen, aber auch von Suharto mit zunehmender Wachsamkeit verfolgt wurde.

Desgleichen entging der Regierung nicht, dass die zunehmende innergesellschaftliche Kritik an der ins Uferlose sich ausweitenden Korruption und die Vernachlässigung des Faktors Armut und nicht vorhandene soziale Gerechtigkeit, die auch als Verstoss gegen die Pancasila thematisiert werden konnte, vom DGI mit offener Sympathie begleitet und unterstützt wurde. Schon nach den ersten massiven Zusammenstössen zwischen Suhartos Sicherheitsapparat und intellektuellen und anderen, sie unterstützenden Demonstranten, insbesondere Studierenden, im Januar 1974 wurde gemunkelt, dass Simatupang nur deshalb nicht mit anderen «Anführern» verhaftet wurde, weil sein Prestige in vorwiegend, aber keinesfalls ausschliesslich älteren Jahrgängen im Militär und in der Gesellschaft immer noch so gross sei, dass Suharto einen solchen Schritt nicht

---

[34] Solahuddin, *Dari NII sampai DI. Salafy Jihadisme di Indonesia* (Vom Islam-Staat Indonesien bis zum Darul-Islam. Salafitischer Jihadismus in Indonesien). Jakarta, Komunitas Bambu, 2011, S. 132.

[35] *Masyumi (alte Schreibweiwse: Masjumi): siehe oben Anm. 20.*

[36] Adnan Buyung Nasution, The Aspiration for Constitutional Government in Indonesia. A Socio-legal Study of the Indonesian Konstituante 1956–1959. Jakarta, Sinar Harapan 1992.

[37] Z.B. Bernhard, Dahm, *Sukarnos Kampf um Indonesiens Unabhängigkeit. Werdegang und Ideen eines asiatischen Nationalisten.* Frankfurt/Main-Berlin, Alfred Methner Verlag 1966, u. a. S. 244 ff.

wagte. Simatupang hatte sich in den vorangegangenen, vor allem in den Universitäten ausgetragenen Debatten und Diskussionen mit den Studierenden immer wieder sehr freimütig geäussert. Nach dem Ende der Demonstrationen und Suhartos Gegenschlag fragte er einmal in kleinem Kreise und innerlich zutiefst verwundet, ob es diese Republik sei, für die er und seine Generation bereit gewesen waren, ihr Leben als Guerillas gegen die zurückgekehrte Kolonialmacht zu opfern. Die Stimme der Jugend, die ihre Aspirationen über ihre Zukunft, wie sie selbst sie sich vorstellte, zu Gehör bringen wollte, verstummte weitgehend. Die Intellektuellen zogen sich in ihre Zirkel zurück, und Suharto war für einige Zeit damit beschäftigt, die bisher letzte messianische Bewegung, die sich auch noch gegen ihn persönlich gerichtet hatte, mit Stumpf und Stil auszurotten.[38]

Ein neues Verständnis der Pancasila

Ein neues Spannungsfeld tat sich nahezu gleichzeitig, nämlich 1978, auf, als der damals zusammentretende «Volkskongress»[39] den von der Regierung vorbereiteten (bereits erwähnten) *Leitfaden zur Belebung und Ausführung der Pancasila*[40] (P-4) zu Gesetzesrang erhöhte und später von der Regierung zunächst alle politischen, später (1985) auch alle gesellschaftlichen ein-

---

[38] Vgl. Olaf Schumann, Staat und Gesellschaft im heutigen Indonesien, zuerst erschienen in: *Die Welt des Islams 33 (1993), 182–218, wieder abgedruckt in: O. Schumann, Selbstverständnis und Fremdwahrnehmung. Religionsforschung im interreligiösen Kontext*, hg. von Klaus Hock, Münster, LIT, 1999, 100–130, hier 119ff.

[39] *Majelis Permusyawaratan Rakyat* – MPR, das nach der damals gültigen Verfassung ein Jahr nach allgemeinen Wahlen zusammentrat, um den Rechenschaftsbericht der alten Regierung zu hören und anzunehmen, dann die allgemeinen Richtlinien für die Regierungspolitik in der nun begonnenen Legislaturperiode festzulegen und einen neuen Präsidenten mit dem Auftrag zu wählen, für die Durchführung dieser Richtlinien zu sorgen. Er selbst bestimmte die Minister als seine «Gehilfen», und das gewählte Parlament (*Dewan Perwakilan Rakyat* – DPR) hatte lediglich Beratungsfunktion, ebenso wie der «*Volksraad*» in der kolonialen Vergangenheit. Mitglieder des MPR waren die gewählten Parlamentarier und eine etwa gleich grosse Anzahl von Vertretern aus den Provinzen und anderer Interessengruppen. Erst Abdurrahman Wahid verfügte als Präsident (1999–2001), dass das MPR einmal jährlich zusammentreten und über die von der Regierung geleistete Arbeit debattieren sollte.

[40] Siehe oben.

schliesslich der religiösen Organisationen per Gesetz zu einer Klausel in ihrer jeweiligen Verfassungsurkunde verpflichtet wurden, die Pancasila «als einziger Grund (*satu-satunya asas*) in ihrem gesellschaftlichen, nationalen und staatlichen Leben in Indonesien» anzuerkennen. Bevor das auch die Kirchen betreffende Gesetz 1985 erlassen wurde, entstand in den PGI-Kirchen eine heftige Debatte darüber, ob in einer kirchlichen Grundordnung ein solcher letztlich staatsrechtlicher Passus Aufnahme finden dürfte. Da nach 1 Kor 3,11 Jesus jedoch der «einzige Grund ist, auf dem die Kirche gebaut ist», wurde hier das Wort «*dasar*» gewählt, das nicht nur im indonesischen Bibeltext, sondern auch in der Verfassung des DGI steht. Beide Worte, *asas* und *dasar,* bedeuten dasselbe. Der Unterschied liegt lediglich darin, dass das Wort *asas* ursprünglich aus dem Arabischen stammt, während *dasar* malaiischen Ursprungs ist. Die Hoffnung, dass sich die Politik mit dieser etymologischen Spitzfindigkeit und einem «doppelten Grund» der Kirchen zufrieden gäbe, erfüllte sich nicht. In einem Gespräch, das Nababan als Generalsekretär des DGI mit dem Innen- und dem Religionsminister führte, fragte er diese, ob die Regierung verlange, dass die Christen den Vers 1 Kor 3,11 aus der Bibel zu entfernen hätten. Das auf keinen Fall, war die Antwort, aber man möge doch nach einem Ausweg suchen. So wurde dann im PGI beschlossen, dass in Paragraf 2 einer jeden Kirchenordnung 1 Kor 3,11 als Grund der Kirche festgeschrieben werde, und dann in einem zusätzlichen Paragrafen die Kirche als «christliche Organisation» «im Lichte von Paragraf 2» die Pancasila als Grundlage (*asas*) im «gesellschaftlichen, nationalen und staatlichen Leben» annehme. Diese Formulierung wurde schliesslich von der Regierung angenommen, aber die tiefe Abneigung Suhartos gegen die widerspenstigen Christen und besonders gegen Dr. Nababan als einer ihrer Wortführer blieb.

Aber auch viele Kirchenmitglieder fanden die Einmischung der Regierung als zu weit gehend. Vor allem fragten sich nicht wenige der älteren Kirchenglieder, warum jetzt dieses Theater um die Pancasila inszeniert werde. Seit Gründung der Republik standen sie alle hinter der Pancasila, verteidigten sie gegen innere und äussere Feinde und identifizierten sich mit ihr als Ausdruck ihrer nationalen Identität und Solidarität. Mit Ausnahme jener Gruppen, die sich schliesslich ausserhalb der Republik platzierten und gegen diese kämpften, wie die islamischen Darul-Islam-Gruppen oder die von Christen geleitete «Republik der Süd-Molukken», haben auch interne Gegner oder Kritiker nie die Pancasila-orientierte Grundlinie ihrer Organisation in Frage stellen können. Doch trug diese Debatte offensichtlich noch einmal zur Verstimmung des Präsidenten bei. Die Einladung, wie üblich an der für 1984 vorgesehenen kommenden Vollversammlung des DGI in Ambon teilzunehmen und dort eine Rede zu halten, wurde abgelehnt. Die Delegierten auf der Vollversammlung akzeptierten die Erklärung, dass der Präsident wegen Arbeitsüberlastung die Einladung nicht habe annehmen können.[41]

Als schwer akzeptierbar galt jedoch die praktische Auswirkung, dass es Suharto in erster Linie um die Akzeptanz der in P-4 festgelegten Interpretation der Pancasila gehe, nicht jedoch um die eigentliche, in mancher Unklarheit der Formulierung eben auch für unterschiedliche Interpretationen offene ursprüngliche Form derselben. Als Stein des Anstosses galt inbesondere die Tendenz in P-4, die fünf Prinzipien nicht als gleichwertig miteinander verbunden zu betrachten, sondern in hierarchischer Weise Prinzip eins an die Spitze und die anderen vier darunter, aber ohne Verbindung miteinander, zu stellen. Dieses Verständnis wurde zwar von manchem muslimischen Pancasilaisten geteilt, traf jedoch auf massiven Widerspruch anderer Verfechter der Pancasila wie etwa Simatupang oder A. Wahid, für die die religiöse Dimension zwar wichtig, aber nicht dominierend sein sollte; Staat und Religion sind eben nicht dasselbe, und im Pancasila-Staat stehen die religiösen (Prinzip 1), nationalen (Prinzip 2 und 3) und sozialen (Prinzip 4 und 5) Anliegen gleichwertig und konzeptionell aufeinander bezogen nebeneinander.

---

[41] Vgl. den Berichtsband von der Vollversammlung: *Yesus Kristus Kehidupan Dunia. Harapan dan Keprihatinan Bangsa dan Gereja Memaski Akhir Abad ke-20* [Jesus Christus: das Leben der Welt. Hoffnung und Sorgen von Volk und Kirche vor dem Ende des 20. Jahrhunderts], Notulen SR ke-X, Ambon/Maluku 21.–31. Oktober 1984, 22–24. Das von der PGI herausgegebene Protokoll der entscheidenden Sitzung des Zentralausschusses des DGI im August 1984, deren Ergebnisse der Vollversammlung zur Beratung und Beschlussfassung vorgelegt wurden, ebd. 397 ff.

In all diesen Krisen und Auseinandersetzungen mit der Regierung um grundsätzliche ideologische, nationale und soziale Fragen, von denen manche allerdings auch eine Portion von theologischem Gehalt in sich trugen, standen die Spitzen des DGI im Rampenlicht, insbesondere der Generalsekretär Dr. S. A. E. Nababan (von 1967–1984). Auf der Vollversammlung in Ambon wurde er zum Allgemeinen Vorsitzenden[42] der – inzwischen umbenannten – PGI gewählt; nach der neuen Struktur wurde das damals ein Fulltime-Job. Es ist bemerkenswert, dass in der Amtsperiode der 1984 gewählten PGI-Leitung von 1984–1989, dem Zeitpunkt der nächsten Vollversammlung, die Leitung der PGI nur zweimal vom Staatspräsidenten empfangen wurde: einmal 1986 noch im Zusammenhang mit der Diskussion um die Position der Pancasila in der Grundordnung der Kirchen einschliesslich der PGI, und das zweite Mal 1989, als dem Präsidenten die Einladung zur nächsten Vollversammlung der PGI in Surabaya überreicht wurde. Beim zweiten Treffen war Nababan allerdings nicht mehr dabei, denn 1987 war er von der *Synode Godang* der HKBP zum Ephorus gewählt worden und musste deshalb von Jakarta nach Tarutung umziehen. Als Nababan auf der Vollversammlung der PGI 1989 wiederum für das Amt des Allgemeinen Vorsitzenden kandidierte, bemühte sich die Regierung erfolgreich, diese Wahl zu verhindern. Stattdessen wurde Prof. Dr. Sularso Sopater, wie Suharto ein Javane, in dieses Amt gewählt und garantierte einen für Suharto angenehmeren Umgangsstil. Diese Vollversammlung fand auf dem Komplex des Marine-Oberkommandos in Surabaya statt. Einer der Gastredner war Abdurrahman Wahid.

---

[42] Zur Erklärung: An der Spitze von DGI/PGI stand der Allgemeine Vorsitzende (*Ketua Umum*), früher halbzeitlich, nun vollzeitlich besetzt. Ihm zur Seite standen drei Vorsitzende, von denen in der Regel jeder sich im Besonderen um die Belange je eines der drei Hauptabteilungen kümmerte: soziale und gesellschaftliche Aufgaben, Fragen des kirchlichen Lebens und der ökumenischen Einheit sowie Erziehung und Unterricht. Daneben gab es den Generalsekretär mit einem Stellvertreter und einen Schatzmeister, ebenfalls unterstützt von einem Stellvertreter. Sie alle waren Mitglieder des Exekutiv-Ausschusses, dem noch einige wenige andere Mitglieder angehörten, der möglichst etwa einmal pro Woche tagte und für die laufenden Geschäfte die Verantwortung trug.

Tatort: Der Distrikt Tapanuli (Nord-Sumatra)

Nababan also blieb in Tapanuli. Dort regierte er mit eisernem, für manche wohl allzu eisernem Besen.[43] Auch hier ging es ihm, wie einst im DGI, um eine effektivere und disziplinertere Arbeit sowohl in der Gemeindeleitung als auch hinsichtlich der sozialen und diakonischen Programme der Kirche. Unterstützt wurde Nababan schon bei seiner Wahl zum Ephorus vor allem von einer Reihe von jüngeren Theologen und ihrem Anhang in den Gemeinden, die bereits die vorangegangene Krise in der HKBP in den 1970er-Jahren am eigenen Leibe gespürt hatten. Diese Krise wurde durch die Aspirationen von Dr. h. c. T. D. Pardede hervorgerufen, der ein beachtliches Wirtschaftsimperium mit u. a. einigen Hotels aufgebaut, sich als Mäzen des Fussballclubs von Medan einen guten Namen in der Bevölkerung erworben hatte und zum Zeitpunkt, als die damalige Krise eskalierte, Präsident der in Medan und Pematang Siantar gelegenen «Nommensen Universität» der HKBP war. In seiner Lebenshaltung war er tief in der batakschen Adat und ihrem Normensystem verankert, das dann auch sein Kirchenverständnis und seine Amtsführung gewissermassen als «Häuptling» prägte. Sukarno hatte ihn einst als Musterbeispiel für einen «einheimischen»[44] Unternehmer bezeichnet. Seine Amtszeit war durch um sich greifende Korruption gekennzeichnet. Als er sich durch Eingriffe in die Ämterbesetzung auch der damaligen Theologischen Fakultät bemächtigen wollte, kam es zum Bruch: Im Frühjahr 1975 zogen etwa die Hälfte der Studierenden mitsamt einigen Dozenten aus dem Campus aus und erhielten in der Folgezeit in verschiedenen Lokalitäten diverser in Pematang Siantar ansässiger Kirchen einen notdürftigen, aber engagierten Unterricht; der Zugang zur fakultätseigenen Bibliothek wurde ihnen versperrt. Unterkunft erhielten die meisten bei Gemeindegliedern. Erhebliche Unterstützung erhielten sie von Dr. Nababan, der damals Generalsekretär des DGI war. Diese durch die Erfahrungen des «Seminars im Exodus» (*Seminex*) geformten Studierenden und späteren Pfarrer waren es vor allem, die sich 1987 «vehement für ihn (sc. Nababan) eingesetzt ...»

---

[43] D. Becker, *op. cit.,* 131 ff.

[44] *Pribumi*, im Unterschied zu den chinesisch-stämmigen Unternehmern, die zumeist geschäftstüchtiger als die Einheimischen sind.

hatten.[45] Sie hatten schon im Studium die verhängnisvolle Macht der Adat kennen gelernt und waren von daher offen gegenüber Nababans Reformplänen innerhalb der Kirche.

Unter den folgenden Ereignissen, die in besonderer Weise zusätzlichen Zorn Suhartos gegenüber Nababan hervorriefen, sei nur eines hervorgehoben, nämlich der Protest der Bevölkerung gegen das 1988 begonnene «Indo-Rayon-Projekt» in der Nähe von Porsea, nicht allzu weit entfernt vom Ufer des Tobasees und inmitten der vormals bewaldeten Randgebirge,[46] der in einer Protestdemonstration batakscher Frauen vor dem Parlamentsgebäude in Jakarta seinen Höhepunkt erreichte und ungewöhnliche Aufmerksamkeit in der indonesischen Öffentlichkeit fand. Anlass für diese Reaktionen war die umfassende und gründliche Umweltzerstörung, die dieses Projekt, eine Zellstofffabrik, verursachte: Nicht nur wurden die Berghänge kahlgeschlagen, sondern auch sämtliche Wasserläufe grossräumig vergiftet. Damit wurden auch die Sawahs (Reisfelder) und andere landwirtschaftlich genutzten Flächen unbrauchbar. Die Versorgung mit Trinkwasser sorgte für weitere Probleme. Und, wie üblich in solchen Fällen: Schadenersatz vollzog sich im Wesentlichen im rhetorischen Bereich. Es war das erste Mal in der Geschichte der HKBP, dass von Gemeindegliedern veranstaltete Protestaktionen diesen Ausmasses gegen die Regierung von der Kirchenleitung, und das war in diesem Falle in erster Linie der Ephorus, mit Nachdruck unterstützt wurden. In der Regel galten Angriffe auf die Regierung, entsprechend der Adat, als ungehörig.

Doch war die Sachlage nur die eine Seite der Angelegenheit. Firmenbezeichnungen, die das Element «Indo-» in sich enthielten, deuteten in der Regel darauf hin, dass sie offiziell zwar Staatseigentum waren, de facto jedoch zum Wirtschaftsimperium des Präsidenten und seiner Familie gehörten. Kritik in diesem Bereich wurde als Angriff auf die persönliche Integrität des Präsidenten bewertet und geahndet. Mit seiner Haltung bot Nababan also genügend Anlass, um seine Beseitigung von der politischen

---

[45] D. Becker, *op. cit.*, 137 f.
[46] Ebd.,156.

bzw. gesellschaftlichen Bühne zu betreiben. Um das zu erreichen, wurden auch innerkirchliche Gegner Nababans herangezogen.

Der Staat als Friedensmittler?

«Herangezogen»: von wem? In der Berichterstattung wurde zumeist von «der Regierung» gesprochen, um den Ereignissen, die sich im Vorfeld, während und nach der «Wahlsynode» im November/Dezember 1992 abspielten, einen Anschein von Legalität zu geben. Tatsächlich befanden sich die massgebenden Akteure in Gruppierungen, die eher dem verfassungsrechtlichen «Halbdunkel» zuzurechnen, d. h. dem Befehl des Präsidenten direkt zugeordnet und mit verschiedenen Geheimdiensten verbunden sind. Besonders hervorgetan hat sich die Führung des «Bakostanasda»[47] unter Generalmajor Pramono, der die meisten der gegen die Verfassung der HKBP verstossenden Massnahmen angeordnet hatte, um sicherzustellen, dass nur regierungsgenehme Pfarrer in leitende Positionen der Kirche gewählt oder ernannt wurden, die dann ihrerseits für die Ausschaltung missliebiger Amtsinhaber in den Gemeinden zu sorgen hatten. Die innerkirchliche Aufsicht darüber hatte Dr. Sountilon N. Siahaan als Generalsekretär der HKBP, dessen enge Beziehungen zu Dr. Habibie die Staatsführung informativ auf dem Laufenden hielt und Sorge dafür trug, dass dem Teil der HKBP, der sich ihm unterstellte, die Sympathie der Regierung erhalten blieb. So wird der Vorwurf an Dr. Siahaan begründet, dass er sich im Hinblick auf die HKBP zum Erfüllungsgehilfen Dr. Habibies im Rahmen von dessen Generalauftrag, in den gesellschaftlichen Organisationen die Ausschaltung der gegen Suharto opponierenden Gruppen zu bewerkstelligen, mache.

Damit trat «der Staat» nicht, wie es ihm nach modernem Staatsverständnis zustünde, als Vermittler und Agent einer angestrebten Versöhnung zwischen die konfligierenden Parteien auf. Vielmehr präsentierte er sich selbst als Partei, und dazu noch als Partei, die nicht lediglich die Interessen des einen oder beider Konfliktgegner vertrat, sondern letztendlich die eigenen, vertreten durch die Personifikation der Staatsmacht, den

---

[47] Siehe Anm. 14.

Präsidenten. Kriterium für die Unterstützung war die ideologische und politische Linientreue, aber diesen Sachverhalt galt es durch Druck und Propaganda zu vertuschen. Damit hatte «der indonesische Staat» seine eigene Bestimmung als «Staat», nämlich unparteiisch für Gerechtigkeit und das Wohlergehen *aller* seiner Bürger zu sorgen, verraten. Dass der indonesische Staat unter der Herrschaft von Präsident Suharto zum Zeitpunkt der HKBP-Krise nicht mehr in der Lage war bzw. auch nicht sein wollte, seiner Neutralitätspflicht nachzukommen, hätten Dr. S. N. Siahaan und seine Gefolgschaft wissen müssen. Wenn sie es jedoch wussten, dann sind sie auch mitverantwortlich für die Folgen, die diese Allianz nach sich zog. Wiederholt sind «Gegner», auch Pastoren und Studenten, vom Militär inhaftiert und gefoltert worden.

Im selben Jahr, in dem die HKBP-Krise offen ausbrach (1992), hatten in Indonesien allgemeine Wahlen stattgefunden, in denen die von Dr. Habibie dirigierte «proportionale Demokratie» zur Anwendung kam. Die Sympathien der «Regierung» waren klar verteilt, und gegebenenfalls wurde mit Gewalt dafür gesorgt, dass die «richtige» Seite an die Macht kam. Wo Gewalt auf diese Weise eingesetzt wird, bleibt es bei der Anwendung von Gewalt. Das haben beide Seiten der HKBP in den folgenden Jahren schmerzlich erfahren. Somit stellt sich die Frage, ob es wirklich der interne Konflikt war, der die HKBP in das blutige Szenario stürzte, dem sie sich in den Jahren nach 1992 gegenübersah. Inwieweit waren hier auch äussere Drahtzieher am Werke, denen, zur Erlangung ihrer personbezogenen Ziele, letztlich jedes Mittel recht war? Dieser Blick nach aussen exkulpiert allerdings keineswegs die HKBP: Die Art, wie sich die Krise seit dem Amtsantritt von Dr. Nababan 1987 als Ephorus aufbaute, hätte rechtzeitig die auch in der batakschen Adat vorhandenen Mechanismen zur Konfliktüberwindung aktivieren müssen, selbstredend auch christliche Prinzipien[48] im Umgang mit «dem Gegner», um dadurch heuchlerischen Friedensmaklern von aussen von vornherein den Zugang zu verwehren und

---

[48] Nach Fertigstellung des Manuskripts erhielt ich Kenntnis von der Amsterdamer Dissertation von Binsar Jonathan Pakpahan, *God Remembers. Towards a Theology of Remembrance as a Basis of Reconciliation in Communal Conflict,* auf die ich nachdrücklich hinweisen möchte.

damit zu verhindern, dass die Krise ausser Kontrolle gerät. Stattdessen wurde von einer Seite die Staatsmacht als Helferin eingeladen, die Staatsmacht, deren Charakter inzwischen hinreichend bekannt war. Und sie entschied über Sieger und Verlierer.

Die Kirche gehört sich wieder selbst

Die Ereignisse nach dem Sturz Suhartos im Mai 1998 scheinen diese Sicht der Dinge zu bestätigen: Bereits ein Jahr nach dem Fall Suhartos und der Betrauung Habibies mit anderen Aufgaben und damit dem Ende seiner Rolle als Oberaufseher über die gesellschaftlichen Entwicklungen, wodurch Dr. Siahaan seinen wichtigsten Mentor verlor, drängte es in beiden Flügeln der HKBP auf eine Versöhnungssynode und die Wahl einer gemeinsamen neuen Kirchenleitung. Aus eigener Kraft, und ohne die «selbstlose» Hilfe der Regierung, gelang dieser Plan.

Diese Beobachtung lädt einen Augenblick zum Verweilen ein. Ähnliche Erfahrungen wurden auch in anderen Regionen in Indonesien gemacht, die von kommunalen Auseinandersetzungen heimgesucht worden waren, dass nämlich die jeweiligen Ortsbevölkerungen sehr viel besser ohne die «wohlmeinende Hilfe» von aussen angereister Regierungs- oder Militärvertreter zu wirkungsvollen Akten der Versöhnung kamen als mit deren «Hilfe». Doch darauf weiter einzugehen würde den Rahmen dieses Beitrages sprengen.[49]

Damit hat die HKBP gezeigt, dass in ihr in der Tat starke Kräfte vorhanden sind, die zu einer funktionierenden zivilen, gesitteten Gesellschaft erheblich beitragen könnten. Hat damit der oben genannte Student mit seinem Votum Recht? Teilweise «ja», aber zu einem grossen Teil «(noch) nicht». Die Potenzen dafür sind zweifellos da, aber sie können (noch) nicht in Anwendung kommen, weil die Neigung zur Introvertiertheit nach

---

[49] Zur Situation auf Halmahera, Nord-Molukken, beispielsweise vgl. meinen Beitrag Christliche Kirchen in Ost-Indonesien (Halmahera). Der religiöse Hintergrund kommunaler Konflikte, in: Hans-Martin Barth und Christoph Elsas (Hg.), *Religiöse Minderheiten. Potentiale für Konflikt und Frieden*, Hamburg, EBV 2004, 44–64; Heiko Landwehr, *Reziprozität von Religion und Gewalt*, Frankfurt/Main, Lembeck, 2007, z. B. S. 66 ff.

wie vor vorherrscht und die in Nord-Tapanuli wohnenden Nachbarn, die z. B. nicht der toba-batakschen Adat-Gemeinschaft angehören, nicht in ihr Gesellschafts-Verständnis integrieren kann. Diese Haltung steht im Konflikt zu den Prinzipien einer Zivilgesellschaft, zu der alle Angehörigen gleichberechtigt und gleichwertig ihre Vorstellungen beizutragen haben. Das Gefühl (ob realistisch oder nicht, sei dahingestellt), in Nord-Tapanuli die Bevölkerungsmehrheit zu stellen und damit die Gesellschaft «entscheidend» zu prägen, behindert zweifellos die notwendige Öffnung. Zweifellos ist die Toba-Batak-Kirche Teil der Adat-Gemeinschaft in Tapanuli, sie ist aber nicht ihre alleinige Vertreterin. Und selbst die gesamte Adat-Gemeinschaft ist nicht identisch mit der Zivilgesellschaft der Region. Als Teil kann sie nur dann wirken, wenn sie sich im gesellschaftlichen Bereich den anderen gegenüber öffnet und mit ihnen gemeinsam die gesellschaftlichen Anliegen beregelt.

Und noch ein zweiter Hinderungsgrund sei genannt: «Pluralität» wird in Indonesien mit Vorliebe als «Gruppenpluralität» verstanden, vgl. oben Habibies «proportionale Demokratie». Damit wird ein Grundprinzip der zivilen Gesellschaft ausgehebelt, demzufolge alle Bürger als mündige und gleichberechtigte Staatsbürger behandelt werden, unabhängig von ihrer Gruppenzugehörigkeit. Zwischen Staatsbürger und Staat gibt es keine Zwischeninstanz, oder, wie es in der Präambel der indonesischen Verfassung heisst: die Souveränität liegt beim Volke. Damit wird auch dem traditionellen Verständnis der Adat-Gemeinschaft widersprochen. Zur Klärung der Definitionen müsste das Buch von Ferdinand Tönnies, *Gemeinschaft und Gesellschaft,* wieder einmal, trotz seines Alters, herangezogen werden.[50]

---

[50] Ferdinand Tönnies, *Gemeinschaft und Gesellschaft,* 1887; Neudruck: *Gemeinschaft und Gesellschaft. Grundbegriffe der reinen Soziologie,* Darmstadt, Wissenschaftliche Buchgesellschaft, 1979.

Adat-Gemeinschaft versus Zivilgesellschaft(?)[51]

Das Gefühl jedoch, Majorität zu sein, kann nicht der einzige Grund für die Neigung zur Exklusivität sein, denn dort, wo Batak-Gemeinden als Minderheit leben, findet sich dasselbe Phänomen einer kulturellen und gesellschaftlichen Distanzierung zur Umwelt. Ich möchte zum Abschluss dieses Beitrages nicht allgemein auf die Folgen für die «Ökumene vor Ort» in anderen Regionen Indonesiens eingehen, sondern erwähne ein Konfliktfeld, das in den letzten Jahren gelegentlich auch die Aufmerksamkeit der internationalen Presse auf sich gezogen hat: die Bedrängnisse, denen sich – keineswegs ausschliesslich, aber doch auch in grosser Anzahl – Batak-Gemeinden in West-Java bei der Ausübung ihres Gottesdienstes in ihren Kirchen gegenübersahen, und die bis hin zur Brandschatzung reichten.[52] Auch hier ähnelten sich die Szenarien: Ein Mob von Anwohnern und anderen, zumeist verstärkt durch radikal-islamische Gruppen, die wer weiss woher kamen, forderten das Ende gottesdienstlicher Handlungen in der Umgebung und den Abriss ihrer Kirchen, weil die umwohnende Bevölkerung zu ihrer Errichtung ihr Einverständnis nicht erteilt habe, die Anlieger jedoch nach der Rechtslage vor dem Bau religiös genutzter Immobilien ihr Einverständnis erklären müssen. Das sei nicht geschehen, und alle Versuche in der Vergangenheit, der Rechtslage zum Sieg zu verhelfen, seien verhindert worden. Die Radikalen, die die Gewalttätigkeiten initiierten, traten nun als Beschützer der Bevölkerung auf und verhalfen ihr zu dem, wozu die staatlichen Organe nicht bereit waren: zu ihrem Recht. So schien es wenigstens.

In der auch im Ausland kolportierten «öffentlichen Meinung» stand hier vor allem die Frage im Vordergrund, ob – angesichts der zumeist tatenlosen Zuschauerrolle der Regierung und ihrer Ordnungsorgane – die

---

[51] Vgl. dazu meinen Beitrag «Adat und Moderne – ein Widerspruch?» in der in Anmerkung 12 genannten Festschrift für Lothar Schreiner, *Injil Dan Tata Hidup – Evangelium und Lebensordnung*, a. a. O., S. 387–420.

[52] Nach einer Aufstellung der PGI im Dezember 2007 sind allein in den Jahren von 2004–2007 in 111 Gemeinden verschiedener Kirchen in West-Java Kirchen oder andere gottesdienstliche Räume ganz oder teilweise zerstört und/oder die Gemeinden gewaltsam an der Durchführung des Gottesdienstes gehindert worden, *Berita Oikoumene* (PGI Jakarta), Jan./Febr. 2008, 21–27.

von der Verfassung garantierte Religionsfreiheit, immerhin ein Menschenrecht, noch in Geltung sei. Die hier vorgebrachten Argumente dürften weithin bekannt sein, sie interessieren hier jedoch nicht weiter. Bei genauem Hinsehen oder Hinhören schienen nämlich ein oder mehr Elemente in der Wahrnehmung zu fehlen. Die Spannungen waren ja nicht neu, sondern hatten bereits eine längere Geschichte hinter sich. Was also waren die tieferen Hintergründe für ihr Entstehen und für ihr derzeitiges Eskalieren?

Einige Studenten aus Nord-Sumatra, die sich auf eine *Fact-finding-Tour* nach West-Java begeben hatten, fanden recht schnell heraus, was zu vermuten war: dass die Spannungen bereits in die Zeit zurückreichen, in der das Land, auf dem einige dieser Kirchen standen, selbstverständlich unter den damaligen korruptiven Bedingungen erworben wurde. Im Umkreis aller grösseren Städte, vor allem um Jakarta herum und den für Industrieprojekte vorgesehenen Nachbarstädten der Hauptstadt in West-Java, wurden im Namen oder unter dem Schutze der Regierung Ländereien in grossem Massstab aufgekauft, wobei den ehemaligen Besitzern lediglich Minimalpreise angeboten und oft nicht einmal diese bezahlt wurden. Wenn von solchen Ländereien, die bei guten Beziehungen noch relativ günstig von Nachkäufern erworben werden konnten, einige zum Bau von Kirchen benutzt wurden, war ein Konflikt mit der Nachbarschaft – den ehemaligen Besitzern – vorprogrammiert. Doch war es damals in der Regel aussichtslos, Rechte irgendwelcher Art, und sei es nur die Auszahlung eines angemessenen Preises, über einen Rechtsweg einzufordern. Die Spannungen schwelten also vor sich hin, bis, angesichts der Passivität der derzeitigen Regierung in Bezug auf von islamistischen Terrorgruppen verübte Gewalttaten – andere religiöse Gruppen wie die Ahmadiyya traf es noch viel schlimmer –, diese Terrorgruppen auch hier auftraten und sich als Verfechter der legitimen Ansprüche des Volkes anboten, von Ansprüchen also, die eigentlich von der Regierung oder den Gerichten geregelt werden müssten, wozu diese jedoch nicht in der Lage oder nicht willens oder beides nicht sind. Damit hilft die Regierung den Radikalen, sich quasi den Nimbus von Robin Hood zuzulegen (den Vergleich würden sie selbst wohl ablehnen). Kein Wunder, dass sie Zuspruch erhalten. Den damit indizierten Rechtsverfall – parallel zum Verfall des Rechtsbewusstseins – hat jedoch die Regierung selbst zu verantworten, desgleichen die zunehmende Popularität der radikalen Gruppen innerhalb der marginalisierten Bevölkerung.

Ordnung im eigenen Haus – und mit der Nachbarschaft

In dieser Situation hätten die HKBP-Gemeinden, und mit ihnen andere, denen Ähnliches widerfuhr, die Gelegenheit, auch in einer Minderheitensituation einen Aspekt von Zivilgesellschaft zu praktizieren. In der Regel präsentierten sie sich in ihrer Nachbarschaft als Fremdkörper mit wenig zivilen bzw. bürgerlichen Beziehungen zu ihren Nachbarn. Das dadurch gestärkte Fremdheitsgefühl wird von den Radikalen selbstverständlich genutzt, und auch darin werden sie von Regierungsinstitutionen wie z. B. dem von der Regierung eingesetzten «Rat der indonesischen Muslimgelehrten» (*Majelis Ulama Indonesia – MUI*) unterstützt, der etwa die üblichen Nachbarschaftsbesuche zu den grossen Feiertagen durch eine *Fatwa* (Rechtsgutachten)[53] zu unterbinden suchte. Dass sich viele Muslime nicht daran hielten, zeigt die Bereitschaft zu guten oder zumindest zu besseren beiderseitigen Kontakten innerhalb der Bevölkerung. Trotz der Bemühungen radikaler Gruppen und ihrer Sympathisanten in der Regierung, sich die Konfliktherde zu erhalten und sie bei Gelegenheit für ihre Zwecke auszunutzen, ist der Wille zu zivilem Zusammenleben stark. Es liegt auch an den Christen, Bereitschaft zu zeigen, über die tatsächlichen Ursachen der Spannungen und Möglichkeiten ihrer Beseitigung gemeinsam zu beraten. Auch hier wäre dann darauf zu achten, dass wie auch immer gemeinte «Hilfe von aussen» möglichst auch draussen bliebe und sich die direkt Beteiligten miteinander einigen. Die Christen pochen in der Regel bei diesen Auseinandersetzungen auf das Grundrecht der Religionsfreiheit, das auch in der indonesischen Verfassung garantiert ist. Das mag seinen Sinn gegenüber den Radikalen haben, für die es «Rechte der anderen» nicht gibt. Von der Sache her sind hier oft aber noch andere Dimensionen des Rechts tangiert, die ebenfalls Beachtung verdienen und gegebenenfalls in ziviler Selbsthilfe direkt von den Betroffenen geregelt werden können.

---

[53] Eine *Fatwa* ist ein von einem oder mehreren dazu befugten Islamgelehrten erteiltes Rechtsgutachten. Keinesfalls darf sie als «Urteil» missverstanden werden.

Mit dem Fall Suhartos haben sich die Prioritäten des öffentlichen Interesses verschoben. Nicht mehr der «Aufbau des Pancasila-Staates» steht im Vordergrund, sondern das Verlangen nach einem wirkungsvollen zivilen Rechts- und Regierungssystem, innerhalb dessen auch die Religionsfreiheit ihren festen Ort hat, jedoch nicht als isolierter Topos. Wenn es gelänge, die Kirchen aus ihrem lähmenden Minderheitenkomplex zu befreien – das geschieht in Indonesien unter Hinweis auf das dritte Prinzip der Pancasila – und ihre materiellen, vor allem aber auch mentalen Potenzen zum Aufbau einer offenen zivilen Gesellschaft einzusetzen, dann könnte jener Student in Pematang Siantar (der inzwischen längst Pfarrer ist) doch noch Recht haben, dass die HKBP zwar nicht «die», aber wohl ein integraler und dynamischer «Teil der» Zivilgesellschaft ist, in Tapanuli sowohl als auch in anderen Gegenden, wo ihre Gemeinden in der Minderheit sind. Und andere Kirchen nicht minder.

Doch dazu bedürfte es wohl zuvor eines einschneidenden Paradigmenwechsels in der einheimischen Theologie. Nicht die stets aufs Neue geforderte «Inkulturation» des Evangeliums, die schliesslich zu seiner Vereinnahmung und Bevormundung durch die Adat führt, kann die Kirchen aus ihrer Introvertiertheit befreien, sondern die positive, kreative, kritische und realistische Auseinandersetzung nicht nur mit der Regierung, sondern mit dem gesamten kirchlichen und gesellschaftlichen Kontext, zu dem auch die Adat gehört. Die Kultur gilt es «zu taufen», und nicht umgekehrt die Adat zur Richtschnur für das Evangelium zu machen. Vielleicht gelingt es der HKBP, auf Grund ihrer schlimmen Erfahrungen diesen Schritt zu wagen und mit ihren Nachbarn gemeinsam die Überwindung der anstehenden Kontroversen zu beraten.

Derzeit scheint es allerdings zu diesem Schritt noch weit zu sein. In einer Verlautbarung der HKBP-Pfarrer in und um Bekasi von 2009 wird wieder auf die in der Verfassung Indonesiens garantierte Religionsfreiheit verwiesen und die Gemeinden werden aufgefordert, alle von Polizei, Militär und bewaffneten Sondereinheiten getroffenen Massnahmen zur Sicherung der öffentlichen Ruhe und zum Schutz des gottesdienstlichen Lebens zu unterstützen. Die Regierung und alle gesellschaftlichen «Komponenten», die sich um die Gestaltung einer gerechten, fortschrittlichen und

wohlhabenden Gesellschaft bemühen, sollen ins Fürbittengebet eingeschlossen werden. Dies sind die alten, aus der Suharto-Zeit bekannten
Redegewohnheiten. Die Aufforderung, sich aus eigener Initiative um eine
Verbesserung der Beziehungen zur gesellschaftlichen Nachbarschaft zu
bemühen, taucht in der Verlautbarung nicht auf.[54]

Abkürzungen

Bakostanasda	*Badan Kordinasi Stabilitas Nasional dan Daerah*, Koordinationsbehörde für die nationale und regionale Stabilität
Bappenas	*Badan Perencanaan dan Pengembangan Nasional*, Amt für nationale Planung und Entwicklung
BPK	*Badan Penerbit Kristen Gunung Mulia*, Christliches Verlagshaus
CSIS	*Center for Strategic and International Studies*
DGI	*Dewan Gereja-gereja di Indonesia*, Rat der Kirchen in Indonesien (von 1950–1984, siehe PGI)
DPR	*Dewan Perwakilan Rakyat*, Rat der Volksvertretung, Parlament
GKJTU	*Gereja Kristen Jawa Tengah Utara*, Christliche Kirche aus Nordmitteljava
HKBP	*Huria Kristen Batak Protestan*, Christlich-Protestantische Toba-Batak-Kirche
ICMI	*Ikatan Cendekiawan Muslim Indonesia*, Verband muslimischer Intellektueller in Indonesien
IRM	*International Review of Mission* (Genf)
IMC	*International Missionary Council*
Masyumi	*Majelis Syuro Muslimin Indonesia*, Beratende Versammlung der Muslime in Indonesien (Name einer seit 1960 verbotenen Partei)

[54] Vgl. «Pernyataan Sikap Pendeta HKBP se Kota/Kabupaten Bekasi» (Meinungsäusserung der HKBP-Pfarrer in der Stadt und dem Distrikt Bekasi), in: *Berita Oikoumene*, Edisi khusus 2010, S. 40. *Berita Oikoumene* ist das offizielle Nachrichtenorgan der PGI in Jakarta.

MAWI	*Majelis Agung Waligereja Indonesia,* Oberster Rat der katholischen Kirchenprovinz Indonesien
MPR	*Majelis Permusyawaratan Rakyat,* Volkskongress
MUI	*Majelis Ulama Indonesia,* Rat der Religionsgelehrten in Indonesien
NGO	*Non-governmental organization*
NU	*Nahdlatul Ulama,* Renaissance der Religionsgelehrten
ÖRK	Ökumenischer Rat der Kirchen
P-4	*Pedoman Pengamalan dan Penghayatan Pancasila,* Leitfaden zur Praxis und Verinnerlichung der Pancasila
PGI	*Persekutuan Gereja-gereja di Indonesia* (seit 1984, siehe DGI), Gemeinschaft der Kirchen in Indonesien

Olaf Schumann, geboren 1938 in Dresden, studierte evangelische Theologie in Kiel, Tübingen und Basel (1959–1964) und Islamologie in Tübingen und Kairo (1963–1966). Von 1966–1968 Deutschlektor an der Universität Assiut, Oberägypten. 1970 Ordination zum Pfarrer in der Evang.-Luth. Kirche Schleswig-Holsteins und 1972 Promotion zum Dr. theol. in Tübingen. – Ende 1970 wurde er auf Einladung des «Rates der Kirchen in Indonesien», Jakarta, von der Basler Mission als wissenschaftlicher Mitarbeiter nach Jakarta entsandt. Sein Forschungsgebiet: die Geschichte des Islam in Südostasien, die christlich-muslimischen Beziehungen in Indonesien, Fragen des interreligiösen Dialogs. Gleichzeitig wurde er zu Intensivkursen in Religionskunde an verschiedene theologische Hochschulen in Indonesien und in anderen Nachbarländern eingeladen. 1981 Berufung zum Professor für Religions- und Missionswissenschaft durch die Universität Hamburg an ihren Fachbereich evangelische Theologie. 1989–1992 Beurlaubung zur Wahrnehmung einer Gastprofessur an der Theologischen Hochschule Jakarta. Nach der 2004 erfolgten Emeritierung zog er nach Kota Kinabalu, Sabah/Malaysia. Am dortigen *Sabah Theological Seminary* Aushilfe mit Kursen zur Religionskunde. – Publikationen zu Themen aus dem Islam, dem interreligiösen Dialog, allgemeiner Religionsgeschichte, Religionen und Staat/Gesellschaft in Deutsch, Indonesisch, Englisch, Niederländisch.

STS, P.O. Box 11925, Kota Kinabalu 88821, MY-Sabah, Malaysia;
Olafschumann@gmx.de

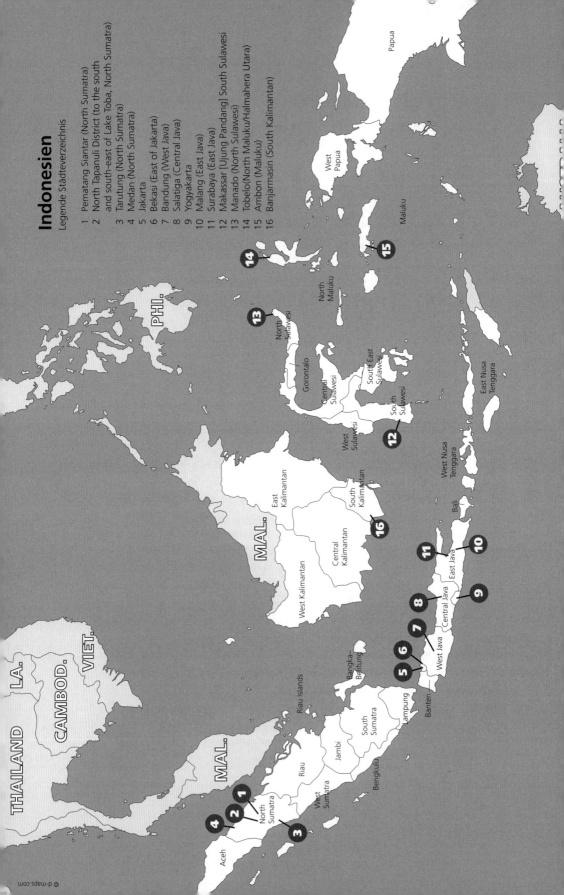

Indonesien

Legende Städteverzeichnis

1 Pematang Siantar (North Sumatra)
2 North Tapanuli District (to the south
  and south-east of Lake Toba, North Sumatra)
3 Tarutung (North Sumatra)
4 Medan (North Sumatra)
5 Jakarta
6 Bekasi (East of Jakarta)
7 Bandung (West Java)
8 Salatiga (Central Java)
9 Yogyakarta
10 Malang (East Java)
11 Surabaya (East Java)
12 Makassar [Ujung Pandang] South Sulawesi
13 Manado (North Sulawesi)
14 Tobelo(North Maluku/Halmahera Utara)
15 Ambon (Maluku)
16 Banjarmasin (South Kalimantan)

THAILAND

LA.

CAMBOD.

VIET.

MAL.

MAL.

PHIL.

Aceh

North Sumatra

West Sumatra

Riau

Jambi

Bengkulu

South Sumatra

Lampung

Bangka-Belitung

Banten

West Java

Central Java

East Java

Bali

West Nusa Tenggara

East Nusa Tenggara

Riau Islands

West Kalimantan

Central Kalimantan

South Kalimantan

East Kalimantan

West Sulawesi

Central Sulawesi

Gorontalo

North Sulawesi

South Sulawesi

South East Sulawesi

North Maluku

Maluku

West Papua

Papua

© d-maps.com

On the Future of Asian Theology: Public Theologizing

Felix Wilfred

Zusammenfassung

Der Autor ist ehemaliger Professor für indische Studien an der Universität von Dublin, Irland, delegiert von der Regierung Indiens. Im ersten Teil seines Beitrags hebt der Autor einige charakteristische Merkmale hervor, die asiatische Theologie erworben hat. Er hält die Notwendigkeit fest, sich in eine neue Richtung eines vertieften interaktiven Dialogs zu bewegen, bei dem Theologie auf die Themen und Anliegen der Öffentlichkeit zu antworten sucht und in Zusammenarbeit mit anderen Kräften der Zivilgesellschaft dadurch eine wirklich öffentliche Theologie wird. Durch ihre Ausrichtung auf die Förderung des Gemeinwohls über Grenzen hinaus wird sie sich als glaubwürdig erweisen und für andere in der multireligiösen Situation Asiens als bedeutsam erscheinen. Die Zukunftsaussichten einer asiatischen Theologie werden davon abhängen, inwieweit sie eine öffentliche Theologie wird. In diesem Kontext setzt sich der Autor mit der Frage der Öffentlichkeit auseinander mit Bezug auf Habermas, Rawls und andere und differenziert diese Auseinandersetzung mithilfe der Öffentlichkeit, wie sie in Asien unter anderen soziopolitischen und religiösen Verhältnissen verstanden und gelebt wird.

Asian theological reflections have been quite original, and even radical. They have contributed to enliven the life of the Christian communities and also make them open to the realities of the Asian societies, cultures and religious traditions. There has been as well quite a significant impact of Asian theological reflections at the global level. Some of the more open positions regarding the role of other religions, for example, to be found in the Roman documents owe in no small measure to the sustained reflections of Asian theology and of the Federation of Asian Bishops' Conferences (FABC). The force of Asian theology and its innovative character came in the open at the Asian Synod in the many interventions of the bishops.[1] They reflected a theology rooted in the experience of the Asian continent in dialogue with religions, cultures and the poor of Asia – the triple dialogue announced by FABC.

In the first introductory part of the article I intend to quickly recall the spirit of Asian theological pursuit and some of its main characteristics. While they mark a significant achievement, there is also the need to move forward. The second part of the article then goes to show that this new direction probably has to be the development of an Asian public theology.

Part I: The Spirit of Asian Theology

Reading into the various theological efforts in Asia in the past decades and going through the documents of FABC and of Christian Conference of Asia (CCA), I find certain convergence of concerns and shared perceptions. Asian theologizing has certain quality which may not be always explicitly articulated but could be found underlying. This quality of Asian theologizing I wish to present briefly, instead of going into specific issues.

Sense of Divine Mystery

One of the important things Asian theologies imply is the sense of the inexhaustible mystery of God. This has been conveyed differently whether Asia deals with Christology, mission or theology of religions. This sense of the divine mystery inspires Asian theologies not to follow paths of exclusion but of integration and inclusion. This sense of mystery is also behind the spirit of pluralism that characterizes Asian theologies. This pluralism is not simply a reaction to dogmatism, but something born of the realization that the mystery of God is endless and innumerable are the ways in which it comes to expression. Asian theologies celebrate this pluralism and have tried to understand Jesus Christ and Christian faith from this perspective.

---

[1] Cf. Peter Phan (ed.), *The Asian Synod. Texts and Comments,* New York, Orbis Books, 2002. See also Felix Wilfred, The Reception of Vatican II in a Multireligious Continent, in: *Concilium* 2012/3, 116–121.

The Turn to the Subject in Mission

Asian approach to mission is inspired by the sense of mystery, as well as the importance of the *subject* in mission. The people, their aspirations, their perceptions are important. Mission is not simply a teleologically oriented project. People are not object of mission, but subjects. It is they who in freedom appropriate faith, a process set in particular social, political and cultural processes within their history. Hence it is important to enter into the world and know the story of their experience of faith and understand the expressions they give to it at various levels. There is an effort today to rewrite mission history by foregrounding the subjecthood of the people. Moreover, the realization of the presence of God in peoples, cultures, religious traditions, etc. have contributed to view mission in a unique manner by the Asians. It became very evident during the preparation as well as in the various interventions of bishops during the Asian synod.

Integral Understanding of Salvation and Liberation

Asian theological efforts show more and more an integral understanding of salvation. It means the well being of the whole person without any dichotomy of body and soul, and the welfare of all without distinction of caste, class, religious belonging. Moving towards salvation implies progressive liberation from all that maims, corrodes or negates life in any form. It is a freedom from whatever binds the self as much as the society and the world. Integral salvation and liberation imply that there are no two histories – one history of salvation and the other of the world moving on parallel lines. Some would even oppose one to the other. There is but one single history which all the peoples share across borders and boundaries, testifying to the universality of God's grace and dealings.

Realization of Diversity and Pluralism

Asian theology is infused with the positive affirmation of diversity and spirit of pluralism, not only as a fact but as a value to be fostered. Few continents have such diversity as Asia in its composition of peoples, cultures, traditions and the variety of gifts of nature. The traditional recognition of pluralism and value of a life of harmony resist trends of uniformity and homogenization. There is no attempt to streamline all this diversity into one common point of unity. There is a mystical feeling that all the differences and plurality we experience meet somewhere and are somehow interconnected, though we are not able to identify the bonds that bind them together. Asian theologies have cultivated this spirit of millennial diversity and pluralism of the continent. It is this which also inspires Asian theology to recognize the infinite faces of the divine mystery.

Pluralism derives also from the fact that human beings are subjects and their perception of reality and their judgments are shaped by their differing world-views experiences, diverse contexts, histories, etc. This realization has led Asian theologies to view the diversity of perspectives not as a hindrance but as a great enrichment to the life of faith.

There is today a feeling of threat whenever pluralism is talked about. It derives from a false conflation of pluralism with relativism. FABC has clearly distinguished the two.

Λ pluralism which claims that all point of view of reality are of equal value surely ends up in relativism. When a point of view lacks a common reference to reality, it amounts to the mere opinion of the subject who holds that opinion. When each and every such point of view that is cut off from a common reference to reality is assigned an equal value, then it amounts to relativism. In other words, relativism holds that there are many truths which vary according to the subjects who hold different opinions of reality … The affirmation of plurality rests on the human search for an underlying unity that enables us to understand reality better. Many Asian philosophies and theologies have shown the unity and harmony behind pluralism.[2]

---

[2] Office of Theological Concerns of FABC, Document on: Methodology: Asian Christian Theology 1.1. For the text see, Vimal Tirimanna (ed.), *Sprouts of Theology from the Asian Soil. Collection of TAC and OTC Documents (1987–2007)*, Claretian Publications, Bangalore, 2007, 258–259.

Partnership in Salvation and Liberation

If all the people in their diversity of cultures, traditions and religious paths participate in the single salvation, they become partners in salvation and liberation. People of different religious traditions converge to experience and bear witness to the grace of God, and God's salvation. They engage themselves in bringing about ever greater freedom to the human family and for the protection and flourishing of nature and all of God's creation. Religious traditions are not opposed to each other but are partners in the project of God's salvation and liberation. This is also true of the many secular movements at work among Asian peoples.

Practicing of a Different Theological Methodology

Theology is not simply a learning of faith-propositions or interpretations of the same. Conscious of this fact, Asian theology follows a method of dialogue and mutuality. Its methodology is not aimed at simply communicating the truths of faith but dialoguing with the larger world. Asian theological orientation is not marked by any sense of closure and easily attained certainties, but rather is imbued with the spirit of a movement. The images of journey, pilgrimage could be more aptly characterize Asian theologizing than images of frames and architectures. In fact, Asian theologizing has broken the conventional frames and architectures as it moves into new avenues of reflection and travels on untrodden paths.

Such being the nature and orientation of Asian theology, it has called for also a significant transformation in theological methodology. This methodology can be characterized as dialogical and open-ended, experiential and transformation-oriented. The integral character of Asian theologizing has come out also in the fact that it does not rely simply on reason. Reason is not the sole instrument, theology involves other faculties and dimensions of human life. The sources of this Asian theologizing includes the religious traditions of the neighbours of other faiths, the riches of cultures as well as the new forces at work in the life of the Asian peoples. These realities of the context, as rightly pointed out by the document of the Office of Theological Concerns (OTC) of FABC, form part of the resources of theology along with Scripture and tradition.[3] Asian theologians have been using these resources in their theological endeavours, and this has made a difference and has given a distinctive character to their theologizing. OTC sums up the Asian methodology when it states:

> The Asian way of doing theology is historically rooted and concrete, a method in which we learn to face conflicts and brokenness, a method we value as one of liberative integration, inter-relatedness and wholeness, a method that emphasizes symbolic approaches and expressions, and is marked by a preference for those at the periphery and «outside the Gate» (Heb. 13:3).[4]

Part II: Moving in a New Direction

Developing an Asian Public Theology

In spite of the innovative character of Asian theology, it is a fact that theological reflections have remained mostly internal to the Church and its pastoral needs. I am not saying that the concerns of the world and society are absent. But the point is that these are treated as realms or fields for the application of faith and theology. It has been more a theology in service of public life. The understanding of the nature of theology is basically the same, while the applications differ.

Public theology represents a new genre in theology, so to say. It affects the understanding of theology itself and the way it is pursued. In the context of multireligious and multicultural societies with fast transformation in the field of culture, economy, politics, etc., theology needs to interrogate itself regarding its responsibilities to the larger world. Traditional theology tends to cut everything – the world, society and culture – to its size, reminding us of the Procrustean bed! Asian public theological reflection needs to be open-ended and should begin from the world.[5] It will endeavour to respond with others to the question and issues thrown up

---

[3] Cf. Vimal Tirimanna (ed.), *Sprouts of Theology from the Asian Soil ... op. cit.*

[4] *Op. cit.*, 343.

[5] This project could benefit by the approach of public sociology, cf. Dan Clawson et al., (eds), *Public Sociology*, Berkeley, University of California Press, 2007.

from the life-situation of the people and societies. Such a theology can be characterized as public theology which needs to be promoted increasingly. At the root of this theology is the conviction that the greatest challenge to Christian faith today is to interpret and practice the Kingdom of God in the world.

To understand more closely what is meant by public theology, it is better to see what it is not, and how it distinguishes itself from other related forms of theologies. First of all, we need to draw a distinction between *theology for public life* and *public theology*. The former speaks about faith-motives and convictions for involving oneself as a believer in the affairs of the world – politics, economy, culture, violence, war and peace, etc. It is a discourse within the Church about the world.

> Theology of public life takes as its primary audience, Christian believers unsure of the religious fruitfulness of civic engagement; and it argues to them that they can become better Christians, and their churches better Christian communities, through understanding and participating in public life as an ascetical process of spiritual formation.[6]

From a methodological point of view, in theology for public life, theology is already made and then applied to public life. Though it talks about issues in the world outside the boundaries of the Church, yet it is a discourse meant for consumption within the Church. On the other hand, in public theology, the concrete life-situation and the questions emanating from it are taken seriously, and an effort is made to respond to them in faith – a faith that understands itself in relation with others and not as a private matter. It is a theology strongly based on God's creation and on the Kingdom of God which have no boundaries. Besides, in public theology we try to create a discourse and language which is understandable for others, and therefore can be shared with them. This new language breaks forth when we hold aloft the truth of creation and the great vision of the Kingdom of God.

---

[6] Charles Mathews, *A Theology of Public Life*, Cambridge, Cambridge University Press, 2007.

How come that, even though theology speaks about the world, history and various issues affecting the society, yet it remains a discourse within the Church? Why does this isolation happen? It could be explained in great part by the fact of the strong clericalization theology suffers from. Theology is not only pursued by clerics, but is also mostly oriented to the training and education of the clerics. Hence it looks to me that along with the vision of the Kingdom of God, there need to take place a process of de-clericalization so that theology be freed to see and identify the presence and action of God in the society, world and history. Then theology will not speak about these realities within the clerical or clerically-conditioned milieux, but will become really a discourse about God in relationship to the world with a language the world understands and grasps as something relevant and meaningful.

Public theology is related to but different from *liberation theology*. This latter theology broke the privatization of religion and made its way to the public realm. The motivation for praxis of liberation came from Christian roots, and the methodology and tools of analysis were by and large Marxian in character. Public theology incorporates the concerns of liberation theology but its approach is much wider and its premises lie in the kind of relationship of religion to common good. Some comrades may be sceptical of public theology, and wonder whether it is an attempt to hijack liberation theology, and even a conspiracy of capitalism! The point we need to remember here is that liberation is the goal to which God's Word is beckoning us. Moving towards that goal calls for continuous rethinking of our analysis of the society and the tools we use to uncover oppression and bondage. In today's world of globalization we live in a much more complex society than was the case with the feudal society or industrial society of the past. The manifold forms of oppression today may not be adequately accounted for by a social analysis in terms of labour-capital conflict. Think of the issues of women, environment, ethnic minorities, immigrants, etc. Consequently, the analysis of the past requires a thorough revision in present-day circumstances of globalization. Public theology will explore new methods to assess the nature of oppression with regard to specific issues and questions, and seek a multipronged approach to overcome them.

Public theology is also different from a theology relating to public life pursued by Protestant *neo-orthodoxy*, as for example, by John Milbank, Max Stackhaus and others.[7] Here we have a theology of Barthian inspiration, rather than a contextual theology bearing upon culture and society. This theology concerns itself with public life so as to make it conform to transcendental values, to the Kingdom of God, to God, who is "totally the other" and who challenges and judges the world.[8] It rests on the assumption that instead of God's Word coming in encounter with the world, it is the world which needs to conform to God's Word.

Public theology refers to a theology that focuses on questions and issues that are public in nature and touches everyone across borders. In the process, it frees itself from doctrinaire moorings that have no or little bearing on the shared life and history with others in a society or polity. Since public theology needs to be done differently depending on the concrete situation, it cannot but be *contextual*. Public theology culls out from tradition and sacred sources those elements and insights that could contribute in the concrete context to the wellbeing of the people and of nature. This is a theology which has a language that is inherently dialogical and is ready to cooperate with all forces contributing to common good, something we understand when God's Kingdom becomes the point of reference. The ideal of God's Kingdom will serve also as the point of reference to distinguish a good theology from a mediocre one. Public theology firmly based on this ideal will serve to prune dominant theologies, and convert them to the core of faith and what is most important.

Public theology is concerned about the world, the history and what pertains all. As such, it calls for some basic reflections. Since it is a theology through and through in dialogue with the world and history, we are led to the fundamental question of how to relate religion and the public realm. Public theology cannot escape this issue. As I noted earlier, to create a form of theology and a theological language which others can under-

---

[7] See the forthcoming volume, Felix Wilfred – Daniel Pilario – Erik Borgmann (eds.), *Orthodoxy in Postmodern Times (Concilium 2013/5)*.

[8] Cf. John Milbank – Catherine Pickstock – Graham Ward (eds.), *Radical Orthodoxy*, London, Routledge, 1999.

stand and perceive as relevant and meaningful, we need to clear the ground of this relationship of religion to society and public life. In other forms of theology, such a question may not figure at all, or only marginally. Here in public theology it becomes a crucial issue. Even more, effective construction of public theology – whether in the East or West – will depend on how this question of religion and public life is broached. We shall begin from the case of the West.

The Western Case

In the last couple of decades there has taken place a shift in the perception of the relationship between religion and public life. With the decline of the thesis of secularization and the progressive abandonment of the thesis of religion as private, there have come about new equations between religion and public life. Instead of going into an analysis of how this has taken place, what I intend to do is to examine two most significant voices in the West – Jürgen Habermas and John Rawls – whose position on the relationship of religion to public life has become the core issue in public theology today, and at the same time most vigorously discussed and debated.

From Denial to the Recognition of Public Role for Religions

We could identify three phases in the thinking of Habermas in relation to religion: a) Suppression of religion through communicative reason, b) coexistence of religion and reason, c) cooperation of both for upholding the gains of modernity. The new turn to the third phase can be discerned in his works since 2001: *The Future of Human Nature, On Faith and Knowledge, Between Naturalism and Religion*. In the third phase of his thinking, Habermas shows his openness to the contribution of religion to the public sphere, challenging the claims of a narrow secularity. He notes:

> (S)ecularized citizens may neither fundamentally deny that religious convictions may be true nor reject the right of their devout fellow citizens to couch their contributions to public discussions in religious language.[9]

[9] As quoted in Maureen Junker-Kenny, *Habermas and Theology*, London, T&T Clark, 2011, 137; see also William Outhwaite, *Habermas*, Cambridge, Polity, 2007, 157 ff.

By way of example, I may adduce here how Habermas shows the importance of Christian doctrine of creation for the strengthening of human dignity and rights. He also sees its importance in addressing biomedical technological issues such as the genetic enhancement. Theological beliefs could throw light on this intricate question and contribute to the present and future wellbeing of humanity.

The Question of «Comprehensive Doctrines»

John Rawls speaks of *"comprehensive doctrines"* and *"overlapping consensus"*.[10] By comprehensive doctrines he means articulated systems of thought or explanations that claim to give a full-range of ultimate explanation of the world, nature, society, bearing upon their origin, value, their future, etc. And this is done by philosophy, religion, moral beliefs, etc. In simple terms, comprehensive doctrine means a theory of everything. Religions are habituated to present such a theory of everything – about God, humans, the world and so on. These comprehensive doctrines shape the way we look at the world, others and ourselves.

To be able to understand Rawl's political theory and his conception of the role of religion in relation to public life, we need to grasp how he transforms Kant's ideal of moral autonomy (*Critique of Practical Reason*) in an inter-subjective manner. Here is a question of abiding by those laws and arrangements that find acceptance among all concerned in a polity on the basis of their public use of reason. Moral autonomy is not simply a matter of freedom from coercion; it has a necessary reference to the other and to the public. This moral autonomy is linked to political autonomy. A religious group is politically autonomous not simply when it is free from any coercion with regard to the profession and practice of its beliefs, but when it is able to abide by what the common good requires and what finds acceptance among all concerned in a particular society. In this sense, religious freedom today needs to be defined not in isolation from the other, but in relation to the other and to what concerns the general good of all concerned.

---

[10] Cf. John Rawls, *Political Liberalism*, New York, Columbia University Press, 1993.

Religion and Public Reason

In the context of the discussion on public theology, a question of paramount importance is the relationship of religion to public reason.[11] Here is an issue that allows a wide interpretation but also raises many intricate questions. Contribution to public reason means that religious traditions do not get bogged down by their internal convictions and belief-systems but raise their heads above and hold before their eyes the general interest of the people. It would also involve a kind of translation into secular language of those beliefs that have public significance. The beliefs and convictions held by religious groups require to be supported by public reason, if they are to have any role in public life. The creation narrative of the Bible, for example, can support the equality of woman which is a secular issue in the polity. The same creation story can be deployed to support the cause of human rights. According to Christian belief, human beings are endowed with dignity since they have been created in the image of God. The question then is, should religions be stripped off their beliefs to reach a common ground of neutrality where they could enter into conversation with other similar religious groups. Don't we lose, in this way, the richness the religious beliefs, myths and symbols contain? Why not the religions carry these roots with them and enter into conversation with others, and thus through a mutuality that touches deeper chords reach consensus and understanding? This is a point which some Western theologians like Linda Hoggen and Nigel Biggar contends, when responding to the position of Rawls and Habermas in relation to public reason or overlapping consensus. Linda Hogan notes, for example: "[A] fundamental flaw in the idea of public reason lies in the manner in which it requires the speaker and listener to believe both the self and the other to be, or to act as though he or she is *rootless*."[12]

---

[11] Cf. John Rawls, *The Law of the Peoples Revisited*, Cambridge MA, Harvard University Press, 2001, 129–180 (The Idea of Public Reason Revisited).

[12] Nigel Biggar – Linda Hogan (eds.), *Religious Voices in Public Places*, Oxford, Oxford University Press, 2009, 223.

The Normative and the Factual

The positions of Rawls and Habermas are at the level of the normative, and are abstracted from concrete context. They follow a procedural reasoning in determining the relationship of religion and public sphere. But the factual reality does not correspond to this theorizing. As a matter of fact, in many European countries, there are the so-called established religions. The clearest example is that of UK. There, the bishops form part of the House of Lords. Similarly in the Scandinavian countries Lutheranism is the established religion. In these cases as well as in Germany, Belgium and Holland what we find is a kind of accommodation of religion and its continuing role in the public sphere. It is expressed in different forms, such as state-funding for educational institutions managed by Catholics, Protestants, Calvinists, etc., and collection of tax for the Church by the state.[13]

Situation in Asia

We do not want to begin the discussion from a normative and procedural plane, but rather start from the empirical situation of differences in the relationship of religion to public life, as it obtains in Asia. Looking at the empirical reality, we could identify three basic types in regard to the relationship of religion to the public sphere.

1. Religion Controlled by Centralizing State Authority

This is the model we could identify in the so-called "socialist countries" (China, Vietnam, Myanmar, North Korea, etc.). While religions are allowed freedom for worship and for carrying out certain limited activities, they are strictly controlled, so that they do not become any threat to the centralized authority. Such a situation allows little room for religions to play any effective role for common good and welfare of the whole society, going beyond their religious confines.

In the case of China, we need to refer to the cultural revolution of Mao Zedong. One of the ideological components of this revolution is the belief that religions are counter-revolutionary forces, and against national

---

[13] Cf. José Casanova, *Public Religions in the Modern World,* Chicago, The University of Chicago Press, 1994.

goals.[14] Along with the bourgeoisie, religions also need to be suppressed for the growth of the country, so it was argued. The ideology of Cultural Revolution viewed religion as an enemy to be fought against. Senseless destruction of religious places of worship and symbols followed. The reforms of 1978 in that country allowed, indeed, some space for the existence of religions, but under the watchful eyes of the state authorities. The vicissitudes in the relationship of the Chinese state with Vatican illustrates the various shifts in the position of the state.[15]

Zhibin Xie who has researched on the public role of religion in China enumerates three important reasons for greater role of religion in public life, in the future.[16] First of all, there is the traditional religious character of Chinese societies which is to be seen today also in the revival of religion in that country. Secondly, religious groups show increasing interest in participation in public life, which also involves dissent and protest. Thirdly, according to Zhibin Xie, with greater democratization in Chinese political life, there will be room for the voices of different religious groups to be heard. The view of this author may sound optimistic. What is important to note is that even in a centralized Asian country like China, the prospects of religion playing public role has become increasingly greater.[17] This calls for a theology of public life attuned to this new situation. The historically inherited models from the West may not respond to the unique nature of the relationship of religion and public life in China.

[14] In the case of Christianity, it was viewed also as a tool of imperialism and as an ally of the nationalist Kuomintang – an alliance to fight against atheistic communism.

[15] Cf. Eric O. Hanson, *Catholic Politics in China and Korea*, New York, Orbis Books, 1980.

[16] Zhibin Xie, *Religious Diversity and Public Religion in China*, Burlington, Ashgate Publishing Company, 2006, 2.

[17] A few years ago, there took place a conference in Singapore precisely on the issue of the role of religion in public life. The unique character of this conference is that some high-level state authorities and representatives of state institutions like the Chinese Academy of Social Sciences participated. The speeches and papers presented reflect clearly the state recognition of a positive role for religions, and this is defined as contribution to the harmony of the society. «Harmony of the society» is often an euphemism to say that religions should not act in a manner that upsets the system, the ways of the state. The papers of this conference are collected and published as a volume: Michael Nai-chu Poon (ed.), *Pilgrims and Citizens: Christian Social Engagement in East Asia Today*, Singapore, Atf Press, 2007.

Christians in China and other countries with centralized rule are in a dilemma, of having to contribute to the common good and public life and at the same time not conforming uncritically to the state and its policies. It is from this situation that we need to think of Christianity vis-à-vis the public sphere. It is very complex. For some Christian groups, especially from among the Protestant Churches, things seem to be rather simple: Religion contributes to public life by aligning with the state and its programmes, and one speaks about «common ground» of national goals where state and Church converge.[18] Public role of religion here ends up in endorsing and promoting uncritically the programmes of the state and the goals of the society it defines. We see then how urgent and important is a reflection on public theology in such contexts.

2. Established Religions

We have in Asia also situations in which religions openly determine politics and public life. There are many variants to this model. Heavy determination of politics and public life by Islam can be seen in Pakistan, Indonesia, Malaysia, Bangladesh, etc., and somewhat tenuous intervention of Buddhism in politics and public life in Thailand. In these countries, one could hardly separate majority religion from public life. On the contrary, in many respects it defines public life. Sri Lanka has not made Buddhism the state religion, but the constitution gives it «foremost place». In some of these countries with established religion, like in Pakistan, certain public offices cannot be held by any person other than a Muslim. The state support and preferential treatment of a particular religion conditions the scope for other minority religious groups. Often it is the case that the role in public life is reserved to the established religion, and other religious minorities are tolerated in the practice of their religion, but may not claim any intervention in the public sphere.

---

[18] Cf. Philip Wickeri, *Seeking the Common Ground. Protestant Christianity, and Three-Self Movement and China's United Front*, New York, Orbis Books, 1988; cf. also Jason Kindoop – Carol Lee Hamrin (eds.), *God and Caesar in China: Policy Implications of Church-State Tensions*, Washington, Brooking Institution Press, 2004.

3. Principled Distance

In this model, the secular is understood as non-privileging of any one religion by the state. Religions are allowed the freedom of worship and the freedom to propagate and be engaged in social and developmental activities, without prejudice to public order, morality and hygiene. We have such a model for example in India, Philippines, South Korea, etc. This model allows in theory the possibility of religions coming together and jointly contributing to the promotion of common good. But in reality this does not seem to happen. For, religions and religious bodies are often in conflict with each other to secure greater power and privileges for their own groups. Therefore, there is endless discussion and debate on secularism, as for example in India.

All the three models and the underlying situations we have seen lead us to the conclusion that we in Asia urgently need a public theology in new terms, in fresh and unique contexts.

Asian Debate on Religion in Public Life

Unlike in the West, there has been relatively little debate in Asia on religion in relation to public life in its various aspects and dimensions. The discussion has been almost exclusively focused on religious freedom and the understanding of secularism. This is clearly the case of India. Some intellectuals like Ashis Nandy, T. N. Madan debate this often in a polemical manner against the Western concept of the secular.[19] They maintain that in India religion has an important role to play. But then, there are but few constructive theories and suggestions coming out from these circles as how and in what manner religion could play a role in public life in a multi-religious society. The discourse in this matter needs to be initiated and advanced. Let me put forward a few thoughts and views in this regard by way of a foreword to Asian public theology.

---

[19] For the discussion on their views, see Rajeev Bhargava (ed.), *Secularism and Its Critics*, Delhi, Oxford University Press, 1998.

The Understanding of Public – Cultural Determination

When we speak of public theology in Asia, we need to be also conscious of the way "public" is understood and defined. This has important consequences for the role of religion in general, and Christianity in particular, vis-à-vis the Asian societies. Here is something which distinguishes Asian approach to the understanding of public and public theology. Hence, not only the history of relationship of religion to state is different from the West, but different also is the way public comes across to peoples of the Asian continent. Everyday experience shows that what the Western cultural world would consider private is blatantly public for Asians, and the reverse is also true. The cultural determination explodes the conventional demarcation between the public and the private. Without going into the details of the cultural determination, we may say that religion in Asia is *both public and private*. In a certain sense it is private; in another sense it is public. It is the intermingling and criss-crossing of the two that is something uniquely Asian.

Difference in the Understanding and Approach to Religion

As I noted, public theology presupposes the current debate on the role of religion in the public sphere. The discussions in the West on this question may trigger our reflections, but may not be able to come to terms with the Asian situation. One important reason for this is the fact that the concept of religion in Asian traditions has been quite different from the dominant conception of it in the West. To cite an example, religion is not viewed in Asia as a set of beliefs or doctrines, but as a way of life – a path, a journey. Religion is embedded in the culture and daily life of the people as the folk traditions of Asia manifests. This makes it already extremely difficult to create any "wall of separation" between religion and public life. But the point is that often the Constitutions of States do not reflect this Asian reality of religion, but seem to be attuned to the Western understanding of religion.

Moreover the relationship of religion to state and public life has had a different trajectory in the West which may not be replicated in Asia. This trajectory, to put it summarily, had three stages: the distinction between the Church and the state; separation of the two; and finally marginalization of the Church and religion from public life as of no consequence.

Public theology will go deeper into the relationship of religion and public life in Asian societies, and its contextually different histories. This history is by and large one of *accommodation of religion in public life* as the development of Indian secularism shows. This type of Asian accommodation cannot be fitted into any three stages of the Western trajectory.

Political Justice

In the context of our present discussion, by political justice I mean the rightful participation of various segments of the society with their different conceptions of good life in the construction of the common good. Since religions in a very significant way determine the outlook on life and values, it is important that religious groups also play a role in contributing to the common good which means that they go beyond the interests of the respective groups. This way of considering breaks the framework of *minority and majority*.

A second related question concerns specifically Christianity and its participation along with other religious groups for the public good. The difficulty with Christianity is that it is viewed as religion "foreign" to Asian societies. So, the question is, should a foreign religion like Christianity be considered on a par with other religious traditions and therefore having a share with others in deliberating on public good. This issue gets accentuated where there is an established religion. *Christianity is not viewed as a partner in the deliberation for common good.* The problem then is how Christians and Christian communities bring to bear upon the public life, the values and ideals which they believe are important and necessary for the general welfare of the people. The same attitude and practice of exclusion exists in practice also for Christianity in India in spite of a secular Constitution and the absence of any established religion.

The principles of democratic governance which recognize equal rights to individuals and groups would go against any such exclusion. But then, here historical memory overtakes any theory of equal participation. The alleged connivance of Christianity with the colonial rule makes many citizens sceptical about the participation of Christians and their contributing to the welfare of the nation. There is an undercurrent that a religious group cannot participate in the common good unless it subscribes to the nationalist expectations. This is how a Chinese writer expresses himself on this point:

> Chinese Christianity should participate in the cultural enterprise of Chinese nationalism in order to achieve a "common outlook" by abandoning its insistence on being seen as "different".[20]

But in fact, "foreignness" and being "different" alone does not seem to be sufficient reason for the exclusion of Christianity from being part of a national dialogue on common good. For, the same societies have had no difficulty to accept Western science and technology as contributing to the welfare of the nation. And in the case of China, it is not only science and technology; its ideology of Marxism was a Western import, but then it has been deployed to construct the political framework, ironically, when socialist systems have been abandoned in the West – in its place of origin.

Public Accountability of Religions

Public theology calls for an internal critique within Christianity. It raises a crucial question: What is being discussed as theology in the Churches, how relevant is it to the public? Public theology makes theology answerable to the people, and in this way justifies its interpretation of God's Word for today. When there are conflicts between religions, it is a clear sign that their theologies have failed in their mission. However much they may explain and interpret the truths of religion, when theology does not bear upon public life, it is a failed theology. Such a theology is not only irrelevant, but could be most dangerous. Views maintained at theological level have serious social and political consequences.

For any religion to have significance beyond the pale of its believers, it needs to demonstrate what contribution it could make to the well-being of all. Sometimes the claim is made that by the very announcement of its faith, Christianity contributes to humanity. That could be a well-

---

[20] Chin Ken Pa, What is Sino-Christian Theology?, in: *Concilium* 2008/2, 91.

meant statement. But often this is stated as a protective cover against undergoing any influence from the society and the world, as a refusal to learn from the world. What needs to be said is that Christianity cannot limit itself to expounding doctrines and beliefs which have universal scope, but needs to show how those beliefs concretely affect the life together in the public realm and contribute to the common good.

Public Theology and the Strengthening of Democratic Process

Democracy as a value and as a mode of governance is indispensable for sustaining a society in equity with full recognition of every segment and group in the polity. It is the antidote to exclusion which is the root cause of injustice. The understanding of collective life and community presupposed in democracy (understood as a process and culture) as well as the dignity of human person and human rights it implies, reflect Christian faith as found in the belief in creation and its understanding of human being and human community. Such being the case, public theology could contribute significantly to strengthen the democratic process. This contribution will be at the same time one towards social justice. Unfortunately, we have not reflected on this aspect in Asia. There is a lot to do along these lines.

Widening the Scope of Religious Freedom

This is a presupposition for a meaningful public theology in Asia. Religious freedom has many dimensions. Unfortunately, it is often reduced only to the relationship of a particular religious group to the state. Obviously, this is still a major issue in several parts of Asia. Religious freedom is not to be viewed simply as freedom from the coercion of the state enjoyed by a particular religious group for its activities in conformity with its beliefs and convictions. *Religious freedom needs to contribute to the attainment of public good* through forging relationship with other groups – both religious and secular. Public theology could help in the development of a deeper understanding of religious freedom and its practice.

There are various kinds of restraint on religious freedom. In India, religious freedom, according to the Constitution, is to be exercised with-

126

out any prejudice to public order, morality and hygiene. But we need to spell out the positive contribution the freedom of religion enjoyed by a religious group needs to make. The freedom of one religious group needs to be related to other religious groups and all of them together point to the attainment of common good. Here is then the *horizontal strengthening of religious freedom* as freedom for something which goes beyond the interests of a particular group. In other words, a religious group has real religious freedom when the space is open for it to be able to freely engage with others in the pursuit of the wellbeing of the entire community. I would say that this wider understanding of religious freedom is a necessary presupposition for public theology.

The wider understanding of religious freedom challenges the control of religion by the state as well as the established religion, or the idea of official religion which can be discriminative and curtail the freedom of other groups, and hence stunting the potential they have for contributing to common good. Public theology in Asia will address the issue of religious freedom as a necessary condition to bring out the contribution of religious groups to the larger community and to common good.

Conclusion

To speak of public theology is to speak of the future of Christianity in Asia in multicultural and multireligious societies in the larger horizon of the Kingdom of God. In these societies there is need to foster communion and build inclusive communities. Theology will help in this project by taking up for its praxis and reflection issues of common interest that affect everyone. This will help theology to be truly catholic in its original sense of comprising all, and it will not have the mark of being a sectarian enterprise limited to the faith-life of the Christian community. Asian Public theology will tell us what it means to live and understand the Kingdom of God in dialogue with the realities and experiences of this continent.

Public theology is a challenge to traditional theological pursuit, which had mostly the Christians and Christian community as its focus. Traditional theology, by its claim to be a science, it was thought, had come to the public realm in the comity of other sciences. Today, when the understanding and approach to science in general has undergone a sea change and when it operates with new epistemological premises, it would be futile to believe that the public character of theology is acquired by proving it to be a science in the traditional understanding.

Today, theology acquires public character because it relates to the reality of public life with peoples across religious borders and boundaries. It starts with experiences that go beyond the Christian communities, and it asks what contribution it could make to sustain and enhance the quality of public life. This way of pursuing theology could have great repercussion in rethinking its methods and sources.

Public theology will be pursued differently in Asia and in the West which have differing histories of relationship of religion to society and to the public realm. However, dialogue and conversation among public theologies of Asia and the West could be enlightening and mutually beneficial. But we need to be also aware of the fact that there is a certain asymmetry here. Whereas in the West, public theology has been object of reflection since the last few decades, it is only just now that Asian public theology is beginning to emerge. Asian public theology could be stimulated by the Western discussion, and could go deeper into a reflection on the role of religion in general and theology in the multi-religious and pluri-cultural societies of Asia.

Felix Wilfred is Professor Emeritus and Dean of the Faculty of Arts at the State University of Madras. He was also Professor and head of the department of Christian Studies in the same university. Dr. Wilfred is the President of the International Theological Review Concilium. He has been a member of the Vatican International Theological Commission and visiting professor in several universities, including the University of Frankfurt, University of Nijmegen, Boston College, Ateneo de Manila and Fudan University, China. He was recently appointed by the Government of India to the newly endowed Chair of Indian Studies at the University of Dublin, Ireland. Besides numerous publications in different languages, most recently he has edited The Oxford Handbook of Asian Christianity, a massive work dealing with major debates and themes, and the status of research in the area, and the work is due for publication shortly.

Asian Centre for Cross-Cultural Studies, 40/6a Panayur Kuppam Road, Panayur, Sholinganallur Post, Chennai – 600119, India.
felixwilfred@gmail.com

Bolivia: ¿Un Estado Laico?

Matthias Preiswerk

Summary

The relationships between religion and state that are subject to a process of change are highlighted with the example of Bolivia. The notion of secularism (worldliness, freedom from Church) is presented in the manner in which it appears in the state constitution and in the new regulations for education. As a special case the changes are presented as they should be realized in the religious education in elementary schools. In many countries of Latin America the new practice led to conflicts between the secular-oriented states and the churches regarding the formulation of laws concerning sexual rights and the right to procreation, abortion and marriage between people of the same sex.

Bolivia, uno de los países de América Latina con mayor densidad poblacional indígena tiene desde hace unos pocos años un Estado laico: un cambio muy significativo para un país que, además, ha pasado de ser una República a un Estado plurinacional. El cambio de una Constitución ¿implica, a corto o largo plazo, modificaciones en la mentalidad y en la vida cotidiana de la gente?, ¿será más bien una interpretación más cabal de lo que ya viven las personas en particular en sus relaciones con su tierra y territorio, con sus cuerpos, con sus diferentes orígenes étnicos, culturales, históricos, económicos, de género?

De manera más limitada me preguntaré qué significa pasar a un Estado denominado «laico» para un país que, por siglos y a través de relaciones unilaterales con la iglesia católica, se ha ocultado a sí mismo su extrema diversidad religiosa. Además discutiré la pertinencia del adjetivo laico dentro de una sociedad cuyo funcionamiento (incluso estatal) está atravesado por mentalidades, prácticas, tradiciones y símbolos profundamente religiosos.

Para no quedarme en generalidades y abstracciones, limitaré las preguntas anteriores al campo educativo: una esfera en la que cualquier Estado se cruza siempre con el campo religioso. Mostraré que la Educación Religiosa Escolar (ERE) se ha vuelto en los últimos años un campo de batalla entre cierta concepción del Estado laico e iglesias de las más diferentes tradiciones. Esta tensión es fuerte aunque no sea tan conflictiva como otros temas que aparecen en la agenda política de los Estados que empiezan a afirmar su condición laica: derechos sexuales y reproductivos, aborto o matrimonio igualitario.

¿CÓMO SALIR DE UNA MENTALIDAD DE CRISTIANDAD?
Las iglesias como instituciones tutelares

Con matices diferentes, creo que la pregunta sobre la perduración de una mentalidad de Cristiandad se aplica a la gran parte de los países de América Latina y del Caribe. Efectivamente estas sociedades han estado viviendo durante siglos bajo regímenes de Cristiandad con o sin concordato con el Vaticano. Dicho de manera corta y esquemática, la iglesia católica ha funcionado por mucho tiempo como una institución tutelar, un adjetivo que, significativamente, se usa de la misma manera para calificar la condición de las Fuerzas Armadas. La iglesia sería una institución encargada de cuidar y defender a la Nación de las agresiones y contaminaciones que podría sufrir particularmente en lo moral y en lo espiritual[1]. La iglesia católica como garante de una determinada forma de vivir, definida y aplicada desde fuera y por encima del Estado mismo pero con traducciones y aplicaciones jurídicas, a veces drásticas.

En un país como Bolivia, el Estado laico irá buscando poco a poco romper esta dependencia e intromisión pero se encuentra confrontado a dos dificultades mayores. Dificultades internas en la medida en que no

---

[1] Resulta curioso observar que en América Latina, las llamadas Secretarías de «Cultos» están insertas en tres tipos diferentes de Ministerios: en el de Relaciones Exteriores como en Bolivia, en el del Interior o en el de Justicia, como en Ecuador y Perú por ejemplo. Estas inserciones son altamente simbólicas. Como si lo religioso estuviera ligado a un asunto extranjero, ajeno de alguna manera a lo nacional y por ende normado por relaciones diplomáticas. O como si estuviera relacionado con un tema de seguridad nacional en el último caso. Hilando un poco más la paradoja de lo religioso como ajeno, llama la atención que, en Bolivia, los grupos que tienen que ver con las cosmovisiones propias a estas tierras, no aparecen en la lista del año 2010 de 341 grupos del Registro Nacional de Asociaciones religiosas en la Dirección de Cultos http://www.rree.gob.bo/webmre/documentos/servicios/d27.pdf

tiene a disposición un capital simbólico suficientemente amplio y estructurado como para sustituir el conjunto abigarrado de símbolos, sentidos, «valores», *habitus* construido a lo largo de siglos y aglomerados debajo del manto de la tradición católica occidental. Dificultades externas porque la estructura católica institucionalizada y profundamente internalizada se resiste, a veces violentamente, a perder un sitial que le otorgaba el papel de Madre. Dificultades también de orden jurídico en la medida en que la iglesia católica ha logrado ser reconocida como «persona colectiva de derecho público»[2] lo que le da acceso a grandes privilegios[3] que no comparte con otras iglesias y religiones.

Cristiandad de sentido común

Es notable observar cómo el régimen y la mentalidad de Cristiandad perduran en afirmaciones que se confunden con cierto sentido común y que, sin embargo, corresponden cada vez menos a la realidad empírica. Todavía se escucha con frecuencia decir que Bolivia es un «país católico», negando por ejemplo el crecimiento rápido de otras expresiones cristianas y de amplios sectores de la población que, debajo de una identidad impuesta, siguen con una práctica religiosa, cosmovisión y espiritualidad profundamente ancladas en tradiciones prehispánicas. La fórmula anterior da lugar a una cantidad de silogismos: si Bolivia es católica, la o el ciudadano boliviano lo es también; por lo tanto es legítimo que las leyes del país traduzcan y apliquen una moral católica y que la escuela, con su misión de transmitir conocimientos y valores, se encargue de comunicar esa fe específica.

Insistiré sobre el hecho de que la mentalidad de Cristiandad está profundamente internalizada por grandes sectores evangélicos que sueñan con quitarle a la iglesia católica el sitial y los privilegios heredados. De esta manera se encuentran con mucha frecuencia en declaraciones y prédicas evan-

---

[2] Es también persona de derecho internacional por las relaciones diplomáticas que mantiene con el Vaticano, como Estado.

[3] En Bolivia las iglesias cristianas no católicas están equiparadas jurídicamente hasta el momento a unas especies de ONGs religiosas que no acceden a liberación de impuestos, convenio s con el Estado, invitaciones a actos públicos, entre otras cosas.

gélicas expresiones tales como «sociedad occidental y cristiana»[4], «nación cristiana», «leyes o instituciones cristianas», «gobierno cristiano», etc.

La mentalidad de Cristiandad contra el Estado laico

Los proyectos de Ley de derechos sexuales y reproductivos, la legalización del aborto (aun en caso de violación por ejemplo) y el matrimonio igualitario chocan frontalmente con la tradición y con la mentalidad de Cristiandad. En América latina, cuando estos temas entran al debate parlamentario y público, desencadenan reacciones de gran violencia simbólica[5].

Los conflictos en torno a la sexualidad y al control sobre los cuerpos tienen traducciones diferentes a lo largo de los años. Por ejemplo hace unos treinta años atrás, cuando eran muy pocos los Estados latinoamericanos que podían abrirse a la laicidad, uno de los temas álgidos era el del control de la natalidad. Entonces, contrariamente a lo que pasa ahora con los derechos sexuales, el aborto o el matrimonio igualitario, el control de la natalidad lograba juntar en un mismo frente a sectores ideológicos y políticos diametralmente opuestos tales como jerarquía eclesiástica e iz-

---

[4] Una expresión amplia y tristemente reivindicada por todas las dictaduras militares latinoamericanas.

[5] A título de ejemplo las palabras del Cardinal de Argentina, Mgr. Bergoglio, en una carta dirigida a las hermanas carmelitas de Buenos Aires en 2010: «*No seamos ingenuos: no se trata de una simple lucha política; es la pretensión destructiva al plan de Dios. No se trata de un mero proyecto legislativo (éste es sólo el instrumento) sino de una movida del Padre de la Mentira que pretende confundir y engañar a los hijos de Dios*» http://infocatolica.com/?t= noticia&cod=6783. Paralelamente la Alianza Cristiana de las Iglesias Evangélicas de Argentina, después de la aprobación de la ley declara: «*ACIERA considera que claramente se ha establecido un nuevo orden social apartado de los fundamentos del cristianismo, y que no distingue entre libertad y libertinaje. Los tiempos anticipados por la palabra de Dios llegan inexorablemente y la acción de la Iglesia de Cristo, Santa y en comunión con Él, deberá cumplir su función de alertar sobre el pecado, presentar el mensaje de salvación en Cristo a todos los seres vivientes y tomar autoridad espiritual sobre autoridades, principados y potestades que operan en las regiones celestes, en el Nombre de nuestro Señor Jesucristo, sabiendo que ante Él se doblará toda rodilla en el cielo, en la tierra y debajo de ella, y toda lengua confesará que Jesucristo es el Señor.*» http://www.iglesialcs.cl/newweb/index2.php?option= com_content&do_pdf=1&id=195. Además de las coincidencias entre la jerarquía católica y los sectores evangélicos más conservadores, se logró constituir coyunturalmente una especie de frente de credos monoteístas, incluyendo a judíos y musulmanes.

quierda radical: se mezclaba la «defensa de la vida» con la lucha contra un imperialismo conspirativo interesado en impedir el crecimiento de «masas revolucionarias». Volveré más abajo sobre esta especie de ecumenismo que determinadas acciones estatales logran consolidar entre sectores religiosos o ideológicos antagónicos.

Para contrastar con lo anterior, hay que recordar que, en otras circunstancias y contextos, las iglesias y grupos religiosos pueden tener otros focos de debate o de confrontación con el Estado más allá de lo concerniente a la sexualidad y a la educación. Me refiero por ejemplo a la objeción de conciencia (derecho de no servir al Estado cuando se trata de matar al prójimo), a la lucha contra la pobreza, a la preservación del medio ambiente, a la equidad de género, a la seguridad alimentaria, a la lucha contra el armamentismo, etc. Parece que, en la mentalidad latinoamericana de Cristiandad, estas luchas no tendrían mayor relación con la identidad cristiana y no serían exigencias a plantear a los Estados con la misma urgencia como la referida a la moral sexual.

LA NUEVA CONSTITUCIÓN BOLIVIANA: ¿LAICA O MULTIRRELIGIOSA?
Antecedente
Antes de referirme a la nueva Constitución aprobada por un referéndum el año 2009 menciono brevemente lo que se mencionaba sobre lo religioso en la versión de 1967 incluyendo las diversas correcciones que llevaron a la de 1995[6], antecedente inmediato del actual texto constitucional.

ARTÍCULO 3º. – Libertad de Culto

El Estado reconoce y sostiene la religión católica, apostólica y romana. Garantiza el ejercicio público de todo otro culto.

Las relaciones con la Iglesia Católica se regirán mediante concordatos y acuerdos entre el Estado Boliviano y la Santa Sede.

En las circunstancias de entonces el sostenimiento a la religión católica se concretizaba, además de lo ya indicado en el plano jurídico, a través de un apoyo económico a algunos sacerdotes y diócesis así como en el reconocimiento de ítems para los profesores de religión. Si bien ese apoyo no era

---

[6] Esta versión, en su introducción, tuvo la virtud de introducir y reconocer por primera vez el carácter multicultural y plurilingüe de Bolivia.

muy significativo en relación con los aportes de la iglesia en el campo educativo, se trataba de un reconocimiento y sostenimiento más simbólico, mediante la simbiosis ya mencionada.

Hasta la llegada al poder de Evo Morales ese artículo fue el centro de todos los enfrentamientos entre la jerarquía católica y las otras iglesias cristianas. La primera lo defendía a rajatabla mientras que las otras no encontraban la forma de hacerse reconocer en igualdad de condiciones y de derechos. Ambas resistían con fuerza a la idea de un Estado laico, introduciendo consciente o inconscientemente una amalgama entre laicidad y laicismo. Sin embargo dentro de la Asamblea Constituyente la iglesia católica como los grupos evangélicos más representativos se vieron obligados a asumir de una y otra manera el discurso sobre la laicidad; la jerarquía católica para no perder todo, las otras acudiendo a la tradición protestante de separación entre Iglesia y Estado.

¿Una Constitución laica?

En primer lugar recalco el hecho de que, aunque tanto el ciudadano de a pie como las autoridades estatales dicen que Bolivia se ha vuelto laica, esta palabra no aparece en ninguna parte del nuevo texto constitucional. Al contrario en los párrafos introductorios referidos a sus fundamentos, se explicitan unos cimientos relacionados con creencias tanto religiosas como no religiosas. El Preámbulo inicia con una declaración que calificaría de poético-telúrica:

> *En tiempos inmemoriales se erigieron montañas, se desplazaron ríos, se formaron lagos. Nuestra amazonia, nuestro chaco, nuestro altiplano y nuestros llanos y valles se cubrieron de verdores y flores[7]. Poblamos esta sagrada Madre Tierra con rostros diferentes, y comprendimos desde entonces la pluralidad vigente de todas las cosas y nuestra diversidad como seres y culturas. Así conformamos nuestros pueblos, y jamás comprendimos el racismo hasta que lo sufrimos desde los funestos tiempos de la colonia.*

---

[7] Se podría calificar el lenguaje de animista cuando se otorga a montañas, ríos, lagos la capacidad de erigirse, desplazarse, formarse o a las diferentes regiones ecológicas del país (chaco, altiplano, valles, etc.) la calidad de cubrirse de verdores y flores.

Termina con referencia a diversas creencias:

> *Cumpliendo el mandato de nuestros pueblos, con la fortaleza de nuestra Pachamama y gracias a Dios refundamos Bolivia.*

El lenguaje utilizado nos indica que el nuevo Estado boliviano no se erige sobre los modelos clásicos de la laicidad. Efectivamente, la refundación de Bolivia se basa en tres tipos de creencias.

- La primera es de tipo no religioso: la referencia al «mandato de nuestros pueblos» está relacionada con las luchas de los movimientos sociales. Estos se empoderaron notablemente a partir del año 2000 mediante las luchas por el agua y por el gas, provocaron una crisis del modelo de Estado anterior, la expulsión de un presidente y la victoria abrumadora del MAS en las elecciones democráticas del año 2005.
- Las dos últimas son de tipo religioso:
  - «la fortaleza de nuestra Pachamama»: referencia más obvia a las religiones andinas pero no así a las religiones de las tierras bajas,
  - «gracias a Dios»: fórmula genérica que se puede probablemente asimilar aquí con el Dios cristiano.

Sin embargo y contrastando con lo anterior, se puede afirmar que, a pesar de no definirse como laico, el texto constitucional describe varias de las características de un tal Estado. Lo mostraré con algunos artículos.

> *Artículo 4. El Estado respeta y garantiza la libertad de religión y de creencias espirituales, de acuerdo con sus cosmovisiones. El Estado es independiente de la religión.*

La nueva constitución respeta explícitamente la libertad religiosa y su «independencia» de la religión[8]. Más abajo el texto se refiere a la prohibición de toda discriminación:

> «*fundada en razón de sexo, color, edad, orientación sexual, identidad de género, origen, **cultura,** nacionalidad, ciudadanía, idioma, **credo reli-***

---

[8] El hecho de hablar de «independencia» y no de «separación» entre religión y estado podría, tal como lo mencionaron algunos sectores evangélicos, introducir ambigüedades favorables tanto a la iglesia católica como a las religiones andinas. La primera no perdería todos sus privilegios y las segundas podrían ser acogidas en espacios estatales, algo que menciono más abajo.

gioso, ideología, filiación política o filosófica[9], *estado civil, condición económica o social, tipo de ocupación, grado de instrucción, discapacidad, embarazo, u otras que tengan por objetivo o resultado anular o menoscabar el reconocimiento, goce o ejercicio, en condiciones de igualdad, de los derechos de toda persona.» (Artículo 14/II)*

Lo mismo se expresa de manera positiva en Artículo 21 cuando se garantiza la: *autoidentificación cultural; la privacidad, intimidad, honra, honor, propia imagen y dignidad;* **la libertad de pensamiento, espiritualidad, religión y culto,** *expresados en forma individual o colectiva, tanto en público como en privado, con fines lícitos.*

La libertad de conciencia incluida implícitamente en los dos artículos recién citados aparece explícitamente más abajo a propósito del tema religioso en la escuela:

> *En los centros educativos se reconocerá y se garantizará la libertad de conciencia y de fe y de la enseñanza de religión, así como la espiritualidad de las naciones y pueblos indígena originario campesinos, y se fomentará el respeto y la convivencia mutua entre las personas con diversas opciones religiosas, sin imposición dogmática. En estos centros no se discriminará en la aceptación y permanencia de las alumnas y los alumnos por su opción religiosa. (Artículo 86)*

Las citas anteriores nos permiten plantear que la Constitución apunta a un tipo de laicidad que trata de integrar e incluir a lo religioso en una perspectiva pluralista o multirreligiosa y que de ninguna manera se opone a lo religioso en una línea modernista y secularizante. Estas características serán precisadas y profundizadas en la nueva Ley de Educación.

RELIGIONES Y LAICIDAD EN LA NUEVA LEY DE EDUCACIÓN

El nombre de esta Ley viene de dos destacados educadores: Avelino Siñani (aymara) y Elizardo Pérez (urbano mestizo) que idearon la Escuela-Ayllu de Warisata en el altiplano paceño, un hito para la educación indigenista en América Latina en la primera mitad del siglo XX.

---

[9] El resaltado es mío y busca señalar los campos de la existencia en los que intervienen más explícitamente unas creencias, sean religiosas o no.

No pretendo sintetizar los contenidos ni siquiera la filosofía del documento en su conjunto. Introduce sin duda cambios radicales en el sistema educativo tradicional boliviano. Recoge propuestas y discursos de política educativa producidos durante las últimas décadas por las principales organizaciones populares e indígenas, ongs, iglesia católica y otras.

Calificativos de la educación

La principal novedad consiste en calificar a la educación boliviana como laica, algo que debe ser ubicado e interpretado a partir del contexto tanto literario como ideológico del texto de la Ley.

El Artículo 3 del Capítulo II desarrolla las Bases, fines y objetivos de la educación. En seguida llama la atención una acumulación y reiteración impresionante de adjetivos que, en determinadas lógicas y culturas, podrían aparecer contradictorios cuando no antagónicos. Las Bases de la educación están descritas acudiendo en los catorce incisos del mismo artículo a no menos de treinta y tres adjetivos calificativos que se sitúan en varios registros y con diversos acentos.

Político

1. *descolonizadora, liberadora, revolucionaria, anti-imperialista, despatriarcalizadora y transformadora de las estructuras económicas y sociales*

2. *comunitaria, democrática, participativa …*

3. *universal …*

7. *inclusiva, asumiendo la diversidad …*

12. *promotora de la convivencia pacífica …*

Cultural o culturalista

1. *orientada a la reafirmación cultural de las naciones y pueblos indígena originario campesinos, las comunidades interculturales y afrobolivianas*

8. *intracultural, intercultural y plurilingüe …*

Educativo o pedagógico

3. *se desarrolla a lo largo de toda la vida […]*

4. *única, diversa y plural […] erradicando las diferencias entre lo fiscal y privado, lo urbano y rural …*

5. *unitaria e integradora […]*

138

10. *científica, técnica, tecnológica y artística, […] desde la cosmovisión de las culturas indígena […], en complementariedad con los saberes y conocimientos universales*

Económico

9. *productiva y territorial, orientada a la producción intelectual y material, al trabajo creador y a la relación armónica de los sistemas de vida y las comunidades humanas en la Madre Tierra, […]*

Ético

13. *Con referencia a diferentes principios éticos de los pueblos originiarios, al Vivir Bien y otras expresiones propias tanto a las tierras altas como a las tierras bajas.*

Educación laica

Transcribo integralmente los dos incisos directamente relacionados con las creencias y la problemática religiosa:

6. *Es laica, pluralista y espiritual, reconoce y garantiza la libertad de conciencia y de fe y de la enseñanza de religión, así como la espiritualidad de las naciones y pueblos indígena originario campesinos, fomenta el respeto y la convivencia mutua entre las personas con diversas opciones religiosas, sin imposición dogmática, y propiciando el diálogo interreligioso.*

11. *Es educación de la vida y en la vida, para Vivir Bien. Desarrolla una formación integral que promueve la realización de la identidad, afectividad, espiritualidad y subjetividad de las personas y comunidades; es vivir en armonía con la Madre Tierra y en comunidad entre los seres humanos.*

Finalmente el Artículo 3 sobre Fines de la Educación vuelve sobre el carácter laico:

6. *«Desarrollar una educación laica y pluralista que permita el conocimiento de historias religiosas universales, la espiritualidad de las naciones indígenas originarias y del pueblo boliviano y respete las creencias como base del derecho individual y comunitario.»*

Retomando el texto de la Ley en su integralidad, señalo los énfasis y la frecuencia de determinados adjetivos y expresiones relacionados directa o indirectamente con las interacciones entre culturas, religiones y creencias:

- La categoría más utilizada, retomando lo que ya está en la nueva Constitución, es la dupla intra e intercultural acompañada generalmente de plurilingüe. Entre adjetivos y sustantivos aparecen más de veinte veces[10].

- El Vivir Bien (*suma qamaña en aymara y sumak kawsay* en quechua), principio o esquema económico, social, cultural ético-político presentado como alternativo al sistema capitalista, industrial, occidental aparece diez veces.

- Espiritual y espiritualidad aparecen ocho veces.

- La Madre Tierra (expresión más incluyente que Pachamama) aparece ocho veces.

- Cosmovisiones, cuatro veces.

- El adjetivo laico aparece dos veces.

- El sustantivo religión o religiones no aparecen mientras que el adjetivo aparece dos veces.

- El adjetivo interreligioso una vez.

---

[10] Los conceptos intraculturalidad e interculturalidad merecen una definición pormenorizada lo que no deja de ser significativo en un texto de ley, Capítulo III, Artículo 6:

I. *Intraculturalidad: La intraculturalidad promueve la recuperación, fortalecimiento, desarrollo y cohesión al interior de las culturas de las naciones y pueblos indígena originario campesinos, comunidades interculturales y afrobolivianas para la consolidación del Estado Plurinacional, basado en la equidad, solidaridad, complementariedad, reciprocidad y justicia. En el currículo del Sistema Educativo Plurinacional se incorporan los saberes y conocimientos de las cosmovisiones de las naciones y pueblos indígena originario campesinos, comunidades interculturales y afrobolivianas.*

II. *Interculturalidad: El desarrollo de la interrelación e interacción de conocimientos, saberes, ciencia y tecnología propios de cada cultura con otras culturas, que fortalece la identidad propia y la interacción en igualdad de condiciones entre todas las culturas bolivianas con las del resto del mundo. Se promueven prácticas de interacción entre diferentes pueblos y culturas desarrollando actitudes de valoración, convivencia y diálogo entre distintas visiones del mundo para proyectar y universalizar la sabiduría propia.*

El hechizo de los adjetivos

La acumulación y reiteración de adjetivos tienen un cierto efecto hechizante y de encantación al margen del riesgo de que algunas expresiones puedan anularse entre sí. Algunas palabras llegan a ser como fetiches o comodines ideológicos que podrían dar pie a las interpretaciones más diversas: de lo ancestral a lo posmoderno, de lo folklórico a lo intercultural, de lo dogmático a lo interreligioso. Dentro de una lógica moderna algunos adjetivos se contradicen entre sí por ejemplo cuando, en una misma frase, se califica a la educación de «laica y espiritual». Sin embargo considero que en el contexto cultural y boliviano la expresión denota más bien una tensión creativa y sugerente aunque no explicitada ni trabajada todavía.

Para interpretar correctamente el texto habría que analizar el modo según el cual fue producido. Desde la política tanto sindical como indígena se procede generalmente a crear aprobaciones por añadidura: en vez de alcanzar consensos posiblemente imposibles y sin poder imponer una posición sobre la otra, se suman las diferentes propuestas o adjetivos de sectores socio-culturales y políticos contrapuestos. Se podría comparar este procedimiento con el que caracteriza la producción de algunos textos y declaraciones eclesiásticas[11].

Finalmente es fundamental recalcar que los políticos, representantes de movimientos sociales e intelectuales orgánicos que redactaron este documento coinciden en propuestas culturales generales pero no se interesan por el tema religioso en sí; mucho menos manejan categorías ligadas a ese campo específico. Se crean malentendidos con los responsables de las diferentes expresiones religiosas cristianas y con los teólogos porque estos abordan y leen categorías como laicidad y espiritualidad con otros lentes.

Para concluir se puede afirmar que la nueva Ley de Educación marca un cambio radical en relación con lo planteado e implementado por la del año 1994. Esta ruptura se expresa con evidencia a nivel filosófico, epistemológico, político, sociológico, antropológico y pedagógico. Sin embargo al mismo tiempo arrastra contradicciones y dificultades que difi-

---

[11] Lo menciono en el artículo «Ecumenismo y Educación Teológica en Aparecida» p. 49 a propósito de la redacción del documento de la V Conferencia del CELAM. VV.AA. 2007 Y *después de Aparecida, ¿qué?* Verbo Divino, Cochabamba.

cultaron seriamente la implementación de la Ley anterior. La principal consiste en pretender elaborar e implementar un cambio radical en la educación de todo un país al margen – cuando no en contra – de algunos de sus actores decisivos como el magisterio en primer lugar. Por otra parte, en un Estado precario y pobre como el boliviano, la educación en general no ha podido sostenerse al margen del apoyo de iglesias y de organismos internacionales, el mismo que ahora está mermando gravemente[12].

HACIA UNA NUEVA EDUCACIÓN RELIGIOSA ESCOLAR

Al igual que los otros temas que provocan conflictos entre el Estado y las iglesias, el de la ERE representa en Bolivia una especie de volcán que tiene erupciones de frecuencia e intensidad variables. Basta a veces la declaración de un Ministro, el anuncio de alguna jerarquía eclesiástica para que los ánimos se caldeen y que el debate se polarice.

Antes de mencionar y analizar los nuevos rumbos que toma o podría tomar la ERE en el contexto de la nueva Constitución y de la nueva Ley de Educación, recordemos de manera rápida y sintética el estatus y algunas características generales de esta práctica educativa altamente extraña. Efectivamente puede desatar conflictos de mucha intensidad entre Estado y jerarquías eclesiásticas a pesar de ser una de las materias que menos le importa al escolar boliviano (y, probablemente, latinoamericano en general).

Antes de la reforma neoliberal

Al margen de un análisis histórico más amplio, se puede anotar algunas características generales de la ERE hasta el año 1994. Me limitaré a la educación fiscal ya que la situación de los colegios privados dependientes de iglesias representa un caso particular diferente.

Por mucho tiempo la materia de lleva el nombre de Clase de religión lo que, para el sentido común, es una referencia obvia a la religión católi-

---

[12] No existe relación alguna entre los recursos económicos internacionales conseguidos para la Reforma educativa de 1994 con el financiamiento de la actual.

ca[13]. Se trata por lo tanto de una educación claramente confesional o, mejor dicho, monoconfesional si se asume que existen otras confesiones en Bolivia. De manera general esa clase de religión combina la transmisión de conocimientos religiosos particulares y específicos a la tradición católica con la iniciación a esa misma fe y, aún, con la preparación a determinados ritos. En este sentido se puede afirmar que el espacio escolar se vuelve terreno de evangelización, y que la clase de religión corresponde técnicamente a lo que convendría nombrar una catequesis escolar. Era muy frecuente que, en los colegios fiscales bolivianos, la clase de religión fuera utilizada para la preparación a la primera comunión católica por ejemplo.

Lo anterior que refleja a cabalidad la mentalidad de Cristiandad, satisface a muchos hogares que delegan a la escuela la responsabilidad de una educación religiosa familiar que ellos no quieren asumir o no saben cómo enfocar.

Lo anterior, salvadas honrosas excepciones, tenía un nivel teológico y didáctico extremadamente bajo que explica en parte el poco interés de las y los estudiantes por una materia que, en escala de importancia, disputa su lugar con educación cívica, educación física y artes.

Buscando levantar el nivel de la materia la iglesia católica, a partir de la década de los noventa propició dentro de sus Normales la formación de profesores de religión acreditados por las autoridades estatales competentes. Siguiendo el ejemplo apareció una Normal adventista con el mismo propósito. Estas instancias ya fueron cerradas por el actual Gobierno.

Con la Reforma neoliberal

La Reforma educativa de 1994 es de cuño modernizador y hasta neoliberal en la línea de las reformas ya introducidas en Chile y Colombia. Sus autores, siguiendo a sus pares a lo largo y ancho de América Latina, esperaban sustituir la tradicional materia de Religión por una de «Ética y moral» o de

[13] En Bolivia como en muchos países de América Latina determinados sustantivos no requieren de ningún adjetivo calificativo para expresar una particularidad dentro de la diversidad. En conversaciones o en artículos de prensa, cuando se habla de la iglesia o de la embajada todo el mundo entiende que se hace referencia a la iglesia católica o a la embajada norteamericana.

«Valores»; una perspectiva secularizante que, si aborda lo religioso, lo hace solamente desde la perspectiva de la ética. Se puede observar que sus iniciadores no logran desplazar ni reequilibrar el peso de lo religioso en la educación nacional. Efectivamente la jerarquía católica de inmediato, usando las íntimas relaciones que mantenía con los gobiernos neoliberales de turno, logra no solamente evitar la laicidad y la secularización de la educación boliviana sino reforzar de alguna manera su confesionalidad. De esta manera, la Ley de Reforma educativa legitima la hegemonía de la educación religiosa católica en la escuela pública, aunque introduzca la posibilidad de una diversificación[14]. Que estudiantes y/o padres de familia puedan acceder a una educación religiosa de otro cuño confesional nunca se implementó. Tampoco se conocen casos en los que los educandos que no «estuvieran de acuerdo con la religión impartida» (léase católica) en el colegio hubieran solicitado y conseguido dispensa de la clase de religión para acudir a una materia de «formación ética y moral». La no obligatoriedad de la enseñanza católica, probablemente deseada por la Reforma del 94, no prosperó.

Desde el año 1999 el nombre oficial de la materia religiosa dentro del programa oficial se vuelve «Religión, Ética y Moral»: una cooptación del vocabulario secularizante de la Reforma, reabsorbido en perspectiva católica. La iglesia católica logra además aumentar la carga horaria de la clase de religión a dos horas semanales en todos los ciclos. Al mismo tiempo se dan avances significativos en la producción de documentos de la Conferencia Episcopal de Educación de cara a una apertura confesional pero profesores de religión no buscan ni pueden salir de la confesionalidad.

En el Estado plurinacional

Si la Reforma educativa fracasó en su intento de «relocalizar» a la educación religiosa confesional fuera de la escuela, el Gobierno del MAS en sus

---

[14] **Artículo 57°.** *En los establecimientos fiscales y privados no confesionales se impartirá la religión católica; y en los privados confesionales, la religión acorde con su naturaleza confesional. En ambos casos, si no se estuviera de acuerdo con la religión impartida en el establecimiento, se podrá solicitar el cambio de la materia de religión por la materia de formación ética y moral, que podrá ser atendida por cualquier profesor del establecimiento capacitado para el efecto.*

inicios, no tuvo mayor suerte para disputar la hegemonía religiosa educativa señalada. El primer Ministro de Educación, apenas instalado y en el marco de la descolonización, propuso sacar la religión católica y cristiana de la escuela para reemplazarla por clases de historia de las religiones ancestrales, algo que desatará un verdadero conflicto de Estado[15].

La nueva Constitución y la nueva Ley de Educación ofrecen un techo muy rico y abierto para imaginar e incentivar nuevos tipos de ERE en perspectiva incluyente y no confesional. Por otra parte son insignificantes los sectores que reclaman la simple supresión de lo religioso en la escuela pública. A pesar de ello no se logra, hasta el momento, abrir un espacio de debate y de construcción colectiva para un nuevo currículo. Los esbozos y productos alcanzados reflejan una tensión no resuelta entre tendencias y actores con competencias dispares. Esquematizando la situación existen por un lado algunos actores católicos capaces de elaborar un programa confesional más o menos abierto e incluyente y, por el otro, técnicos del Ministerio (con formación más sociológica y filosófica que pedagógica y de las Ciencias de la Religión) que velan por una coherencia ideológica dentro del currículo global en construcción. Esta dinámica pasa de lo participativo formal a imposiciones del Ministerio[16]; va acompañada por sucesivos cambios de nombre para llegar a llamarse desde 2010 «Valores, Espiritualidades y Religiones»[17] en el marco del nuevo currículo del Siste-

[15] La siguiente anécdota resulta significativa. El 30 de julio de 2006 se reúnen en la ciudad de Cochabamba las tres mayores autoridades del Poder Ejecutivo: Presidente, Vice-Presidente, Ministro de la Presidencia con las tres máximas autoridades del catolicismo boliviano: Cardenal, Vice-Presidente y Secretario de la Conferencia Episcopal para tratar del tema de la clase de religión, como si se tratara de algo de vital importancia para la sociedad boliviana. Los resultados apagan la tensión pero son francamente insignificantes ya que no van más allá de la reafirmación de la libertad religiosa.

[16] Para ilustrar lo anterior se puede mencionar la convocatoria pública que se hizo en 2008 para consultores encargados de elaborar una primera propuesta de currículo. Esta primera licitación fue ganada por una religiosa y un sacerdote católico que elaboraron un proyecto confesionalista, poco contextual y menos inculturado: una propuesta mucho más retrógrada que la que la iglesia católica elaboró bajo el techo de la anterior reforma educativa. Este proyecto curricular fue desechado rápidamente.

[17] Esta materia está ubicada en el área de Saberes y Conocimientos que se encuentra a su vez dentro del campo Cosmos y Pensamiento.

ma educativo plurinacional. Llama la atención el hecho de que la materia, finalmente, desparece del ciclo de Primaria apareciendo solamente en los últimos cursos de Secundaria. El objetivo general del área está formulado en los siguientes términos:

> «*Desarrollamos valores éticos, morales y espirituales de las naciones indígena originario campesinas, afro-bolivianas y comunidades interculturales a partir de las manifestaciones de espiritualidad, religiosidad y la historia de las religiones, mediante la investigación y el análisis crítico, respetuoso y armónico de la diversidad existente para el ejercicio pleno de la libertad de conciencia y de fe sin imposición dogmática.*»

Esta formulación tiene un sesgo culturalista e indianista claro que se traduce en las propuestas temáticas del currículo correspondiente.

Estos documentos, conocidos apenas en círculos restringidos, no fueron debatidos todavía por instancias religiosas, eclesiales o educativas y, se desconoce aun como se implementarán, cómo se capacitará a las y los docentes respectivos, qué materiales educativos se producirán, etc. En síntesis la situación es potencialmente conflictiva en la medida en que, por falta de diálogo corre el riesgo de crear nuevas polarizaciones entre un Ministerio que defiende posturas políticas y actores educativos que, bajo diferentes proyectos y sensibilidades, buscan un espacio de reflexión y vivencia religiosa.

Frente al temor de que el nuevo Estado sustituya la todavía dominante mentalidad religiosa de Cristiandad por una hegemonía indígena/andina, las y los profesores de religión católica[18] y quienes pertenecen a otras confesiones o denominaciones están desorientados.

A falta de un diagnóstico empírico sobre lo que pasa realmente en las clases de la nueva materia se puede emitir algunas hipótesis:

---

[18] Anteriormente, los profesores de religión integrados al magisterio se constituyeron en un Consejo Nacional de Profesores de Religión, Ética y Moral. A partir de 2010 se reconfiguran bajo la Asociación de Maestros de Valores, Espiritualidades y Religiones. Asumen el nuevo nombre de la materia al tiempo de reafirmar una postura tanto corporativista como confesional que contradice en los términos los objetivos y lineamientos establecidos por el Ministerio.

- Las y los docentes católicos o evangélicos que enseñan más por vocación siguen en una tarea evangelizadora de baja intensidad (con acentos más rituales, doctrinales o bíblicos según los casos).
- Las y los docentes que necesitan preservar su puesto laboral propician por el momento una enseñanza religiosa de bajo perfil, con referencias a textos, autores y novelistas de moda que apuntan a una moral individualista con tintes espiritualistas tipo Paulo Coelho y otros textos de crecimiento personal. Renuncian a la transmisión de una doctrina confesional y fomentan una concepción de lo religioso encerrado al ámbito privado, una cultura globalizada, la invisibilización de lo político, etc.
- Son todavía insignificantes los intentos de construir una educación multirreligiosa que apunte al ejercicio de un diálogo intercultural e interreligioso desde la vivencia de la diversidad de creencias de sus integrantes.

En síntesis el espacio escolar público boliviano no ha logrado implementar aún la apertura y las perspectivas abiertas por los textos legales y puede en cualquier momento volver a ser escenario de polarizaciones y querellas entre Estado y religiones.

Proyecciones

Para terminar este estado de la cuestión de la ERE en Bolivia señalo algunas de las soluciones o búsquedas que se presentan en otros contextos cuando se busca integrar la dimensión de las creencias (religiosas o no) a la educación en general.

- Propuestas educativas confesionales que desde la afirmación de la identidad propia van al encuentro de otras creencias para buscar un diálogo al margen de cualquier tentativa de integración o cooptación.
- Yuxtaposición y convivencia pacífica entre diferentes propuestas y programas de enseñanza religiosa relacionados con diferentes credos y tradiciones religiosas y/o filosóficas.
- Explicitación y análisis de la diversidad religiosa en perspectiva fenomenológica, acudiendo a las Ciencias de la Religión, dentro de

una materia que se llame «Enseñanza del hecho religioso» por ejemplo. El riesgo consiste en presentar lo religioso de manera algo aséptica, pasando al lado de las experiencias vivenciales como del impacto socio-político que tiene cualquier sistema de creencias.

- Una perspectiva llamada transversal en la que lo religioso está abordado y absorbido dentro de las otras áreas del saber, con el riesgo de que se difumine o, al contrario, de que pretenda nuevamente aparecer como saber normativo y unificador.

- Educación multirreligiosa y pluralista con puntas hacia el diálogo interreligioso. Conocer algo de las creencias del otro es una condición necesaria para llegar al respeto y a la tolerancia religiosa pero no suficiente. Falta todavía crear y propiciar espacios de silencio, escucha, debate, convivencia e investigación sobre la diversidad religiosa y de creencias.

Es en Brasil donde más se ha avanzado en esta última perspectiva. Según mi punto de vista este planteamiento corresponde al contexto religioso boliviano y estaría en conformidad con la letra de los documentos legales mencionados más arriba. Además parte de la apuesta según la cual la escuela como espacio ciudadano, es un lugar formativo en el que el ensayo y error es todavía posible contrariamente a lo que pasa en las luchas políticas o religiosas dentro de la sociedad en general.

CONSTRUIR LA LAICIDAD DESDE LA DIVERSIDAD RELIGIOSA
Nuevas interacciones entre Estado, iglesias y religiones

Quiero volver en este último aparte al concepto de la laicidad para percibir mejor su adecuación o desfase con el contexto de un país como Bolivia. Antes de hacerlo recordaré con pinceladas gruesas y rápidas algunas de las cosas que cambiaron en el país y otras que se mantienen en cuanto a las relaciones entre Estado y religiones.

- La mentalidad de Cristiandad perdura y se manifiesta todavía tanto en el sentido común como en las mentalidades de las principales iglesias, incluyendo a muchos llamados nuevos movimientos religiosos que apuntan, a veces sin saberlo, a sistemas teocráticos.

- La iglesia católica tiene, en las circunstancias políticas actuales, un perfil más bajo que en los tiempos de las democracias pactadas a pesar de que el Estado no le haya quitado prácticamente ninguno de las prerrogativas con las que ha contado históricamente[19]; sigue siendo persona de derecho público y de derecho internacional, un estatus que no comparte con ningún otro grupo religioso.

- Las dirigencias eclesiásticas evangélicas después de haber luchado por la separación entre Estado e iglesias pelean ahora contra varios fantasmas por ejemplo el de una descristianización del país a favor del fortalecimiento de las «idolatrías» del pasado o el de persecuciones en contra de la fe evangélica.

- El liderazgo de algunas iglesias evangélicas y ecuménicas minoritarias, renegando de sus posturas a favor de la separación entre Estado e iglesia han llegado a cumplir en los últimos años un papel de legitimación religiosa e ideológica del Gobierno con el riesgo de verse intrumentalizadas políticamente[20].

- Otras iglesias evangélicas con un pasado menos abierto a la política y al ecumenismo organizan actos litúrgicos invitando al Presidente[21].

- Han aparecido y se han multiplicado manifestaciones culturales y religiosas ancestrales en muchos ámbitos y acontecimientos del Estado. La primera celebración de este tipo se realizó en Tiwanaku el día anterior a la posesión del Presidente Morales. De manera frecuente, aunque menos pública, se celebran en Palacio de Gobierno como en otros despachos ministeriales ritos andinos.

[19] Otro resabio anacrónico es el «Convenio de asistencia religiosa a las fuerzas armadas y policiales» vigente todavía.

[20] En la firma de un convenio interinstitucional el Presidente Morales declaró el 28 de septiembre de 2012: «De la Iglesia Metodista no tengo nada que quejarme; aprendo, escucho sus oraciones y bendiciones, siempre han sido en bien […] **es un modelo de iglesia**, para bendecir, para augurar éxito a nuestro pueblo.» (resaltado mío) http://www.la-razon.com/sociedad/Presidente-Iglesia-Metodista-modelo-iglesia_0_1696030448.html

[21] Es el caso de la Asociación de Iglesias de Dios reformadas. El Presidente asistió a una reunión masiva en Semana Santa en el campo de Oruro después de declarar que no iba a asistir a los actos religiosos de la iglesia católica en La Paz. http://www.la-razon.com/nacional/Presidente-enfatiza-igualdad-derechos-iglesias_0_1592840716.html

- Se van propiciando celebraciones ecuménicas e interreligiosas en actos o festejos públicos, tratando de romper la simbiosis entre autoridades políticas y eclesiásticas católicas que se manifestaba antes en Semana Santa, en fiestas patrias (*Te Deum*) u otros aniversarios. Estos intentos que podrían ser un caldo de cultivo interesante para construir nuevas relaciones entre el Estado y las religiones están por el momento, organizados principalmente por el Ministerio de Relaciones Exteriores, como si el Estado estuviera buscando nuevas legitimaciones de orden religioso. Estos fenómenos no se enmarcan en un régimen de Cristiandad pero reproducen, bajo otro signo religioso, el mismo tipo de mentalidad y van sin lugar a duda en contra de la laicidad.

Da la impresión que algunas expresiones religiosas avasalladas a lo largo de los últimos siglos hubieran interiorizado la imagen de las iglesias que las oprimieron a tal punto que tienden a reproducir el mismo esquema de buscar invadir el terreno público por medio de ritos e intervenciones de otro signo religioso.

En síntesis, los textos jurídicos analizados así como la realidad muestran que, en Bolivia, falta todavía mucho para alcanzar una verdadera igualdad religiosa que, más allá de la simple proclamación de la «libertad de religión y de conciencia» permita luchar y superar las desigualdades religiosas inscritas en la historia, en las mentalidades y en las prácticas de todos los actores en presencia.

Un país multirreligioso con un Estado laico

En un contexto como el boliviano, el debate sobre la laicidad pasa por una relectura histórica de las relaciones entre Sociedad y culturas, Sociedad y religiones, Sociedad e iglesias, Sociedad y nuevos movimientos religiosos, Sociedad y creencias no religiosas. Esto implica entre otras cosas la creación de un observatorio religioso en el que confluyan tanto científicos y expertos de la cuestión cultural/religiosa como testigos significativos[22]. En

---

[22] Hablo de Sociedad y no de Estado por el carácter tan endeble de este en el contexto boliviano y hablo de «testigos significativos» que es una categoría más amplia que la de «representantes oficiales» con su carga burocrática.

las circunstancias actuales parece evidente que el Estado no tiene ni voluntad ni competencias para arbitrar conflictos de tipo religioso.

Además, en los países latinoamericanos el concepto de laicidad tiene que integrar la realidad y el concepto de Religión civil como conjunto y sistema del cual se nutren los Estados (en perspectiva populista o no) para consolidar su legitimidad a partir de los símbolos patrios, de una lectura sesgada de su historia, del ocultamiento o subsunción de los mecanismos de poder bajo el concepto de Nación, de diversas místicas y mitos unificadoras, etc.

En perspectiva teórica el debate sobre laicidad, religiones y educación pasa necesariamente por la discusión interdisciplinaria entre teologías[23] y Ciencias de la Religión. La perspectiva teológica corre siempre el riesgo de interpretar y hasta cooptar el concepto de laicidad para compatibilizarlo con sus propios presupuestos. A su vez, la perspectiva de las Ciencias de la Religión corre el riesgo cientista y positivista de una pretendida neutralidad que no existe en ningún campo y menos aún en el religioso. En el contexto boliviano y andino, las Ciencias de la Religión no pueden limitarse a la antropología de la religión por central que fuera esta. Tiene que integrar a todas las otras disciplinas humanas y sociales con sus propias miradas sobre el fenómeno religioso y de creencias.

La laicidad en nuestro contexto es más un concepto que una práctica y no garantiza de por sí la convivencia pacífica ni la tolerancia entre religiones y creencias; además, dista mucho de ser un criterio universalmente aceptado. Efectivamente descansa sobre premisas epistemológicas, creencias con connotaciones históricas y culturales muy marcadas.

La laicidad en Bolivia es más un proyecto que una realidad palpable. Su suerte está relacionada directamente con la posibilidad de:

- Deconstruir y reconstruir el concepto desde el contexto cultural propio para no verse involucrado en una especie de colonialismo laico, sustituto del colonialismo religioso cristiano en sus versiones tanto católicas como evangélicas.

---

[23] Pongo teologías en plural partiendo del supuesto de que cualquier sistema religioso va acompañado de una reflexión teológica (sea formal o implícita) y que cualquier sistema religioso integra una variedad conflictiva de teologías y/o de contrateologías en su seno.

- Encontrar mecanismos para la regulación de los fundamentalismos de todo cuño, incluyendo obviamente tanto los de origen cristiano como los indianistas.
- Establecer una cultura de diálogo y de paz religiosa y de conciencia alimentada por una capacidad de negociación con lo diferente.

En síntesis apuesto a la construcción de mentalidades, prácticas y reflexiones interculturales. A sabiendas de que la problemática no se resuelve acuñando nuevos conceptos ni recargando el sustantivo laicidad con más adjetivos calificativos, me pregunto sin embargo si, en el contexto referido, se podría debatir y ensayar una **laicidad intercultural** ya que hablar de diálogo interreligioso no integra explícitamente a las creencias no religiosas.

Matthias Preiswerk; Suizo-boliviano, vive en La Paz, desde el año 1976. Ha fundado y dirigido diferentes instancias en las que ha desarrollado una práctica siempre en los cruces entre teología y pedagogía:

– Programa de formación cristiana para los colegios metodistas en Bolivia y en la región
– Centro de Teología Popular (espacio de reflexión y formación para agentes de pastoral comprometidos con los sectores populares)
– Instituto Superior Ecuménico Andino de Teología (facultad ecuménica de teología)
– Servicios Pedagógicos y Teológicos (http://www.serviciospt.org)
– Entre las variadas publicaciones que sistematizan su reflexión y práctica están:
  Teología de la Liberación y Educación Popular. 1994. DEI: Costa Rica (Tesis doctoral).

Contratointercultural. Crisis y refundaciónde la Educación Teológica. 2011. Plural, CLAI, Visión Mundial: La Paz, Quito, San José.

Religion und Markt – Gedanken zu einem polemischen Verhältnis

Josef Estermann

Summary

The present article tests out the relationship between "religion" and "market" as it has developed in the cause of neoliberal globalisation. In doing this the author starts with an apparent contradictory tendency of a "religious renaissance" and the institutional crisis of religion. Apart from the strict separation of market and religion, there are a lot of contemporary expressions whereby religion is established in accordance with the market or the market takes on the form of a global "super-religion". The Latin-American liberation theology aims its criticism against the ideological character of the market without diminishing the lasting importance of economy and politics for a comprehensive liberation.

Seit ungefähr zwanzig Jahren erfährt die «Religion» eine Art Renaissance, vor allem in den als «säkular» und «post-metaphysisch» bezeichneten Kontexten, wie es die Regionen sind, die von der abendländischen Zivilisation beeinflusst und vom Geist der Aufklärung, dem Positivismus und einer auf die Spitze getriebenen Wissenschaftsgläubigkeit durchdrungen sind. Bis in die achtziger Jahre des vergangenen Jahrhunderts haben viele «aufgeklärte» Intellektuelle das baldige «Ende der Religion» und den Sieg der Wissenschaft und Technologie in allen Bereichen des Lebens angekündigt. Der Neoliberalismus und die «neu-klassische» Wirtschaftstheorie haben diese Position dahingehend verstärkt, als sie vom «Ende der Ideologien», dem «Ende der Utopie» und dem «Ende der Geschichte»[1] sprachen. Zumindest in den industrialisierten Ländern des Nordens schien das «positive Reich» einer Zivilisation ohne Religion nicht nur wünschenswert, sondern sogar in Kürze realisierbar zu sein.

---

[1] Vgl. Francis Fukuyama, *The end of History and the Last Man*, London, Penguin, 1989. Auf Deutsch erschienen: *Das Ende der Geschichte, Wo stehen wir?*, München, Kindler, 1992.

154

Renaissance des «Religiösen»

Trotzdem sah sich diese Einschätzung schon bald einer Reihe von Anfragen gegenüber, und statt einem langsamen Todeskampf tat sich schon bald eine «Explosion des Religiösen» hervor, das sich wie der berühmte Phönix erneut aus der Asche erhob. Ausser vielen politischen und sozialen Bewegungen begannen auch ganz und gar unverdächtige Intellektuelle wie etwa Habermas und Vattimo[2], die Hypothese der positivistischen Soziologie zu entkräften, die Zukunft der Menschheit sei unausweichlich «säkular» oder gar «unreligiös». Ich möchte einige Ursachen dieses religiösen Booms erwähnen, der sich nicht nur im globalen Norden, sondern auch im Süden und den neuen Grossmächten China und Indien zeigt.

Zuerst soll die postmoderne Kritik an allen Arten von «totalitären Erklärungsmodellen», eingeschlossen Atheismus und Säkularismus, erwähnt werden. Gemäss der postmodernen Sicht hat eine religiöse Haltung und Erklärung der Wirklichkeit denselben Wert und dieselbe Reichweite wie eine wissenschaftliche Haltung und Erklärung. Die Religion ist demnach weder eine «Übergangsphase» auf der Fortschrittslinie der Menschheit (Auguste Comte) noch einfach «Opium des Volkes» (Karl Marx), sondern ein authentischer Ausdruck der menschlichen Sehnsucht, die Welt zu verstehen und umzugestalten, Seite an Seite mit anderen Möglichkeiten und Optionen.

Die allumfassende neoliberale Globalisierung hat bei vielen Menschen zu einer Art «kulturellen Exils» und einer Uniformierung der menschlichen Ausdrucksformen in einer «globalen Kultur» (der so genannten «Coca-Cola-Kultur») geführt und damit unterschiedliche Formen von Anti-Globalisierungs-Reaktionen ausgelöst, die man als «fundamentalistisch» und «vormodern» bezeichnen könnte. Nicht nur in der

---

[2] Zu Habermas, siehe: Jürgen Habermas, *Zwischen Naturalismus und Religion, Philosophische Aufsätze.* Frankfurt a. M., Suhrkamp, 2005. Michael Reder und Josef Schmidt, *Ein Bewusstsein von dem, das fehlt: Eine Diskussion mit Jürgen Habermas,* Frankfurt a. M., Suhrkamp, 2008. Zu Vattimo, siehe: Gianni Vattimo, *Credere di credere,* Mailand, Garzanti, 1996. Auf Deutsch erschienen: *Glauben – Philosophieren,* Reclam, 1997. Gianni Vattimo und Richard Rorty, *Die Zukunft der Religion.* (Hg. von Santiago Zabala.) Frankfurt a. M., Suhrkamp, 2006.

islamischen Welt, sondern auch in den christlichen Kirchen und den indigenen Religionen, aber auch im politischen Bereich zeichnen sich «fundamentalistische» Entwicklungen ab. In diesem Sinne taucht die «Religion» erneut als typisch «vormodernes» und «gegen-aufklärerisches» Phänomen auf. Man könnte als Beispiele die «Priesterbruderschaft Pius X.» («Lefebristen») in der katholischen Kirche, den Jihad-Islamismus, die *Hindutva*-Bewegung in Indien oder bestimmte Spielarten des nordamerikanischen Neo-Pentekostalismus nennen.

Auch sollte auf die wachsende Unzufriedenheit vieler Menschen wegen der Bombardierung der Medien mit Konsumgütern und einem wachsenden Konsum-Materialismus hingewiesen werden, einer Art «Wüstenerfahrung» des modernen und postmodernen Lebens, ohne Orientierung und Ziel, ohne «Geist» und Transzendenz. Und dies weckt in vielen Menschen den «Durst» nach dem Spirituellen, Esoterischen und Religiösen, das sich in so unterschiedlichen Phänomenen wie dem *New Age,* der Tiefenökologie, esoterischen Zirkeln und post-säkularen Theorien kanalisiert.

Allgemein kann man sagen, dass die so genannte Renaissance des Religiösen mit einer tiefgehenden Krise der institutionalisierten Religiosität (vor allem im Fall des Christentums, das die wohl am meisten institutionalisierte Religion ist) und den vielen Krisen, die den Planeten seit rund fünfzehn Jahren heimsuchen, einhergeht. Im Fall des Christentums und der Kirchen der verschiedenen christlichen Traditionen verursacht die Zivilisationskrise des Abendlandes ein Erdbeben, das die ideologischen und konzeptionellen Fundamente desselben erschüttert und das die Notwendigkeit nach sich zieht, die christliche Religion tiefgehend zu «ent-okzidentalisieren».

Der «merkantile» Charakter der Religion

Die Tatsache der Diversifizierung und Pluralisierung des religiösen Phänomens, sowohl in globaler wie lokaler Perspektive, bringt uns auf den Gedanken, dass es sich um eine «Wettbewerbssituation» auf einem symbolischen und rituellen «Markt» handle, auf dem sich unterschiedliche «Angebote» um die «KundInnen» reissen. Auch wenn sich die als «missionarisch» bezeichneten (vor allem monotheistischen) Religionen schon immer in einer Konkurrenzsituation mit einem anderen religiösen Angebot wähnten, das «heidnisch» oder einer anderen Religion zugehörig sein mag, hat doch der schleichende Prozess der «Globalisierung»[3] diesen «merkantilen» Aspekt der Religion in den letzten dreissig Jahren zusätzlich beschleunigt.

In Gegenden, die zuvor religiös ziemlich homogen waren, sind religiöse Angebote aufgetaucht, die als exogen betrachtet werden, wie es aufgrund der verschiedenen Migrationswellen etwa ganz deutlich der Fall von Europa zeigt. Solange die MigrantInnen aus christlichen Kontexten (Süden Europas, Lateinamerika, Schwarzafrika) kamen, gab es keine nennenswerten Probleme des Zusammenlebens und der Integration. Mit den grossen Wanderbewegungen aus Asien und Nordafrika aber stellen sich neue Herausforderungen, welche die christlichen Kirchen über Nacht in eine Wettbewerbssituation katapultiert haben. Etwas Ähnliches kann man auch in den USA beobachten, in diesem Fall allerdings aufgrund der massiven Einwanderungen aus Lateinamerika und der Gefahr, dass der hispanische Katholizismus den Protestantismus, der traditionellerweise für den *American Way of Life* normativ war, überflügeln und beherrschen könnte.

Im lateinamerikanischen Kontext ist der «religiöse Wettbewerb» weder durch die Einwirkung von Islam, Buddhismus oder Hinduismus noch durch die Eroberungen der historischen protestantischen Kirchen[4] gegenüber der katholischen Monopolstellung entstanden, sondern durch die wachsende Ausuferung von Neu-Pfingstkirchen und dem Hereinbrechen von alten indigenen Religionen in scheinbar mono-religiöse Gesellschaften. Zudem entwickelte sich in bestimmten Kirchen wie der katholischen eine gewisse «innerkirchliche Konkurrenz» zwischen einem

---

[3] Hier ist der Begriff wertneutral gehalten und meint einfach den geschichtlichen Prozess der Vernetzung des ganzen Planeten. In den romanischen Sprachen verwendet man dafür den Begriff der «Mundialisierung» (*mondialisation; mundialización*), im Gegensatz zur ideologisch aufgeladenen «Globalisierung» (*globalisation; globalización*).

[4] Darunter versteht man die aus der ersten (16. Jahrhundert) und zweiten Reformationswelle (18. Jahrhundert) hervorgegangenen Kirchen, wie etwa die lutherischen, calvinistischen, methodistischen, presbyterianischen, anglikanischen, baptistischen oder anabaptistischen Kirchen.

konservativen und progressiven Flügel. In einem Land wie Bolivien spiegelt sich die Situation eines stärker gewordenen «religiösen Wettbewerbs» unter anderem im nennenswerten Zuwachs «religiöser Institutionen», die im Religionsdepartement des Auswärtigen Amtes erfasst sind. Während sich in der Zeit von 1827 bis 1959 (also in 132 Jahren) nur 59 neue Kirchen, religiöse Gemeinschaften und Institutionen registrieren liessen, stieg diese Zahl für die Zeit von 1960 bis 1995 (also in 35 Jahren) auf 160 an. Der grösste Teil von ihnen war christlichen (vor allem evangelischen) und para-christlichen Ursprungs (wie die Mormonen, Zeugen Jehovas, Moon-Kirche usw.).

Die «traditionellen» Religionen haben erst vor kurzem das Marketing entdeckt, um ihre Dienstleistungen anzubieten und sich auf dem wachsenden «religiösen Markt» mit Standortvorteilen zu behaupten, aber bis heute bekunden sie eine gewisse Scheu, ihre «Dienste» wie irgendein anderes Produkt auf dem Güter- und Dienstleistungsmarkt zu betrachten und anzubieten. Die neuen Kirchen und religiösen Bewegungen haben dagegen diesbezüglich keinerlei Skrupel und setzen auf alle Instrumente des Marketings, von den Internetplattformen und den sozialen Medien (Twitter, Facebook, Blogs) bis hin zu generalstabsmässig geplanten und millionenschweren Medienkampagnen, dem politischen Sponsoring und allen Werbemitteln, wie sie von jedem Konkurrenten auf dem grossen neoliberalen Markt benutzt werden. Diese Art der «Merkantilisierung» der Religion erreicht in Ländern wie den USA oder Südkorea regelrechte Auswüchse, aber auch in Lateinamerika kann man eine deutliche Zunahme von so genannten «Fernseh-Kirchen» (tele-iglesias) und der religiösen Propaganda durch die Massenmedien (Radio, Fernsehen, Internet) feststellen. In Bolivien und Peru etwa hat sich die Zahl religiöser Fernsehstationen in den letzten zehn Jahren verdreifacht.

Es ist keineswegs neu, dass man die religiösen «Güter» und Dienstleistungen als eine Art Ware betrachtet, die man anbietet und die einer Nachfrage seitens der religiösen «KundInnen», die «Gläubige» genannt werden, entspricht. Die traditionelle katholische Theologie sprach von der «sakramentalen Ökonomie», und auch wenn die Reformation diese Art der «Merkantilisierung» des Religiösen (etwa in der Form des Ablasshandels) aufs Schärfste verurteilt hat, melden die zeitgenössischen evangelischen Kirchen keine Vorbehalte an, ihre Dienste, Segnungen und Gebete zu «verkaufen». Sogar bei den alten indigenen Religionen Südamerikas gibt es eine Form des merkantilen «Tausches» zwischen den vom religiösen Spezialisten (*paq'u, yatiri, altomisayuq*) geleisteten Dienste und einer von den Teilnehmenden in der Form von Geld, Kokablättern, Essen oder Trinken dargebrachten Gegenleistung. Trotzdem aber ist die «Monetarisierung» des Religiösen, wie sie in gewissen Neu-Pfingstkirchen (*Ecclesia, Asamblea de Dios, Cristo Viene* usw.) festzustellen ist, relativ neu und spiegelt den Prozess der Merkantilisierung und Finanzialisierung von absolut allen Lebensbereichen durch den kapitalistischen freien Markt.

Zwei unvereinbare Bereiche?

Es macht den Anschein, als wären die beiden zentralen Begriffe der vorliegenden Debatte, «Markt» und «Religion», vollkommen unvereinbar und inkommensurabel. Sowohl in konservativen wie progressiven Kreisen der christlichen (katholischen und evangelischen) Kirchen ist die Überzeugung noch immer stark verankert, das Religiöse sollte nicht den «Gesetzen» des Marktes, also der Dynamik von Angebot und Nachfrage gehorchen, und auch unter den Befürwortern des freien Marktes gibt es nicht wenige, die zwischen der Dynamik des Marktes und dem Kern dessen, was die Religion ausmacht, eine Unvereinbarkeit konstatieren. Konservative Kreise tendieren dazu, das «weltliche Reich» der Wirtschaft, Finanzen und Politik einerseits (von Augustinus *civitas terrena* genannt), und das «himmlische Reich» der Erlösung und des Heils andererseits (*die civitas caelestis*) strikt voneinander zu trennen. Dagegen beharren progressive Kreise (unter anderem die Befreiungstheologie) auf einem eher dialektischen Verhältnis der beiden Begriffe: die «Religion» soll gegenüber der Ideologisierung des Marktes im Allgemeinen und dem Geld im Besonderen eine kritische Haltung einnehmen, ohne aber die unverzichtbare Rolle der materiellen Güter im Kampf um Befreiung und soziale Gerechtigkeit zu vernachlässigen. Heute kann man eine dritte Position feststellen, welche die beiden Begriffe praktisch deckungsgleich sieht, und zwar als Allianz, die unter dem Stichwort «Religion des Marktes» bekannt ist.

In allen grossen Religionen finden wir Spuren einer tiefgreifenden Kritik der Verabsolutierung der materiellen Güter, vor allem in der Symbolgestalt des Geldes (Mammon). Jesus trieb die Händler und Geldwechsler aus dem Tempel, aber zugleich machte er sich auch zum Anwalt der erwähnten Trennung der beiden Bereiche, wenn er sagte: «Gebt dem Kaiser, was des Kaisers ist, und Gott, was Gottes ist» (Mt 22,15–21). Das Judentum und der Islam (aber auch das Christentum bis über das Mittelalter hinaus) verbieten die Bankzinsen und den Wucher; für den Buddhismus verhindert das Verhaftetsein an materielle Güter die wahre Erleuchtung. Im christlichen Kontext können wir sowohl im Norden wie im Süden in den letzten Jahrzehnten ein wachsendes theologisches Interesse an wirtschaftlichen Fragen entdecken. Die VorreiterInnen der lateinamerikanischen Befreiungstheologie haben den unverzichtbaren Ort des Wirtschaftlichen in der Heilsgeschichte, die als «Befreiungsgeschichte» interpretiert wird, entdeckt und stützten sich bei ihren Analysen der sozialen Ungerechtigkeit und Ungleichheit auf die wirtschaftliche Dependenztheorie und den Marxismus als Kapitalismuskritik. Fast zeitgleich entstand aber auch eine «neoliberale Theologie», welche die neu-kapitalistischen Mechanismen als die beste Art beurteilen, mittels des berühmten *Trickle Down Effects* zu einer inklusiven und gerechten Gesellschaft zu gelangen.[5] Gewisse Neu-Pfingstkirchen haben diese Art Theologie zu einer «Theologie des Wohlstands» weiterentwickelt, die eine direkte Beziehung von Glaube und Geld oder, besser gesagt, von völliger Hingabe (das Wort «Islam» besagt genau dies) und dem wirtschaftlichen Lohn des Wohlstandes herstellt.

Wenn wir die beiden Begriffe etwas näher analysieren, können wir trotzdem grundsätzliche Unterschiede feststellen, und zwar sowohl hinsichtlich der Wirkungsgeschichte wie auch der eigentlichen Zielsetzungen. «Markt» impliziert die Idee eines Austauschs von Gütern oder Dienstleistungen, bei dem das Geld «neutrales» Mittel dieser Art Transak-

---

[5] Der herausragende Vertreter dieser «neoliberalen Theologie» ist der US-Theologe Michael Novak. Siehe: Michael Novak, *Liberation theology and the liberal society,* Washington, D.C.: American Enterprise Institute for Public Policy Research, 1987. Idem (1998): Paulinus.

tionen sein kann, es aber nicht sein muss. Die «Märkte» haben sich seit dem alten Tauschhandel über eine rudimentäre Geldwirtschaft und dem merkantilistischen Modell des Austauschs von «Waren», bis hin zu den «fortschrittlichsten» oder perversesten (je nach Standpunkt) Formen des Finanzmarktes, des Marktes mit *Futures* und den gegenwärtigen spekulativen Nahrungsmittelmärkten weiterentwickelt. Auch wenn die «neu-klassische» Theorie[6] von der Annahme ausgeht, dass die Personen in einem vollständig freien Markt (also ohne Staatsintervention) dieselben Ausgangsbedingungen haben, zeigen die realen Konsequenzen eine total entgegengesetzte Logik des Ausschlusses und eine Neigung zur Nekrophilie. Auf den heutigen Märkten (insbesondere den spekulativen Finanzmärkten) geht es schon längst nicht mehr darum, die Menschen mit den nötigen Gütern für das Leben zu versorgen, sondern die Gewinne zu maximieren, Kapital und (nicht verderbliche) Güter zu akkumulieren und die Standortvorteile bis zum Maximum auszuschöpfen. Die Güter, die Dienstleistungen und noch viel mehr das Geld werden zu Mitteln der Spekulation und zum Transmissionsriemen, um unvorstellbare Gewinne zu erzielen (der so genannte «Casino-Kapitalismus»). Die menschliche Person wird «Mittel» und «Konsument», und im schlimmsten Fall «stört» er einfach die Mechanismen des freien Marktes. Als letztes Paradox tritt der «Tod des Menschen»[7] ein, wie er von der Postmoderne postuliert wird: der Markt funktioniere viel besser, wenn es keine Menschen mit ihren Gefühlen, Vorlieben und Sehnsüchten gäbe, sondern nur produktive und finanzielle Roboter.

Der Begriff «Religion» bezieht sich dagegen auf eine menschliche «Beziehung» zum Unbedingten, was weder Mittel noch Vermittlung ist, sondern Zweck in sich selber, letztes Ziel des Lebens und der Existenz.

---

[6] Unter «neu-klassische Theorie» oder «neu-klassische Schule» versteht man die theoretische Grundlegung der neoliberalen kapitalistischen «Neuen Ökonomie», die Elemente aus der «klassischen liberalen Theorie» (Adam Smith) und den neoliberalen Theorien, die in den achtziger Jahren des vergangenen Jahrhunderts entstanden sind, miteinander verbindet.

[7] Michael Foucault hat diesen Ausdruck geprägt, und zwar in dem Sinne, dass die neuzeitliche Idee des Menschen (Humanismus) schon bald an ihr Ende komme und der postmoderne Mensch ohne zuvor heilige Ideale leben werde.

Diese Beziehung mit dem Heiligen (jede Religion hat ihre eigenen Bezeichnungen für diese Wirklichkeit) ist weder quantifizierbar noch messbar (also «inkommensurabel»), weil sie zum internen Forum einer jeden Person gehört. Erst als Veräusserung dieser persönlichen und existenziellen Beziehung wird die «Religion» zu einem sozialen und kulturellen Phänomen und nimmt (wie das Geld) eine Funktion der Vermittlung und Repräsentation ein, in diesem Fall nicht von materiellen Gütern, sondern von «spirituellen Gütern» wie etwa der Gnade Gottes, der Erlösung, der Erleuchtung, des Nirwanas, dem Reich Gottes, dem Paradies, der Glückseligkeit, der mystischen Schau, oder in anderen Worten: dem «Leben in Fülle». Im Verhältnis zu den spirituellen Gütern werden die materiellen Güter (eingeschlossen das Geld) als «Mittel» und nicht als Zweck an sich betrachtet. Alle Religionen warnen davor, die Mittel mit den Zwecken zu verwechseln, also die materiellen Güter (Gegenstände, Bilder, Geld, Ruhm usw.) an die Stelle des letzten spirituellen Guts (das Göttliche, das Unbedingte) zu setzen, und nennen diese Haltung «Götzendienst». Es gilt sogar als götzendienerisch, wer die Religion mit dem Gegenstand der Verehrung selber («Gott») identifiziert oder den lebendigen Glauben des Menschen mit reinem Ritualismus und religiöser Routine verwechselt.

In diesem Sinne ist auch die Religion ein blosses «Instrument» oder «Mittel» des Menschen, um eine intime und persönliche Beziehung zu dem, was uns im Tiefsten unserer Existenz berührt, aufzunehmen. Die Religion als solche – und noch viel weniger die Kirchen oder Gemeinschaften – erlöst nicht[8], sondern kann ein Weg sein, der uns zur Erlösung führt, aber auch ein Instrument, um die existenziellsten Sehnsüchte des Menschen zu manipulieren und somit zu einem Instrument des Todes zu werden. Religionen sind zwiespältig wie jede sozio-kulturelle Errungenschaft der Menschheit; sie können zu mehr Leben oder zu mehr Tod, zur Befreiung der Völker oder aber zu grösserer Sklaverei beitragen. Hinsichtlich dieses formalen

[8] Vgl. Josef Estermann, "Religion does not redeem: Theological reflections about the role of 'religion' today". In: Voices Vol. XXXV, Nr. 2012/1, New Series. EATWOT (Hg.). *Towards a post-religional paradigm?: EATWOT's Latin American Consultation on Religion – ¿Hacia un paradigma posreligional?: Consulta teológica latinoamericana sobre religión – Para um paradigma pos-religional?: Consulta teológica latino-americana sobre religião*, 71–88.

Aspekts teilen der «Markt» und die «Religion» dieselbe Zweideutigkeit und die Versuchung, sich als Zweck an sich zu betrachten und nicht nur als Mittel. Der verabsolutierte Markt wird zu Gott oder einem Idol (der «sterbliche Gott» von Hobbes), und die verabsolutierte Religion degeneriert zu einem spirituellen Despotismus und einer totalitären Ideologie.

Der Markt als Religion

Wie ich zuvor schon bemerkt habe, gab es in den letzten Jahrzehnten zwei scheinbar gegensätzliche oder gar widersprüchliche Tendenzen: einerseits hat sich die Welt diversifiziert und pluralisiert, auch bezüglich der Religion. Es gibt heutzutage praktisch weder religiös homogene Länder noch mono-religiöse Kulturen. Andererseits hat sich dieselbe Welt reduziert und ist geschrumpft («Weltdorf»), und zwar im Sinne einer Uniformierung des sozialen, kulturellen und religiösen Lebens. Ersteres, eine Frucht der grossen Wanderbewegungen, der Massenmedien, des *Cyberspace* und des globalen Tourismus, ist von den Ansätzen der Postmoderne, des Multikulturalismus und der Plurireligiosität unter dem Slogan «Es lebe die Differenz!» aufgegriffen worden. Das Letztere, Frucht der Ausbreitung der abendländischen Lebensweise durch Handel und Marketing, Werbung und den Werten des Konsums, verdichtet sich in der These der neoliberalen Globalisierung und der «einzigen globalen Kultur». Beide Tendenzen vertreten die These des Endes der bipolaren Welt (Ost und West; Kapitalismus und Sozialismus), und beide verabschieden sich von einer «ethischen» Lektüre der sozio-ökonomischen Wirklichkeit.

Was das Religiöse betrifft, treten die beiden Tendenzen durch die bereits beschriebenen dialektischen Prozesse von Diversifizierung und Fundamentalisierung der religiösen Auffassungen und ihrer Institutionen in Erscheinung. Aber man sollte ein Phänomen besonders beachten, das scheinbar nicht direkt mit dem «Markt der Religionen» zu tun hat, sondern mit dem Markt selber, also mit dem Prozess der «Säkularisierung» und «Ideologisierung» des neoliberalen Systems des freien Marktes, der seinerseits die Konstitution von religiösen Bewegungen und «Theologien des Wohlstandes» beeinflusst. Wenn wir vom «Markt als Religion» sprechen, haben wir es in strengem Sinne mit einer «Zivilreligion» oder «Säkularreligion» zu tun, die sich nicht als ein religiöses Angebot neben anderen, sondern als «Super-Religion» versteht, die letztlich das gesamte symbolische und rituelle Potenzial aller bestehenden Partikularreligionen absorbiert. Dem Schein nach kann jemand treues Mitglied einer etablierten christlichen Kirche sein, aber gleichzeitig diesem neuen Gott huldigen, der von der «Super-Religion» des Marktes inthronisiert worden ist. Diese «doppelte Treue» ist in vielen Kirchen des christlichen Traditionsstrangs und Teilen nichtchristlicher Religionen derart zur Gewohnheit geworden, dass man schon gar kein Problem mehr darin sieht, «zwei Herren zu dienen». Es gibt Kirchen neu-pfingstlerischer Prägung, die das Credo der «Super-Religion des Marktes» *de facto* zu ihrem eigenen gemacht haben (etwa in den verschiedenen Wohlstandstheologien), auch wenn sie de iure eine ausgesprochen fundamentalistische biblische Terminologie und Ritualität beibehalten.

Diese «Religion des Marktes» teilt mit jeder Religion gewisse Merkmale, auch wenn sie grundsätzlich immanent und materialistisch ist. Erstens kennt und verehrt sie ihre eigene Gottheit, nämlich den sakralisierten Markt, eine neue Schicksalshaftigkeit, die dem vermeintlichen «Liberalismus» ihrer TheoretikerInnen *in terminis* entgegengesetzt ist. Dieser Markt vereinigt in sich viele Merkmale des mittelalterlichen Philosophengottes: er ist unfehlbar, allgegenwärtig, allmächtig, unsichtbar, keiner äusseren Einwirkung ausgesetzt, und wird immer wieder für die Erklärung der Probleme des Planeten herbeigezogen (*deus ex machina*) und dabei gerechtfertigt (Mercatodizee). Zweitens vertritt diese globale Religion eine immanente Eschatologie des Konsumparadieses für alle, die mit den grossen Utopien, die in vielen religiösen und philosophischen Traditionen enthalten sind, im Widerspruch steht. Drittens hat sie ihre spezifischen Gotteshäuser (die «Banken» oder «Effektenbörsen» genannt werden), ihr Credo oder Dogma (die neu-klassische Wirtschaftstheorie), ihre Amtsträger (Banker und Spekulanten), ihre Liturgie (die Rituale an den Börsen und die Mantras oder Rosenkränze der Aktienkurse), ihre Theologie (die unsichtbare Hand; der *Trickle Down Effect;* die doppelte Prädestination; usw.) und ihre Heiligen Schriften (Konsens von Washington; normative Dokumente der neu-klassischen Theorie).

Viele der Begriffe der liberalen und neu-klassischen Wirtschaftstheorie verwenden explizit religiöse Metaphern und Verweise. Adam Smith, der geistige Vater des Wirtschaftsliberalismus und Vertreter des aufgeklärten Deismus seiner Zeit, hat die berühmte Metapher der «unsichtbaren Hand» geprägt, die den Markt leiten soll, eine klare Verweisung auf die göttliche Vorsehung, wie sie von den christlichen Kirchen vertreten wird. Das Bild vom *Trickle Down Effect* (auf lange Frist werden alle vom Geldsegen beschenkt werden) des Reichtums ersetzt die alte Konzeption der überfliessenden göttlichen Gnade, die sich über alle ergiesst, auch wenn nicht alle sie annehmen. Etwas Ähnliches vertritt der Neoliberalismus: alle besitzen die unternehmerischen Fähigkeiten und haben die individuelle Freiheit, Privatbesitz zu erwerben («göttliche Gnade»), aber nicht alle machen Gebrauch davon oder weisen sie gar zurück («Sünde»). Zudem spricht man von wirtschaftlichen und finanziellen «Wundern», einem grundlegenden Begriff der Finanzwirtschaft («das Geld wächst»), einem blinden Glauben an den Markt und einer «Heilsgeschichte», die aus den Etappen der «Hölle» von Planwirtschaft und Sozialismus, dem «Fegefeuer» des Sozialstaates und dem «Paradies» der vollständigen Liberalisierung und Deregulierung des Marktes besteht.

Verschiedene Befreiungstheologen (Assmann, Hinkelammert, Jung Mo Sung) haben den Markt als «Götzendienst» interpretiert, also als eine Sakralisierung und Vergöttlichung von etwas Endlichem, das durch den Menschen geschaffen worden ist und zudem Ursache grosser Ungerechtigkeiten und Ungleichheiten ist.[9] Der entscheidende Punkt bei dieser «Religionskritik» des Marktes besteht darin zu zeigen, dass dieser dazu dient, jegliche wirtschaftliche, politische und mediale Macht zu rechtfertigen, wie auch die Ursachen der sozialen Ungerechtigkeiten und Ungleichheiten in der Welt zu «erklären». Deshalb handelt es sich um eine Religion in Händen der Reichen, um die Armen in ihrem Elend zu belassen. Sie hat bei der Masse der Ausgeschlossenen, die weiterhin vom Dau-

---

[9] Vgl. Hugo Assmann und Franz Hinkelammert, *Götze Markt,* Düsseldorf, 1992. Michael Hochgeschwender und Bernhard Löffler (Hg.): *Religion, Moral und liberaler Markt, Politische Ökonomie und Ethikdebatten vom 18. Jahrhundert bis zur Gegenwart,* Bielefeld, Transcript, 2011.

erregen des Reichtums träumen, eine derartige Anziehungskraft, dass sie zum neuen «Opium des Volkes» geworden ist: «auf lange Sicht werden wir alle profitieren, auch wenn wir jetzt noch leiden und ausgeschlossen sind». Sie spiegelt eine traditionelle Theologie des Trostes, der Menschenopfer, der religiösen Rechtfertigung der sozialen Ungerechtigkeiten, der doppelten Prädestination in einem immanenten Sinne. Im Namen des freien Marktes und seinem Gott «Geld» (oder «Gewinn») werden die fürchterlichsten Verbrechen begangen und zwei Drittel der Menschheit vom versprochenen Wohlstand ausgeschlossen.

Die Religion als Markt
Diese Sakralisierung des Marktes in der Theorie und Praxis des neo-kapitalistischen Systems hat ihre Auswirkungen auf das Phänomen des Religiösen als solchem und auf die einzelnen Religionen im Besonderen. Die Logik von Effizienz, Nützlichkeit und Rentabilität hat sich auf das religiöse Leben ausgedehnt, ja sogar bis auf die alten indigenen Religionen. Die Kirchen in Europa funktionieren heute weitgehend als Unternehmen, die bestimme Güter und Dienstleistungen «herstellen», diese auf einem konkurrierenden Markt mittels eines spirituellen Marketings anbieten und daraus Gewinne erzielen, je nach Wirksamkeit und Flexibilität. Man spricht von «Kundenorientierung» und der *Unique Selling Proposition* des eigenen Produktes.

Die Mehrheit der Religionen bietet eine Art von «Parallelwirtschaft» an, oft in den transzendenten Formen der «göttlichen Ökonomie» und deren Heilsgeschichte. Es gibt Theologien, die den anthropologischen Egoismus unterstützen und sogar fördern, und damit zur ideologischen Quelle des Kapitalismus und dem religiösen Impuls, den «Himmel zu erobern», werden. Für diese Art von Theologien ergänzen sich die beiden «Ökonomien» (eine natürliche und eine übernatürliche, um in traditioneller Terminologie zu bleiben) und funktionieren in perfekter Abstimmung aufeinander. Dies ist vor allem der Fall bei den so genannten «Wohlstandstheologien», die meinen, der materielle Wohlstand (natürliche Ökonomie) spiegle und verdichte sich im spirituellen Wohlstand (übernatürliche Ökonomie). Und diese Auffassung ist eigentlich nichts anderes als eine Neuauflage der berühmten These von Max Weber zur protestantischen Ethik und dem Geist des Kapitalismus: «Selig die Reichen, denn ihnen gehört das Himmelreich.»

Andere (progressive) Theologien heben die grundsätzliche Unvereinbarkeit der beiden «Ökonomien» hervor: Die «Logik» von Jesus von Nazareth ist der «Logik» des Marktes und einem ungebremsten Kapitalismus total entgegengesetzt. Evangelische Werte und Tugenden wie etwa Barmherzigkeit, Nächstenliebe, Verzeihung oder Solidarität sind für die neoliberale Theorie und Praxis «Sünden», weil sie die perfekte Ausübung des Marktes beeinträchtigen. In der «Religion des Markes» ist der Mensch zu einem Mittel oder gar einer Störung geworden, während die Mehrheit der Religionen auf der menschlichen Würde als Zweck an sich bestehen. Diese Art von (progressiven) Theologien weist auch die pessimistische und egoistische Anthropologie eines dogmatischen Calvinismus und Kapitalismus zurück; der Mensch ist nicht von Natur aus egoistisch und in ständiger Konkurrenz zu anderen, sondern wird durch die Logik eines Systems, das den Individualismus und die Gier verabsolutiert, dazu gemacht. Die lateinamerikanische Befreiungstheologie fordert, dass eine wahrhaft befreiende und gerechte Wirtschaft für die Armen optiert, also gerechte Voraussetzungen für die Herstellung und Verteilung der Güter schaffen müsste, indem sie dem sozialen Zugang zu den Basisgütern für das Leben Vorrang einräumt. Dazu aber bietet eine neoliberale und kapitalistische Freie Marktwirtschaft nicht die erforderlichen Instrumente, sondern müsste durch ein öffentliches Regime eines regulierenden und fördernden Staates (Mischwirtschaft) ergänzt oder gar von einer sozialistischen Ökonomie ersetzt werden.

Religionen sind – im Gegensatz zum Gegenstand ihrer Verehrung und des Gebets (das Heilige) – menschliche Ausdrucksformen, die immer von kulturellen Kodes, zivilisatorischen Paradigmen, philosophischen Ideologien und Interessen von Gruppen, Ethnien, Völkern und öffentlichen Institutionen überlagert werden. Deshalb können sich die Religionen im Allgemeinen und das Christentum im Besonderen den vorherrschenden Dynamismen in den Bereichen der Wirtschaft, Politik, Wissenschaft, Kultur und anderen niemals vollständig entziehen. Es gibt keine «reinen und unveränderlichen Religionen», sondern nur solche als geschichtliche und kulturelle Manifestationen der Menschheit, die als «Vehikel» oder Vermittlung dienen, um sich mit dem Heiligen in Verbindung zu setzen. Das eigentliche Problem besteht nicht in der Tatsache, dass sich eine bestimmte Religion zu einem bestimmten Zeitpunkt der Geschichte und in bestimmten geografischen und kulturellen Kontexten «inkulturiert», da dies ein normaler organischer Prozess ist. Das Problem besteht in zwei scheinbar entgegengesetzten Tendenzen, die praktisch allen Religionen innewohnen: sich in einem bestimmten Stadium als «normativ», «orthodox» und «einzigartig» zu versteinern, oder sich vollumfänglich und ohne kritische Distanz mit einem bestimmten Kontext zu identifizieren. Die erste Tendenz kann praktisch in allen Religionen beobachtet werden, vor allem den monotheistischen und den «Schriftreligionen», weil sie eine bestimmte Ausformung der Lehre zu «dogmatisieren» trachten (im Falle des Katholizismus vor allem den abendländischen Hellenismus) und somit dem gegenwärtigen Kontext fremde kulturelle Kodes durch die Geschichte mittransportieren (Patriarchat; Essentialismus; Fatalismus; usw.). Die zweite Tendenz kann zum Beispiel bei den postmodernen Religionsformen (eingeschlossen dem Neo-Pentekostalismus) beobachtet werden, da sie den sozio-ökonomischen Kontext derart absorbieren, dass sie letztendlich mit ihm verschmelzen.

Hinsichtlich der Mechanismen des Marktes ist keine Religion immun (wie sie es auch bezüglich der Sklaverei und des Kolonialismus zu seiner Zeit nicht war). Aber eine kritische und befreiende Theologie warnt vor den Gefahren einer «Dogmatisierung» oder «Kanonisierung» des Marktes und einer Einebnung beider völlig unterschiedlicher Logiken in einer einzigen «Religion des Marktes». In der christlichen Tradition pflegt man diese Vorsicht als «prophetische Haltung» der Anklage und der eschatologischen Dialektik zu bezeichnen, kein (politisches, wirtschaftliches, soziales) System, keine Kultur, keine Institution (nicht einmal die Kirche) oder keine geschichtliche Epoche mit dem utopischen Projekt dieser Religion (im Christentum: das Gottesreich) zu identifizieren.

Josef Estermann, Dr. phil. und lic. theol., war von 1990 bis 1998 mit der Missionsgesellschaft Bethlehem Immensee (SMB) in Cusco (Peru) und von 2004 bis 2012 mit der Bethlehem Mission Immensee (BMI) in La Paz (Bolivien) tätig. In der Zwischenzeit leitete er das Missionswissenschaftliche Institut Missio in Aachen (Deutschland). Seit Oktober 2012 ist er Leiter des Ressorts Bildung RomeroHaus in Luzern. Seine Forschungsschwerpunkte umfassen: indigene Philosophie und Theologie der Andenregion, lateinamerikanische Befreiungstheologie, interkulturelle Theologie und Philosophie.

RomeroHaus, Kreuzbuchstrasse 44, CH-6006 Luzern, Switzerland;
josefestermann@hotmail.com

In Memoriam

Tissa Balasuriya OMI (1924–2013)

Fr. Tissa Balasuriya: a loving and gentle rebel in church and society

Fr. Tissa Balasuriya was a Sri Lankan Oblate priest. He was born in a rural Sri Lankan village in 1924, and he died on 17th January 2013. He studied Economics at the University of Ceylon and later Agricultural Economics at Oxford. Having joined the Novitiate of the Oblate Congregation, he was ordained a priest in Rome, obtaining the Licentiate in Philosophy in 1949 and in Theology in 1953. He did post Graduate studies in Theology at the Catholic University of Paris (Institut Catholique de Paris).

Returning to Sri Lanka from Rome in 1953 as a young priest, he helped begin Aquinas University College (Colombo) as the Registrar and later as Rector. He also served as the Asian Chaplain to the International Movement of Catholic Students (IMCS). He left Aquinas University College in 1971 to begin the Centre for Society & Religion (CSR) which in many ways has been his base till his death and is likely to be his lasting institutional legacy.

As Director and Chairperson of CSR, he promoted inter-religious, inter-generation, inter-gender understanding and environmental preservation. He founded and led numerous civil, ecumenical and inter-religious networks, at national and international level, some of which remain active to date. Amongst these are the Citizen Committee for National Harmony, Civil Rights Movement (CRM), People's Action for Free and Fair Election (PAFFREL), the International Forum of Religious for Global Solidarity, the Forum of African Asian spirituality, Jubilee 1998, the Asian Meeting of Religious (AMOR) and the Ecumenical Association of the Third World Theologians (EATWOT).

He was a prolific writer. The last published article that I read was written at the age of 87 in 2011. His articles have been published in local and foreign journals. His major publications include *Jesus Christ and Human Liberation, Eucharist and Human Liberation, Mary and Human Liberation, Planetary Theology, Right Relationships, Globalization and Human Solidarity, Charity in Truth, Sri Lanka Economy in Crisis, Catastrophe – July*

1983, and *Doing Marian Theology*. He was also the editor of *Logos, Quest, Social Justice and Sadharanaya,* published by CSR as well as of *Voices of Third World Theology* (1985–1992).

Fr. Tissa has been called a radical and rebel within the Catholic Church and society. This is perhaps because like Jesus, he never flinched from challenging the rulers and powerful – be they those in government, multinational corporations or church. Unjust socio-economic-political structures were subjected to his harsh criticism. He never sought or accepted any privileges from the rulers.

But what I remember most about Fr. Tissa is his love and his gentleness. I only got to know him personally when he was in his seventies, though I had read his writings and met him a few years before. Amongst my memories of him are: taking me with him to slums in Summitpura in Colombo, getting me involved in conducting discussions on human rights in schools in Colombo, inviting me to a training on organic farming in Kandy. He also invited me to join theological discussions with leading Sri Lankan and other liberation theologians from across the world, in the farm he lived in at Andiambalama, near the Katunayake airport, where I often ended up being the youngest participant. He lived a simple life, had very little personal belongings and mostly travelled by bus and train.

In 2009, I had to present a paper on the Eucharist and Armed Conflict at a conference held in preparation for the plenary assembly of the Federation of Asian Bishops Conferences (FABC) in 2009. The central theme I picked "The Eucharist has to be related positively to human liberation if it is to be faithful to its origins" was from Fr. Tissa's book on *Eucharist and Human Liberation* published in 1977. I had read the book many years before, but could not find it as I was abroad, and when I contacted Fr. Balasuriya, he was very kind to immediately email me a soft copy of the book and to comment and give input to my own paper. On several other occasions, I consulted him about talks I had to give and each time he generously shared his knowledge, experience and thoughts, all free of charge and with a large dose of love.

Even when he was excommunicated by the Vatican with active collaboration of local Church leaders in Colombo, he didn't speak angrily of those who were responsible. "I feel more in communion with the real church and those oppressed" was the sentiment I remember most in my conversations with him from that time. After much debates and discussions, the excommunication was lifted, though the terms were not very clear. But I suspect this was also prompted by outrage the excommunication brought forth within Church and civil groups.

From my days as a teenaged advanced level student, I had been a visitor to CSR. It was here that I and my friends came across critical material on church and society. It was from CSR that we borrowed slides, videos, overhead projectors and other material and equipment for use in the Young Christian Student Movement (YCS) which I was part of. On one occasion, Fr. Balasuriya recommended a film about Oscar Romero, the Archbishop of El Salvador who was killed due to his outspoken condemnation of the military dictatorship. I had never heard of Romero or the film before, but took his advice and showed the film. It remains one of the most challenging and inspiring films I had watched and since then, I had shown this film several times to different groups. – Fr. Tissa and CSR had played an important role in my journey as a human rights activist.

I remember a woman activist sharing that Fr. Tissa was amongst the few in the late 1980s and 1990s that welcomed her together with her young child to CSR. Long before he wrote the book *Mary and Human Liberation* that led to his excommunication, Fr. Balasuriya had been an advocate for women's rights – in society and especially within the Church.

He was a very caring person. Especially in the last six years, he continued to encourage me, but often also cautioned me and warned me of dangers. Having heard of risks I was facing few years back, he had tried to call me, and having failed to get through to me, sent a very short email telling that "I [Fr. Tissa] have very short time to live, but you have more years ahead of you, so be careful". Later on, he invited me to stay with him and promised that he will protect me. His interest in me was not limited to safety and my activism, and he often used to ask me when I would get married and whether he would be invited. He never failed to reply to an email or return a phone call.

I remembered and looked up one of the last emails Fr. Tissa sent me last year, where he had said: "Would it not be a valuable contribution for all the ethnic groups, religious groups and political parties to regret our shortcomings and come together to build a common monument for peace and for the victims of this tragedy of over half a century in our country. The monument can be physical as well as a movement. We can pardon one another, and resolve to build a united Sri Lanka helping the families of the victims dead and alive injured. Ruki please regard this as confidential to you personally, so far. If you and the group mentioned in your letter are initiating something positive like this I could join you for the short time left to me in life." – Unfortunately, the prevailing political situation didn't enable us to initiate this and involve Fr. Tissa. But we hope someday to be able to do this.

Fr. Tissa was and will remain one of my gurus (mentor) – someone who helped me to connect my faith to realities of oppression and injustices around me – in Sri Lanka and beyond.

Some people close to Fr. Tissa found it difficult to work with him, and indeed had disagreements with some of his thinking. Maybe his visions and commitments were too idealist and hard for others to keep up with. And of course, being human as everyone else, he was not perfect. But I'm amongst the many fortunate persons that he had mentored and inspired – through his writings, talks he gave and the personal conversations we had, but most importantly in the simple way he lived and the love he radiated.

I'm very sad I didn't visit Fr. Balasuriya when I was in Colombo the last time, about a week before his death. He was amongst those I wanted to spend some time when I go back to Sri Lanka, to reflect about what I have been doing the last few years and what I planned to do. But that no longer will be possible.

I will miss you, dear Fr. Tissa. But what I learnt from you and what you inspired me to be will remain. May you rest in peace.

(This personal tribute is based on earlier appreciations by the author available at *http://groundviews.org/2013/01/19/fr-tissa-balasuriya-a-loving-and-gentle-rebel/ and http://ncronline.org/news/people/fr-tissa-balasuriya-loving-and-gentle-rebel.)*

Ruki Fernando, Human Rights Activist, Sri Lanka;
rukiiiii@gmail.com

Notes
Beiträge

An Intercultural and Interreligious Encounter – The First Translation of the Confucian Classics

Intercultural and interreligious encounter is a very challenging topic that is discussed everywhere. How it is put into practice, however, is a different story. Whenever one sees and hears information in the media about religiously motivated bloody encounters, one questions the seriousness of everyday discussions on this topic.

The recently published book by Thierry Meynard, *Confucius Sinarum Philosophus (1687)*[1] gives an excellent example of intercultural and interreligious encounter many hundred years ago that was put into practice with enormous energy and determination.

The Jesuits were leading in transmitting Chinese thought to Europe and at the same time immersing themselves into Chinese thinking and culture as they were learning the Chinese language using the texts of the great sages of China, above all Confucius.

I Introduction to *Sinarum Philosophus*

The editor, a well-known scholar in China, presents the first translation of the Confucian classics in three sections. The first section deals with the historical background of the translation, the second consists in the translation of the preface followed by the Latin text and the third section presents the translation of the Daxue and its commentary with the Latin and Chinese texts in juxtaposition.

A dramatic history

In the first chapter of the first section, the author takes the reader along the dramatic historical time of the generation of the translation that begins

---

[1] Thierry Meynard S.J. (ed.), *Confucius Sinarum Philosophus (1687). The First Translation of the Confucian Classics.* Monumenta Historica Societatis Iesu. Nova Series Vol. 6., Institutum Historicum Societatis Iesu, 2011, VII + 449.

with the use of the Confucian classics as teaching materials for missionaries learning Chinese. The whole project falls into the period of the Chinese Rites controversy. Differences with regards to the point of reference of translation, the interpretation of the related texts and the diverse attitudes of groups of missionaries create a rather complicated history of the translation itself. The reader is given very detailed information about the contradictory attitudes between scholars of the various religious communities and even amongst the Jesuits themselves who were the leading force in the whole project, of the political influence of European heads of state, and of some mishaps (such as the loss of documents) that eventually led to the prohibition of the Chinese Rites. One particular point in the context of the liturgical reform of Vatican II is worth mentioning: there were already that time initiatives asking for permission from Rome to use the vernacular in the liturgy in China.

The whole process of the translation lasted about one hundred years. This long period was in many parts very fruitful regarding intercultural and interreligious encounter. Questions were asked such as: What is the point of reference in translating texts, particularly if it concerns texts on ethics or religious attitudes? Is it the background of the translator and his/her philosophical and theological references? Or is it the context of the text itself that is to be translated? Do the texts speak for themselves? Or is it allowed to measure them by classical texts of the translators? These and many further questions were already discussed at that time and – in my opinion – may certainly serve even nowadays as guidelines and principles for people engaged in intercultural exchange, particularly in the field of translation.

Eventually, in 1687, the translation came out under the title *Confucius Sinarum Philosophus, sive Scientia Sinensis*. One controversy – evolving mainly between the Jesuits and the Friars – concerned mostly the questions of practices and their interpretation. This was aggravated by the fact that in this vast country the local practices differed greatly as well as the people themselves: common people and elite. Besides, the problem of understanding the texts sent to Rome made things even more complicated. Thus there was no common ground for serious interpretation; they went so far as to deny the classical Chinese texts anything that the West possessed already, even discrediting these texts as "impious" and "heretical" (23). Against these accusations, the Jesuits used the *Sinarum Philosophus* as an instrument "for convincing Church leaders, political leaders and intellectuals that Confucianism contained nothing contrary to true faith" (23). However, they failed to get the approval of the Chinese Rites and in 1704 the rites were condemned by Pope Clement XI. The good point resulting from the rite controversy was that for the first time "a comprehensive translation and interpretation of Confucian classics (was) available for a wide readership in Europe" (24).

In this context Meynard proposes some general considerations regarding cross-cultural interpretation of texts whereby he characterizes the Jesuit approach in *Sinarum Philosophus* as "an encounter between two living interpretive traditions at one point in history" (27) rather than being able to go back to an "original" Confucius. Therefore, the *Sinarum Philosophus* is not just a translation and interpretation of classical Chinese texts, but at the same time "a discussion between Neo-Confucianism and Western philosophy" (27).

The hermeneutics

In chapters two, three and four the author elaborates on three complementary approaches that are used in *Sinarum Philosophus* in order to develop a hermeneutics of the Confucian texts: a philosophical, a political and a historical approach that are rooted in Chinese hermeneutics.

With regards to the choice of hermeneutics, it is interesting to note that the Jesuits chose the canon of Zhu Xi (1130–1200), the most important Neo-Confucian of China, concealing it however by using other interpreters who were in line with Zhu Xi. The problem was that in Zhu Xi they found materialistic and atheistic tendencies that were not acceptable for either the missionary students or the Western readers. In this context it has to be noted that the Jesuits found exegetical methods that were more developed than in Europe at that time.

The philosophical approach

The author then presents the philosophical approach (chapter three) where he explains in detail the understanding of two complementary concepts: Chinese "philosophy" (containing only moral and political philosophy) and "learning" (scientia), whereby philosophy "stresses the ability to know truth through reason and the discarding of superstition" and learning "emphasizes the systematic feature of the knowledge gained, and its logical coherence" (43).

Under the title "Metaphysical Framework", the reader learns how the Aristotelian-Thomist framework functions in the interpretation of the Neo-Confucian version of the Daxue whereby the categories of the "summum bonum as a transcendental end" and the "causes" (first and final cause) with its degrees are presented. Regarding the charge of pantheism against the Neo-Confucians, the Jesuits emphasized the notion of transcendence. However, the question of immanence and transcendence in Neo-Confucian thinking remains open to this day.

With regards to epistemology, the Jesuits while in the first period recognizing the lack of logic, tried in *Sinarum Philosophus* to present logical features of the Confucian classics. They were convinced that in Europe the texts would be judged according to standards of logic and in addition that there were identical structures of thought across different cultures. In the field of anthropology and morality there was a highly rationalistic interpretation of the texts. There was, in contrast to Chinese thought, an essential difference between the nature of human beings and the rest of creation – while the Jesuits shared the priority of the rational part of the soul over feelings with Neo-Confucianism.

The political and historical approach

In the description of the political and historical approach (chapter four), the author presents the shift from a pure philosophical reading of the classics towards a political and historical interpretation. This shift was followed by the Jesuits. The classics became more and more a manual for rulers. The dedication of *Sinarum Philosophus* to Louis XIV indicates that it might well be that the Jesuits were in this respect influenced by the trends of Renaissance in Europe of writing political treatises for head of states. The teaching of Confucius seemed to be useful for Chinese and European rulers alike. Thus, the Jesuits indirectly exerted quite a strong influence for the establishment of absolute states in Europe. However, according to their understanding, the absolute power always remained limited by the recognition of the authority of the Church in the areas of religion and morality.

The *Sinarum Philosophus*, in imposing the idea of an ideal Chinese political system presented "for the first time, the intellectual and canonical foundations of a secular state" (67) to Europe. In such a political system, religion could enjoy its freedom, thus Christianity in China could benefit. Unfortunately history showed an opposite image. References to historical figures became ever more important – whereby Confucius remained the absolute point of reference even though it was discovered that he was only the transmitter and not the origin of his cultural system.

An interesting feature regarding historical criticism is the fact that the Chinese were using this tool to interpret their texts while at the same time Europe was only starting to use this method for the Bible, inspired by the exposure to the Chinese approach to history (73).

In summary, it can be said that regarding the *Sinarum Philosophus*, "there was no fundamental opposition between Western and Chinese philosophies" (75). Thus "the *Sinarum Philosophus* represents an interesting example of the cross-cultural reading of classics" (74).

2   The Preface of *Sinarum Philosophus* in English
In the second section Meynard presents the English translation of the Preface of *Sinarum Philosophus*.

The four Jesuit authors Prospero Intorcetta, Christian Herdtrich, François de Rougement and Philippe Couplet dedicated their work to Louis the Great (Louis XIV). This has its reason (see above). In a letter to the king – a sequence of praise and adoration – Philippe Couplet presents Confucius giving the king the greatest honour by letting the Philosopher say that Louis XIV was the "Man to be waited for" (84) and totally submitting himself as a servant to the king. Towards the end Couplet implores

Louis XIV to be sure that the *Sinarum Philosophus* gets a place in the collections of the Royal Library and that the work should not only have a famous place in China, but also all over Europe.

2.1 The first part of the preliminary discussion

Origin and purpose of *Sinarum Philosophus*

In preliminary discussion on the "Origin and Purpose of the Work" the author emphasizes that the translation is not meant for the curiosity of western readers but for missionaries going to China. They elaborate on the best way of establishing contact with the Chinese people and how to gain their respect and trust. It is "to practice holiness of life" (90), not to practice any ascetic way or preaching. The encounter with people of another culture even for missionaries takes place first and foremost by way of the concrete life combined with studying in depth the language and reading their literature, and during this period becoming "like children again, among the Chinese, out of their love for Christ" (91).[2] The Jesuits even learnt the four books by heart, so as to show their respect towards the Chinese culture and to gain the respect of the Chinese. In this way they could dissipate the suspicion towards European "barbarian" thinking and gain the sympathy of the Chinese philosophical and political elite, thus easier showing that Chinese and Christian values were not opposed to each other, even more that the Chinese would recognize that "Christian Truths were deduced from their own principles … established by their ancient Kings and sages" (93). With regards to Confucius it meant: "This Philosopher does not contradict the teaching and light of the Gospel" (94). The Jesuits almost canonized a Grand Secretary of the Chinese Empire, Paul Xu Guangqi (1562–1633) who said "that Christianity supplies and completes what is lacking in our Master Confucius and in the philosophy of our literati" (94). This was the gift the Jesuits wanted to give to Louis XIV when they presented to him the *Sinarum Philosophus*.

---

[2] As a long-time missionary to Taiwan the reviewer can only confirm this experience.

The Chinese Classics

The first chapter gives a short presentation of the Chinese Classics. Already at the beginning the authors mention the variety and diversity of texts and their interpreters because there was no authoritative body (as exists in the Catholic Church regarding the translation of the Bible) regulating the choice of the books and their interpretation.

The authors mention the most important books: the *Five Volumes* and the *Four Books*. Even though the *Five Volumes* enjoy higher authority, the *Four Books* are more useful. Then they present in detail the content of the *Five Volumes*. This presentation provides an excellent summary for today's reader. However, the authors then move to the *Four Books*, the works of Confucius and Mencius that are valued the most by the Interpreters and for several important and understandable reasons are translated instead of the *Five Volumes* from Chinese into Latin. The *Four Books* are sometimes used as a reference. The content of the *Four Books* is briefly presented. The first entitled *Daxue* (Great Learning) "teaches the kings how to rule well and successfully" (104); the second with the title *Zhongyong* explains the "perseverance of the middle, i.e. the golden means" (105); the third, *Lunyu*, contains debates of Confucius with his disciples and their speeches on virtues, vices, duties, etc. Finally the forth book is written by Mencius about nature, rites, mores and duties.

In the second chapter the reader hears about the problem of the interpreters of the "classics" who are as many as six hundred, all with their different backgrounds and aims, very often following the rise and fall of dynasties, even experiencing the burning of the books. However, those interpreters who were writing under the Song dynasty were more reliable.

Interlude: Daoism and Buddhism

As an interlude the authors present in chapters three and four two "sects", as the authors call them: Daoism and Buddhism. Because both "sects" are contrary to any Chinese thinking, they are judged by the authors in a devastating way: superstitious, corrupt and perverse, obscure, ambiguous, evil and vicious to the effect that "it appears clearly that the pitiable Chinese empire has constantly declined toward a degenerate state" (114).

However, almost as a by-product, the reader gets quite a detailed description of the origin and content of the teaching of Daoism and particularly of Buddhism.

Schools and philosophers

In chapter five the reader is taken back to the interpreters of the Classics referred to briefly at the end of chapter two. First of all the ideal of Chinese thought is presented in a summary beginning with: "In cultivating and teaching wisdom, prudence and the other virtues, ancient China has always considered the order and constancy of heaven and earth, striving to imitate them thoroughly, with enthusiasm and zeal" (129). On the background of the ideal of Chinese thought, the authors present a number of the so called "modern interpreters" of the Song dynasty (starting in 960 A.D.) that were again devoted to scholarship and education. Of high reputation were Zhou Dunyi and two brothers called Cheng-zi who were, however, surpassed by Zhu Xi (1130–1200). After 1,500 years, where dynasties rose and fell and were obscured by sects of idols, these interpreters revived the teaching of the ancients (Confucius, Mencius a. o.). The *Five Volumes* and other works such as the *Four Books* were newly published. From forty-two interpreters, the authority in this field would be Zhu Xi. However, the Jesuits authors had the impression that those forty-two misinterpreted the ancient teaching in the sense that they only followed Zhu Xi.[3]

The *Yijing*

In chapter six the reader is informed about the *Yijing,* the *Book of Changes* that serves as the principle of interpretation of the ancient books by the modern interpreters. The authors give an excellent and detailed explanation of this book that stands at the beginning of the above-mentioned new edition of the teaching of the Ancients. Related to *Yijing* are the principles of *Ying* and *Yang* as well as the *8 Triagrams* called *Bagua.* Anyone interested in these terms and their meaning will find an admirable explanation in this chapter and in the following chapters seven and eight.

---

[3] A close look at the Jesuit translation shows that they themselves had followed in their translation and interpretation of *Sinarum Philosophus* Zhu Xi (132, footnote 16).

2.2 The second part of the preliminary discussion

Principles established by the ancients and moderns

With the second part of the preface the authors begin with the "explanation about the principles of things, both material and efficient, established by the ancients and moderns" (157) in chapter one. With strong logical arguments from western philosophy the ideas of *Yijing*, particularly the terms *taiji* (principle) and *li* (reason) that are the principles of the modern philosophers are blown to pieces. Contradictions and very unclear statements and comparisons prove that the origin of the whole philosophical construction is empty and void leading people only to atheism. An historical argument is shattering, namely that the ideas of the *Yijing* have been forgotten for almost two thousand years. How can they suddenly be the foundation of all thinking? At the address of these modern philosophers there could be no more devastating final critic: "You wanted to adjust all antiquity to your own infancy and to pull it towards your own thinking by twisting its neck" (164).

Chapter two describes the situation that Ricci met when going to China. It was the sects and idols that were worshipped everywhere, Buddhism, Daoism and a combination of both, that was followed mainly by intellectuals; even Islam was out of place. Ricci had to fight a mental struggle. As a foreigner and thus a "barbarian" he had nothing to credit himself, even less when he presented himself with a foreign message never heard of and "so contrary to the character of this sophisticated and proud nation, which announces things that at first seem incredible: that there is a Man-God and that he is crucified" (168).

How Ricci contemplated about the situation he faced and how he came to terms with it is described in the following chapter. Ricci again and again made comparisons to the degenerating Roman Empire in order to describe the situation of China. How could he address the Chinese in such a situation? Philosophy and the Bible would not work as he was a "barbarian" with regards to philosophy, and the Chinese had older books than the Bible. Ricci turned to the Apostle Paul who amid all the idolatry in Athens started from small facts, an altar to the unknown God and the poetry of the Athenians. In contemplating this Ricci discovered that he would have to study the culture of the Chinese and start from there in order to find some clues that could lead to religion and eventually to Christian faith. So Ricci spent sixteen years in the South of China, living in silence, studying, talking to Chinese friends who had become Christians in order to be able to understand them better. In January 1601, Ricci entered the royal court of Bejing taking along as gifts paintings of Jesus Christ as Saviour and of Blessed Mary and a crucifix. Discussions and sharing began and Ricci cautiously explained Christian faith starting from what was familiar with the Chinese thinking so that "some could confidently affirm that this was the very same thing that the ancient kings and wise men had called and truly worshipped under the appropriate name of *Shangdi* or 'Supreme Emperor'" (174). It is interesting to note that this discovery was formulated some hundred years later in the documents of Vatican II as the "rays and seeds of truth" (e.g. Nostra aetate 2) when the authors of *Sinarum Philosophus* state: "If Mathew himself has found in the records of the ancient Chinese, the seeds and sparks of his own light and religion, then he might pursue that which had laid so long sleeping, as if extinct, be stirred up, and that through the new splendour of a divine teaching, this native light of original truth be rekindled and perfected" (175). However, Ricci was aware of the fact that he could not alienate the people with an excessive novelty as the Christian teaching was; rather human firmness, justice and reason were asked for. This encouraged Ricci to read and study the ancient teachings ever again, trying to reach the depth of them.

Beginning with the fact that China was always closed up against other nations not only geographically but also "in terms of morality, customs and literature" (177), the reader learns in chapter four about the special status of China and its self-confidence compared to the rest of the world. It is best expressed by calling the empire *Tianxia* which means "what is under heaven" in order to show that no nation is superior to it and that it is the oldest, not deriving from any other nation or culture. The reason is that compared to the oldest cultures in the West like the Assyrians, followed by Medes, Persians down to the Greek and Romans, China was in its early time never corrupted by idolatry – this started only with the arrival of Buddhism. In spite of that, "the Chinese seem to have pre-served for much longer than the rest of mankind the knowledge of the true God" (182).

In chapter five proves with several arguments – particularly with the proximity to the time of the Biblical Flood – that the ancient Chinese "cannot proceed from any other nation on earth, but must come from the Patriarch Noah himself, or his sons, or grandchildren" (183). This testifies the fact of the true knowledge of God of the ancient Chinese transmitted by Noah and his descendents. To prove the opposite would be a difficult task.

Even though there were short periods of religious superstition, one emperor after the other is presented in chapter six as an ideal ruler and worshipper of the true God – eighty rulers in all during a time of 1,975 years. Reading the oldest records shows clearly "that a unique and excep-tional providence of God was watching over and protecting the Chinese people among almost all the other nations" (192). No other culture can be compared to it in this respect.

Ancient China is further idealized in the following chapter where more proofs are given that the Chinese knew the true God. While in west-ern cultures venerated gods and goddesses are described as leading im-moral lives, or in some cases beasts are honoured by religious rituals, there was nothing like this in ancient China. On the contrary, ancient China was "led only by natural light" (195), promoting moral virtues, fair government and the rule of good life. All this was possible because there was no regular exchange with other countries. However, later on sects and superstitions (Daoism and Buddhism) destroyed these ancient principles.

Shangdi

In chapter eight the reader finds a lengthy and very interesting analysis of the etymology and specificity of how the ancient Chinese called the true God. The expression *"Shangdi"* is of ancient origin, many hundred years before Abraham was born or the Greek name *Theos* and later the Roman name *Deus* were invented. It seems that one has "to glorify the Ancient Chinese, for they knew, expressed and worshipped the true God under such a name" (208) that corresponds with the notion of God of Thomas Aquinas. However, the Chinese notion of God was present thousands of years earlier. This "Supreme Emperor" (*Shangdi*) was then directly connected with the emperor on earth "who as his adopted son and vicar on earth, made sacrifices" (208). In the same way *Shangdi* ruled heaven, the Chinese emperor ruled the world.

But there were interpreters, the reader learns in the following chapter, influenced by the sect of Daoism who tried to corrupt the true name for God and its connection with the emperor. Thereby the element of "breadth" played an important role. The false interpreters claim "that the God of heaven is like the breadth of a human being" (211).

Thus the golden age of the correct notion of the true God was badly damaged and had to be rejected.

A concentrated intercultural and interreligious discourse is found in chapter ten with the title "Proof from the Examples of St Paul and Church Fathers that Ancient Chinese Could Name the True God" (213). If the missionaries in China used *Shangdi* for God they actually followed St Paul and the Church Fathers. For the Greeks *Theos* should be favoured and for the Romans *Deus*, because by hearing these words the people were able to form an idea about God because the words belonged to their culture even though sometimes misinterpreted. Paul and the Church Fathers would then explain the difference between their notion of their pagan gods and what *Theos* or *Deus* really meant. The missionaries in China did the same with *Shangdi*. This concerns not only the word for God but also principles that are found in different cultures with similar meaning, e.g.: "Do not do to others what you do not want others to do to you."

In chapter eleven Couplet deals with the question as to whether or not foreigners are able to interpret the ancient Chinese texts correctly. There is a Eurocentric attitude in his arguments originating in the idea of a *philsophia perennis* when he writes: "The Chinese Atheists should listen to the European Saints" (219) because nowhere do we find "such a stable philosophy, a philosophy unchanged from the beginning of the world, a truly divine wisdom …" (219). However, Couplet asserts that one has to respect different interpreters but that it is necessary to find the gems in the middle of the corrupted interpretations. In order to achieve this, learning the languages and knowledge of literature has absolute priority together with the reading of the ancient texts themselves. It is not enough rely on interpreters. This was the method of the Church Fathers.

Couplet presents in chapter twelve Ricci's book on Christian Religion which was published in the Imperial court in 1603. In these two volumes the use of the terms for God (*Shangdi* or *Tianzhu*) plays an important role. Many famous Chinese at the Imperial court followed Ricci as well as Jesuit companions who reprinted the books and added other publications on Christian Religion such as Giulio Aleni and Alfonso Vagnone. However, only a few years after Ricci's death, a first persecution occurred in 1615 out of jealousy and hostility against foreigners. A royal edict in 1675 brought the attacks formally to an end.

Conclusion

In conclusion, Couplet summarizes the whole preface emphasizing that the Chinese had a knowledge of the true God and the hope that China would convert to the Christian faith. Then the author adds a quite detailed and dramatic biography of the extraordinary life of Confucius whom he calls the "Father of Chinese Philosophy" (235). An appreciation follows of Confucius as a person and his influence on the thinking, the culture and politics in China. Couplet affirms that Confucius was not influenced by the atheistic influence of Buddhism that came to China at that time, but was very disturbed by these new ideas. The veneration of Confucius is presented as a purely civil and political honour that has nothing to do with religion. But Confucius remains very important for every missionary because of the authority he has among the Chinese. "It would be possible to use his authority to confirm the Christian truth, in the same way as in the past we saw the Apostle of the Nations (St Paul) using the authority of the Greek Poets among the Athenians" (243).

The portrait of Confucius

The English translation of the Preface is followed by a revealing portrait of Confucius that shows him in a western style "Gymnasium". Couplet

190

shows once again his main aim – to promote the intercultural and inter-religious dialogue between China and the West.

2.3 The Latin original of the Preface

It is important that the Latin original follows the English translation of the Preface of *Sinarum Philosophus* because readers mastering the Latin language are thereby not dependent on the English translation, but get an immediate access to the actual work of the Jesuit authors. The introduction by Thierry Meynard remains a great and indispensable help in locating *Sinarum Philosophus*.

3   The first book of the Chinese Learning

The third section presents the translation of *Daxue* (The Great Learning) and its Chinese commentaries and notes into English with the corresponding Latin and Chinese text in juxtaposition.

In this summary and appreciation of the publication, I do not comment the content of *Daxue*. I rather encourage the reader to go him- or herself into the matter. The advantage of the translation presented in three languages allows the reader to compare the notion of the three languages and thus to get deeper into the content of *Daxue* than if he or she is dependent on a translation into only one language. People who are masters in all the three languages will profit from the comparison.

The presentation in three languages is very clear and easy to take in at a glance. However the reader, even if he or she is familiar with the Chinese characters, is simply amazed at the excellence of the translation of the Confucian texts. They are, as is common with classical Chinese texts, written in the shortest possible way. To grasp the idea and the content of the Chinese characters it needs a really thorough study of the language and of the philosophy, history and politics of the context so as to capture the *Sitz im Leben* of the respective Chinese characters. This is exactly what the Jesuits managed to do and thus made with the *Sinarum Philosophus* an unparalleled work in translating these ancient Chinese texts, making them available and above all understandable for western readers.

Contemplating the effort of the Jesuits, the challenge of any person working in the field of intercultural and interreligious dialogue, as missionaries or in the fields of development projects, is to learn the language of the people he or she works with. This is unquestionably of primary importance. Otherwise it is simply impossible to grasp the essence of a culture and thereby the real meaning of what people in a given culture may say and mean. Communication is not only a question of words but also, and even more, a question of the heart. This is important for any person living and working in a different culture. Even more it is essential in the realm of missionary work as faith is the language of the heart.

The book contains an index of names and places and Chinese works mentioned in the *Sinarum Philosophus*. The addition of the Chinese characters to the transliterations in the indices (names of persons and places, Chinese works, subjects, etc.) is a big help for people who master Chinese characters as they are able to precisely identify the meanings. This concerns also the bibliography.

In the index of subjects, it would have been convenient if, with the Chinese terms (e.g. *Li*, p. 432 or *Taiji*, p. 433), the Chinese characters would have been added.

The Chart of Correspondence (434–438) serves as a helpful guide to the three different texts.

For western readers, this study is an excellent introduction into Chinese thinking and culture (including the "sects" of Buddhism and Taoism!) in comparison with the western cultural heritage. It is even more so for readers who are familiar with the Chinese language and the Chinese characters, who will get an even deeper notion of this ancient treasure of China.

Josef Meili SMB, M. A., Kreuzbuchstrasse 44, CH-6006 Luzern, Switzerland; josefmeili@bluewin.ch

The Asians among Us.
Opportune and Challenging Trends for Mission Inter Gentes

In 2010 SEDOS[1] began with a sequence within the annual seminars on the topic "Church". Africa was placed first with *The Prophetic Challenge of the African Churches*. In 2011 followed Asia with the topic *The Asians among Us. Opportune and Challenging Trends for Mission Inter Gentes*. In 2012 Latin America focuses on *Spring of the Poor?*

From May 17–21, 2011, the annual SEDOS residential seminar took place in the formation centre *Casa Divin Maestro* in Ariccia with the topic *The Asians among Us. Opportune and Challenging Trends for Mission Inter Gentes*.[2] About 130 women and men from over 40 religious communities and as many nationalities participated in the seminar.

In his excellent opening speech: *Cultural and Religious Diversity among Asians: reflection from the Churches of Asia,* James H. Kroeger, M. M. gave an overview situation of the Church in Asia from a missiological point of view. Kroeger pointed out some surprising aspects, e.g. regarding statistics. Out of 100 people, 61 live in Asia, 12 in Europe, 13 in Africa, 9 in South America and the Caribbean and 5 in North America (including Canada). The Eurocentric division of the world into "north" and "south" is definitely out of discussion. The cultural and religious traditions of Asia (Hinduism, Buddhism) are hundreds of years older than the Christian tradition. Even though one may divide Asia into East Asia, South Asia, South East Asia and Central Asia, the cultural variety is almost uncountable. The socio-economic situation can be described by three realities: poverty, cultures and religions. These realities are always the point of departure and reference for the theological reflections of the Federation of

---

[1] Servicio di Documentazione e Studi, Via dei Verbiti, I-00154 Roma.
http://www.sedosmission.org

[2] All the talks are available in: SEDOS Bulletin 2011, Vol. 43, No. 5/6; May-June.

193

the Asian Bishops Conferences (FABC). On the level of church leadership, the FABC is surely the richest theological basis in the world. Subject of the triple dialogue with the poor (peoples), the cultures and the religions is the local Church; her main option is: to live is to evangelize!

The following three days were characterized by: See – Judge – Act
See
A sociological view was presented by Pio Estepa, SVD with the title *The Asian Mission Landscape of the 21st Century.* He pointed out three mega-trends that transform the missionary situation of Asia: mega-urbanization, mega-migration, and mediatization.

Mega-urbanization: By 2030 more than 50% of the people in Asia will live in cities of more than 10 million inhabitants; the biggest Asian mega-cities – Tokyo, Jakarta, Mumbai, Delhi, Metro-Manila – have more than 20 million inhabitants. The urbanization is increasing fast. Thereby the economic gain is paid by the ecological destruction of land, air and water.

Mega-migration: Apart from the hundreds of thousands of contract-workers and highly qualified professionals, there are uncountable forced migrants who move to other continents by way of human trafficking or political unrest. The problem of their cultural and religious identity will arise and will be a challenge to themselves as well as for their host-countries.

Mediatization: The electronic audiovisual media reign as the primary channels for information and communication. Thereby the postmodern values of the *person (egoism), pleasure,* the *present* (instantaneous fulfilment of wishes) are produced and enforced. In consequence the fertility rate drops because children become a burden rather than a guarantee of the future.

There are many questions arising from these situations. What does mission of the Church mean in such situations in Asia itself as well as in the host-countries? What does mission *inter gentes* (in the middle of the peoples) mean? How will missionaries be bridge-builders between city and countryside? What does mission mean between the E-Generation (e-mail, etc.) and all those who have no access to such media? How are we missionaries intermediaries between local people and migrants?

Judge

In his talk *A Theology of Mission Appropriate for the Churches of Asia in the 21st Century* Peter C. Phan changed the title of the seminar from *Asians among us* to *We among Asians*, taking into account the vast area of so-called Asia with its immense population compared to the rest of the world. He pointed out that we should also change the terminology used by Vatican II and its following documents (e. g. *Redemptoris Missio 1990)* from *missio AD gentes* that can have a paternalistic undertone to *missio INTER gentes*, even to *missio CUM gentibus*. In the first part Phan asked who these *gentes* actually are. We must not call them *pagans*, because they lived for hundred of years with strong established religions (Hinduism, Buddhism, Taoism) before Christianity began. These religions gave their people meaning in their life and strongly influenced their cultures, societies and politics. Because of this we have to drop the idea that Asia would eventually become Christian. However, this does not mean that mission would become dispensable. It will have an altogether different character than the traditional one as aiming towards conversion and baptism.

Missio inter gentes means that missionaries are bridge-builders. They live in the middle of people of other faiths *(gentes)* and work together with them, giving witness to their faith; in the same way the *gentes* are witness to their faith. So the missionary and the *gentes* do mission and are at the same time missionized. The faith of both sides is challenged and purified. Religious elements are mutually discovered, exchanged and integrated.

Finally *mission cum gentibus* means that the work of establishing the Kingdom of God is a common and shared project of all religions, cultures and peoples. Phan referred extensively to the practice of Jesus in his encounter with non-Jewish people, e. g. the Samaritan leper (Lk 17), the Good Samaritan (Lk 10), the Roman Centurion (Mt 8), the Canaanite woman (Mt 15), the unknown healer (Mk 9). The whole of humanity is called to join in the mission of God that became visible in Jesus of Nazareth. The Church is but a small sign of it.

Act

The practice of *missio inter gentes* was presented in several short talks. Bonnie Mendes described in his talk *Mission Work among Continental Asians* the extremely complex situation of Christian communities in Pakistan. Dialogue with Muslims exists in the cooperation in concrete projects (mutual help regarding catastrophes, human trafficking, protection of environment, work for peace, education, etc.). Mendes presented also a much more differentiated picture of the general situation in Pakistan than what the international media tell and show. His talk was a very helpful political lesson for the participants.

Sr. Dr. Leo Ackermann from Germany introduced the project SOLWODI (Solidarity with women in distress) in her talk *Mission Work among Asians Overseas*. This project deals explicitly with human trafficking on one hand in the continents of origin (Asia and Africa) as well as in the "guest"-continent (Europe). Her talk was a very strong plea to take a radical stand against every form of slavery or exploitation of the weak. Her question at the end accentuated the point: "How can we say that God is love, without making people in need feel His love through our help?"

Finally Dr. Cristina Liamzon presented her work in Italy in her speech *Accompanying and Journeying with Overseas Filipinos*. She mentioned several specific problems of the almost 125000 Filipino migrant workers found also in other host-countries: ghetto-mentality, problem of language and culture, loss of belonging, dissolution of family and partnership bonds, identity-crisis, abuse by employers, etc. Because the majority of the Filipino migrants are Catholics, the Church has a heavy responsibility towards them. Worthwhile mentioning are the goals of empowering migrants: changing mind-sets, building skills, developing networks, articulating dreams, transforming lives …[3]

The seminar showed clearly that religions – in our case particularly Christianity – are present in the public sphere through their members, not just as bystanders, but as agents of changes in societies and politics. It is a question of using and integrating the resources of religions in order to

[3] See SEDOS Bulletin 2011, Vol. 43, No. 5/6, 157.

build societies that function according to Human Rights, thereby promoting the presence of the Kingdom of God. The various talks of the seminar always pointed to the responsibility of the Christian faith towards the world and humanity.

Josef Meili SMB, M. A., Kreuzbuchstrasse 44, CH-6006 Luzern, Switzerland; josefmeili@bluewin.ch

Book Reviews
Buchbesprechungen

Christoph Bochinger (Hrsg.), Religionen, Staat und Gesellschaft.
Die Schweiz zwischen Säkularisierung und religiöser Vielfalt,
Zürich, Verlag Neue Zürcher Zeitung, 2012, 284 S.

Wie präsentiert sich die «religiöse Landschaft der Schweiz» aktuell, welche Dynamiken des Wandels zeichnen sich ab und wie kann das friedliche Zusammenleben unterschiedlicher religiöser und nicht religiöser Menschen gefördert und gestaltet werden? Auf diese Fragen erhoffte sich der Schweizer Bundesrat von der Wissenschaft praxisrelevante Erkenntnisse im Hinblick auf aktuelle gesellschaftliche Herausforderungen. Er gab darum 2005 das ehrgeizige nationale Forschungsprogramm «Religionsgemeinschaften, Staat und Gesellschaft» (NFP 58) in Auftrag, das im europäischen Vergleich bisher einmalig geblieben ist.

Der Syntheseband «Religionen, Staat und Gesellschaft», herausgegeben von Christoph Bochinger, Religionswissenschaftler aus Bayreuth und Präsident der Leitungsgruppe des NFP 58, bündelt die wichtigsten Befunde aus den 28 Teilprojekten entlang den Schwerpunktthemen «Religionsgemeinschaften im Wandel», «Religion und Individuum», «Religion und Öffentlichkeit», «Staat und Religion» sowie «Religion und Sozialisation». In sieben Kapiteln kommen folgende Autorinnen und Autoren zu Wort: Martin Baumann, Jörg Stolz, Luzius Mader und Marc Schinzel, René Pahud de Mortanges, Irene Becci und Christoph Bochinger. Es sind dies Vertreterinnen und Vertreter der Wissenschaft (Religionswissenschaft, Soziologie und Rechtswissenschaft) sowie des Bundesamts für Justiz.

Eine Bestandesaufnahme aller Religionsgemeinschaften und ihrer Entwicklung während den letzten Jahrzehnten macht deutlich, dass den grossen kirchlichen Konfessionen (römisch-katholische und evangelisch-reformierte Kirche) trotz ihres fortschreitenden Mitgliederschwunds, der zunehmenden Alterung ihres Gottesdienstpublikums und der wachsenden Distanzierung der jüngeren Generationen nach wie vor mehr als 60% der Bevölkerung angehören. Dagegen lässt sich bei manchen evangelischen Freikirchen eine beachtliche Tendenz zum Wachstum beobachten und ihre Altersstruktur ist wesentlich jünger und damit zukunftsgesicherter als bei den Grosskirchen. Doch obschon sie ein Viertel aller lokalen religiösen Gemeinschaften in der Schweiz stellen, macht ihre Mitgliederzahl doch bloss ca. 2% der Gesamtbevölkerung aus. Der Islam, der sich in der Schweiz kulturell und religiös sehr vielgestaltig und heterogen zeigt, vereint einen Bevölkerungsanteil von 5–6%, der Hinduismus ist mit ca. 0,7%, der Buddhismus mit ca. 0,3% und das Judentum noch mit ca. 0,2% vertreten.

Die Religionsgemeinschaften sind Teil der Gesellschaft und von deren stetem Wandel mitbetroffen. Die Desinstitutionalisierung, ein gesellschaftlicher Trend, der nicht nur das religiöse Feld ergreift, betrifft derzeit zwar in hohem Masse den christlichen Mainstream. Doch die damit verbundene Emanzipation des Individuums von religiösen Institutionen lässt sich quer durch alle religiösen Traditionen beobachten, besonders stark jedoch bei Jugendlichen und jungen Erwachsenen. Die Veränderung der Religiosität ist wie in allen westeuropäischen Gesellschaften auch in der Schweiz darum vor allem ein Wandel zwischen den Generationen. Die Tatsache, dass ältere Personen oft eine höhere Religiosität aufweisen als jüngere, ist höchstwahrscheinlich nicht nur auf einen Lebenszykluseffekt zurückzuführen, sondern auf gesellschaftliche Rahmenbedingungen. Ältere Personen sind in einer Zeit religiös sozialisiert worden, in welcher die Gesellschaft insgesamt religiöser war. Dies trifft auch für viele Migranten und Migrantinnen der ersten Generation zu. Im Übergang zur Zweit- und Drittgeneration werden die zugewanderten Religionsgemeinschaften in der Regel auch vom gesellschaftlichen Trend der Desinstitutionalisierung erfasst. Hier ist eine Tendenz weg von einer kollektiv-ritualistischen hin zu einer individualisiert-reflexiven Religiosität zu beobachten. Die Distanzierung von traditioneller Religiosität geht allgemein einher mit dem Anspruch nach individueller Entscheidungsfreiheit und Authentizität. Sie ist aber nicht automatisch gekoppelt mit einer Abwesenheit von religiösen bzw. spirituellen Vorstellungen und Praktiken. Diese orientieren sich aber nicht mehr länger an den etablierten Institutionen.

Dieses Abschmelzen der institutionellen Religiosität führt aber nicht zu einem entsprechenden Zuwachs im Bereich der alternativen Spiritualität. Die religiöse Individualisierung begünstigt aber die Entstehung von religiösen Märkten und damit eine weitere Pluralisierung religiöser Sinnangebote innerhalb und ausserhalb der Institutionen, was zu einem Verwischen vormals gültiger Grenzen führt. Gegenbewegungen zu diesen Trends äussern sich etwa als «Rückkehrphänomene» mit oft separatistischen und fundamentalistischen Zügen.

Diese Beobachtungen zum Auseinanderdriften von institutionalisierter und individualisierter Religiosität, zum allgemeinen Bedeutungsverlust der Religion auf der gesellschaftlichen und individuellen Ebene sowie zur wachsenden Pluralisierung des religiösen Marktes werden interessanterweise durch die Beobachtung kontrastiert, dass Religion in der Öffentlichkeit derzeit einen beachtlichen Bedeutungszuwachs erfährt. Religion als Thema ist nicht nur in der Politik, sondern vor allem in den Medien sehr präsent. Jedoch interessieren sich die Medien kaum für Religion «an sich», sie rückt aber vor allem dann in den Fokus, wenn sie mit den Ordnungslogiken anderer Lebensbereiche kollidiert und so zur Erklärung von Problemen und Konflikten herangezogen werden kann. Dabei führen die Darstellungen oft zu polarisierenden Bewertungen der Religionen. Es erstaunt darum nicht, dass gerade der Islam mehrheitlich negativ etikettiert wird, während der Buddhismus eher gute Noten erhält. Die von den Medien vorgenommenen Zuordnungen in «gut» oder «schlecht», «eigen» oder «fremd» führen zu Wertungen und Stereotypisierungen mit exklusivem Charakter, welche die Wahrnehmung der befragten Bevölkerung, die diese Zuschreibungen spiegeln, nachhaltig beeinflussen. Es zeigt sich für die Schweiz, dass Religion zunehmend als Differenzierungs- bzw. Abgrenzungsmarker gerade für kollektive Identität herangezogen wird. Die Wahrnehmung bestimmter Bevölkerungsgruppen, insbesondere von Zuwanderern, als «fremdreligiös» führt aber nicht nur zu klischeehaften und reduktiv-religiösen Identifikationsmustern etwa von zugewanderten national-ethnisch, kulturell und religiös ganz unterschiedlichen Gruppen, sondern umgekehrt auch zu einer Selbstidentifikation bei den Urhebern der Abgrenzungsstrategie, die sich dann umso stärker als «christlich» wahrnehmen.

Die öffentliche Präsenz der Religionen in der Schweiz ist also nicht mit einer «Rückkehr der Religionen» oder einer Aufwertung der Religion als solcher zu verwechseln. Vielmehr scheint sie als Etikett für gesellschaftliche Probleme oder politische Programme zu dienen.

Überhaupt scheinen die Autoren und Autorinnen in der Sache einig zu gehen, Religion als Phänomen und Thema im öffentlichen wie privaten Leben der Schweizer Bevölkerung sei nicht überzubewerten, denn sie entwickle sich zunehmend zu einem Randphänomen mit gelegentlichen Ausnahmeerscheinungen.

Doch die wachsende Wahrnehmung zugewanderter Religionen und Kulturen verlangt nach Beachtung und rückt die Frage der Integration und damit verbunden der Gleichstellung, Partizipation und des friedlichen Zusammenlebens ins Zentrum. Sie entpuppt sich als Doppelfrage, die sowohl auf die Inkorporationsbemühungen der Angehörigen zugewanderter Religionsgemeinschaften als auch auf die von der Residenzgesellschaft geschaffenen rechtlichen, politischen und sozialen Inkorporationsbedingungen zielt. Der Staat vertritt derzeit eine positiv verstandene weltanschauliche Neutralität und sieht sich in zentralen Bereichen einem religionspluralen Inkorporationsregime verpflichtet. Das bedeutet, dass allen Religionsgemeinschaften grundsätzlich die gleichen Rechte und Pflichten zugestanden werden müssen, auch wenn die grossen Konfessionen in den meisten Kantonen nach wie vor die einzigen Religionsgemeinschaften sind, die einen öffentlich-rechtlichen Status geniessen. Diese Haltung der Gleichbehandlung äussert sich unter anderem darin, dass der Staat sich nicht mehr, wie einst, mit einer bestimmten Kirche oder Religionsgemeinschaft identifiziert, sondern Religionsgemeinschaften dann mit Subventionen unterstützt, wenn sie Dienstleistungen in den Bereichen Bildung, Soziales und Kultur übernehmen. Das auf religiöser Neutralität basierende, pragmatisch-utilitaristische «Regime» ist so prinzipiell offen für alle Religionsgemeinschaften, bleibt aber in der Realität hauptsächlich auf die anerkannten christlichen Kirchen konzentriert, die den Löwenanteil der staatlichen Subventionen beanspruchen, obschon sich zahlreiche andere, christliche und nicht christliche Religionsgemeinschaften mit ihren Angeboten für die gesellschaftliche Integration ihrer Mitglieder einsetzen. Auch in politischen Prozessen haben nicht alle Religionsgemeinschaften die gleichen Chancen. Beispielsweise werden die öffentlich-rechtlich anerkannten Religionsgemeinschaften bei relevanten gesellschaftspolitischen Themen systematisch in das öffentliche Vernehmlassungsverfahren (ein Anhörungsverfahren im Vorfeld der Gesetzgebung im Sinne der demokratischen Mitsprache auf allen Ebenen des staatlichen Gemeinwesens) einbezogen, während kleinere Religionsgemeinschaften viel seltener, muslimische Gemeinschaften sogar fast nie als Gesprächspartner beigezogen werden. Sie verfügen in der Regel auch nicht über die nötigen Ansprechpartner und die finanziellen wie personellen Ressourcen, um mit den Grosskirchen mithalten zu können.

Die pragmatisch-utilitaristische Kooperation des Staates mit den Religionsgemeinschaften wirkt auch in die umgekehrte Richtung. Wo der Beitrag der Religionsgemeinschaften nicht mehr gebraucht oder erwünscht ist, versucht der Staat ihre Privilegien abzubauen. Dies lässt sich etwa in den Bereichen Religionsunterricht an den Schulen und Seelsorge in den Spitälern und Gefängnissen beobachten.

Die grundsätzlich religionsplurale (nicht zu verwechseln mit religionspluralistische) Ausrichtung des Staates und seiner Rechtsordnung kann in der Schweiz jederzeit durch das Initiativ- und Referendumsrecht korrigiert und sogar unterlaufen werden. Es ist darum nicht ausgeschlossen, dass die Zusammenschau der rechtlichen und politischen Elemente des Inkorporationsregimes verschiedene, sich im Prinzip ausschliessende Handlungsstrategien im Umgang mit Religion sichtbar macht (siehe Abstimmungsresultate zu Minarettverbots- und Ausschaffungsinitiative, 29.11.2009 beziehungsweise 28.11.2010). Insbesondere jene Kreise, die auf die wachsende religiöse Pluralisierung negativ reagieren, weil sie darin das ideologisch-politische Programm der Vertreter eines religiösen Pluralismus vermuten, können mit ihren politischen Vorstössen die vom Staat intendierte Gleichbehandlung aller in der Schweiz praktizierenden Religionen, die auch dem Autoren des entsprechenden Kapitels am Herzen liegt, verhindern.

Mit der Integrationsfrage stellt sich die Sozialisationsfrage und damit die Frage nach der Bedeutung und Rolle der Religionen bzw. religiösen Sozialisationsinstanzen in der Schweizer Gesellschaft. Die religiöse Sozialisation findet in der Phase der Primärsozialisation vor allem im privaten Bereich statt. Zwar gehört Religion heute nicht mehr zu den wichtigsten Werten, die Eltern ihren Kindern vermitteln wollen. Unabhängigkeit, Selbstständigkeit und Fantasie, aber auch gute Manieren, Sparsamkeit, Gehorsam und Beruf werden der Religion oft vorgezogen. Doch wo sie vermittelt wird, prägt sie nachhaltig das religiöse Zugehörigkeitsgefühl des Individuums, auch während der sekundären und tertiären Sozialisation, wenn die heranwachsende bzw. erwachsene Person in neue gesellschaftliche Bereiche eingeführt, mit neuen Rollen, Werten und Lebensweisen konfrontiert wird und sich im Vergleich mit Vertrautem auch mit anderen Varianten der Wirklichkeitsschau auseinandersetzen muss.

In dieser Lebensphase kommen die staatlichen Bildungsinstitutionen und andere normativ Einfluss nehmende, religiöse und nicht religiöse Einrichtungen und Personen ins Spiel. Diese sehen sich in einem Wettstreit um die Einflussnahme auf Sozialisation und diskutieren etwa über die Frage, wer für den Religionsunterricht zuständig bzw. wie dieser Unterricht zu gestalten sei. Mit der zunehmenden Übernahme der Verantwortung durch den Staat im Bildungsbereich verändert sich die Rolle der Religionsgemeinschaften als Sozialisationsinstanzen.

Neben der Schule sind auch die Bereiche der sozialen Arbeit, der Bildung von Lehrerinnen/Lehrern und des Strafvollzugs Orte, wo Religion in unterschiedlicher Weise relevant werden kann. Zwar handelt es sich bei den zuständigen Institutionen heute meist um säkularisierte und religiös neutrale Einrichtungen, dennoch kann Religion hier zum Thema werden, in der Ausbildung, als Motivation oder als Angebot.

Bildung ist eine Hauptaufgabe staatlicher Institutionen, wenn es darum geht, die religiöse Pluralität im Horizont des Inkorporationsideals wahrzunehmen. Sie dient der Versachlichung und fördert nicht nur einen kompetenten Umgang mit «fremden» Religionen, sondern ermöglicht auch einen reflexiven Umgang mit der «eigenen» Religiosität. Damit einher geht in der Regel eine Schwächung der Bindung an die eigene Religionsgemeinschaft, was sich nachhaltig auch auf die religiöse Sozialisation auswirkt.

Die Projekte des NFP 58 fokussierten die «religiöse Landschaft der Schweiz» und ihren Wandel in den letzten Jahrzehnten mit dem Anspruch, handlungsleitende Erkenntnisse zuhanden von staatlichen Institutionen zu generieren, die letztlich der Integration der Gesamtgesellschaft, d. h. der friedlichen Konvivenz unterschiedlicher ethnokulturell-religiöser Gruppen dienen sollten. Dieser Anspruch floss in die Fragestellungen der Forschungsprojekte ein und beeinflusste deren Perspektivenauswahl auf die soziale Wirklichkeit. So konzentrierte sich die Mehrheit der Untersuchungen schliesslich auf religiöse Minderheiten, auf die Themen Migration und Integration sowie auf die Rolle der staatlichen und nicht staatlichen Institutionen und der Medien im Umgang mit Religion. Forschungsprojekte zu den etablierten christlichen Kirchen und zum nicht religiösen Teil der Bevölkerung waren verhältnismässig untervertreten. Entstanden sind ausführliche Bestandsaufnahmen, Problembeschreibungen und Empfehlungskataloge mit Blick auf das Inkorporationsideal des Staates. Dabei werden die zugewanderten Religionsgemeinschaften und ihre Angehörigen ebenso wie die vorherrschenden gesellschaftlichen Rahmenbedingungen und das Verhältnis der beiden Seiten untereinander berücksichtigt und angesprochen. Neben viel Detailwissen, theoretischen Überlegungen und mehr oder weniger engagierten Schlussfolgerungen werden am Ende des Buches zuhanden des Auftraggebers (Schweizer Bundesbehörden) einige Kerngedanken des Forschungsprogramms formuliert. Sie resümieren, dass Religion sowohl als potenzielle Gefahr als auch als potenzielle Ressource für das gesellschaftliche Zusammenleben nicht überschätzt werden sollte, denn dessen Gelingen bzw. Scheitern ist komplexer, als dass es auf religiöse Wirkkräfte reduziert werden könnte. Aus diesem Grund gilt es auch, spektakuläre Einzelfälle nicht überzubewerten, sondern sie in ein Verhältnis zum gesellschaftlichen «Normalfall» zu stellen. Bei geplanten rechtlichen und strukturellen Anpassungen seitens des Staates soll in Zukunft die eher skeptische Stimmung der Gesellschaft den Religionen gegenüber mitberücksichtigt werden. Hier hat ein Konzept, das in pragmatischer Manier auf die Akzeptanz religiöser Pluralität setzt, bessere Chancen als ein programmatisch-ideologisches Konzept, das einen religiösen Pluralismus anstrebt.

Das Buch beschreibt die «religiöse Landschaft der Schweiz», so wie sie sich heute präsentiert. Die Landschaftsmetapher taucht immer wieder auf und mit ihr die Frage, welcher Aspekt von Landschaft im Zusammenhang mit dem NFP 58 fokussiert werden soll. Geht es hier bloss um eine

Beschreibung der Lage im Sinne einer Topografie des «religiösen Feldes» oder um ein gezieltes Vermessen und Ausmessen von Zonen, motiviert von raumplanerischen Ambitionen? Das Forschungsprogramm beleuchtet vor allem jene sichtbare Seite von Religion, die sich in ihren Sozialformen äussert. Mit der Konzentration auf die organisierte bzw. institutionalisierte Religion und deren Verhältnis zu Staat und Gesellschaft bleiben nicht nur die inhaltlich-ideologische und performative, sondern auch die historische Dimension mehrheitlich ausgeblendet. Wer aber eine Landschaft sinnvoll gestalten will, sollte nicht nur ihr gegenwärtiges Erscheinungsbild kennen, sondern auch um ihre gewachsenen Strukturen wissen. Ob der Blick auf die institutionelle Seite der Religion und die damit verbundene Diagnose des Desinstitutionalisierungstrends in der Schweiz schon dazu berechtigen, einen fortschreitenden Bedeutungsverlust der Religion zu diagnostizieren, ist noch nicht geklärt. Die Frage, ob Religion ihre gesellschaftliche Relevanz tatsächlich nur dann hat, wenn sie sich im herkömmlichen Sinne organisiert und als Gemeinschaft «sichtbar» wird, muss vorerst noch offenbleiben. Gerade im Bereich der fluiden und selbstgewachsenen Gemeinschaften und der neuen Kommunikationsformen, beispielsweise der sozialen Medien, zeichnen sich vielleicht Formen von Vergemeinschaftung ab, die einerseits den individuellen Bedürfnissen der Einzelnen in hohem Masse entgegenkommen und andererseits ein nicht zu unterschätzendes Potenzial auf der gesellschaftspolitischen Ebene mit sich führen. Diese mitschwingende Eigenschaft der sich wandelnden Religionen wurde im NFP 58 nicht untersucht. Es fehlen auch Untersuchungen zu den Freidenkern, den alternativen Spiritualitätsformen und sogenannten Sekten, ebenso Fachperspektiven im Bereich Recht und Geschichte sowie spezifische Untersuchungen zum Genderthema. Zwar zeigt sich der sogenannte «Gender-Gap» in einzelnen Projekten, doch die vorhandenen Daten ermöglichen keine eindeutigen Erklärungen. Der Herausgeber des Buches ist sich der blinden Flecken im NFP 58 bewusst und benennt auch die damit verbundenen Forschungsdesiderate für die Zukunft. Einerseits reduziert der Syntheseband die zahlreichen und vielschichtigen Befunde aus der praxisorientierten Forschung auf zentrale Trends in der gegenwärtigen religiösen Landschaft der Schweiz, andererseits bietet er dem Auftraggeber des NFP 58 konkrete Schlussfolgerungen und Empfehlungen für die gesellschaftspolitische Arbeit. Dass dabei gewisse Verengungen der empirischen Sachverhalte in Kauf genommen werden müssen, liegt in der Natur eines solchen Übersichtswerks. Als Einstieg in die Lektüre bietet sich darum das Schlusskapitel an, denn es ermöglicht eine dem NFP 58 angemessene und kritische Leseart der Befunde.

Eva Baumann-Neuhaus, Dr. sc. rel. et lic. phil. I,
Schweizerisches Pastoralsoziologisches Institut, St. Gallen, Schweiz;
eva.baumann-neuhaus@spi-stgallen.ch

Daniele Waldburger, Lukas Zürcher, Urs Scheidegger,
«Im Dienst der Menschheit». Meilensteine der Schweizer
Entwicklungszusammenarbeit seit 1945. Bern, Haupt, 2012.

Die Publikation zum schweizerischen Engagement bei der Beseitigung von Armut und Hunger in der Welt bietet einen Überblick über ein kontroverses Thema schweizerischer Politik auf nationaler und internationaler Ebene. Im Vordergrund steht nicht eine Aufreihung wichtiger Stationen, sondern in chronologischer Abfolge werden wichtige Momente der schweizerischen Entwicklungszusammenarbeit in ihrem internationalen Kontext aufgezeigt. Der Schwerpunkt liegt in drei Bereichen internationaler Zusammenarbeit des Bundes: Entwicklungszusammenarbeit, humanitäre Hilfe und Ostzusammenarbeit.

Die «Schweizer Spende» genannte Hilfe für das kriegsversehrte Europa bildete den Anfang des schweizerischen Engagements für eine gerechtere und friedlichere Welt. Bereits kurze Zeit nach der Gründung wurde die finanzielle und technische Hilfe auf Asien, Afrika und Lateinamerika ausgeweitet und als eigentliche Aufgabe des Bundes erklärt. Die Entwicklungszusammenarbeit erfolgte in Form von Beteiligung an multilateralen Organisationen wie der UNO oder in Form direkter bilateraler Zusammenarbeit.

Als ein erstes Ergebnis ist festzuhalten, dass die heutige Gestalt der Entwicklungszusammenarbeit in ihrer 60-jährigen Geschichte mehrmals Gegenstand heftiger innenpolitischer Auseinandersetzungen war. Entwicklung als Referenzrahmen trug sowohl zu einer Schärfung des Bewusstseins für globale Zusammenhänge von Reichtum und Armut wie auch für gegenseitige politische, wirtschaftliche und ökologische Verflechtungen bei. Die heutige Ausgestaltung schweizerischer Entwicklungszusammenarbeit ist das Resultat eines permanenten Ringens um die richtigen Antworten auf die Frage nach dem Konzept der Entwicklungszusammenarbeit und/oder nach der Aufteilung des Engagements auf bilaterale bzw. multilaterale Aktivitäten. Die aktuelle Form der Entwicklungszusammenarbeit kann so als Ergebnis eines Lernprozesses verstanden werden.

Die aufschlussreiche Lektüre führt zu zwei grundlegenden Erkenntnissen: Die internationale Zusammenarbeit der Schweiz hat ihre geschichtlich gewachsene Form mehrmals grundlegend verändert, sich aber als verpflichtende und nicht an Dritte delegierbare Entwicklungspolitik profiliert.

Die Tatsache, dass die heutige Ausgestaltung der staatlichen Entwicklungszusammenarbeit mit der früheren «Schweizer Spende» nichts mehr gemeinsam hat, verweist auf grundlegende Veränderungen im Konzept der Entwicklungszusammenarbeit. Trotz unterschiedlicher Auffassungen identifizierte sich eine grosse Mehrheit der Schweizer Bevölkerung mit der Entwicklungszusammenarbeit. Es bestand ein gesellschaftlicher Konsens daruber, dass es Aufgabe der Schweiz sei, einen Beitrag zur Überwindung von Armut und Ungleichheit in der Welt zu leisten und sich für eine gerechtere Welt zu engagieren, die frei von Armut und Krisen ist.

Die breite Unterstützung und Anerkennung der verschiedenen Formen von Entwicklungszusammenarbeit ist allerdings keine Selbstverständlichkeit. Die gesellschaftliche Legitimation der Entwicklungszusammenarbeit musste immer neu erarbeitet und bestätigt werden. Das war möglich, weil sich Schweizer und Schweizerinnen als Teile einer interdependenten Welt verstanden und eine Zusammenarbeit mit anderen Staaten als notwendig erachteten. Solche grundsätzliche Offenheit schloss allerdings eine kritische Haltung gegenüber der Globalisierung und der

Entwicklungszusammenarbeit nicht aus. Die wahrgenommenen Ängste erschlossen Zugänge zu dem, wozu Entwicklungspolitik im Zeitalter der Globalisierung verpflichtet, sowie zu ihren Grenzen und Möglichkeiten.

Als gemeinsame Anstrengung ruft Entwicklungspolitik nach Zukunftsperspektiven für alle Menschen. Weltweite Armut, soziale Gegensätze, mangelnde Sicherheit, Bodenerosion, Verknappung der Wasserressourcen, Migration und Pandemien wie HIV/Aids verweisen auf Probleme, die sich nicht im Alleingang oder mit den Werkzeugen einer traditionellen Politik lösen lassen. Ausnahmslos alle Länder und damit auch die Schweiz sind gefordert, Verantwortung zu übernehmen, weil aktuelle Risiken zu einer Bedrohung für alle werden. In einer globalisierten Welt macht das Ausmass anstehender und ungelöster Probleme klar, eine Lösung ist nicht durch die Industrieländer allein, sondern nur in Zusammenarbeit mit den Entwicklungsländern möglich.

Angesichts der vielfältigen Wechsel ist Entwicklungszusammenarbeit neu zu begründen: Legten früher in einer christlichen Moral begründete Postulate ein Teilen nahe, wird heute Entwicklungszusammenarbeit zur einzig möglichen Investition für die Zukunft unseres Planeten.

Armut und Entwicklungsdefizite haben in den vergangenen Jahren die Staatengemeinschaft bei der Suche nach einem gemeinsamen entwicklungspolitischen Rahmen zusammengeführt. Es scheint ein Konsens darüber zu bestehen, mit welchen Mitteln und in welcher Zeitspanne Armut einzudämmen und ganzheitliche Entwicklung zu fördern ist. Eine Konkretion solcher Überlegungen sind die Millenniumsziele und die Festlegung einer verbindlichen Umsetzung der Entwicklungsziele durch die Konferenz im mexikanischen Monterrey. Bei der Ausgestaltung dieses entwicklungspolitischen Rahmens hat die Schweiz aktiv mitgewirkt. Sie orientiert sich an den von der Völkergemeinschaft festgelegten Zielen.

Die Lektüre hinterlässt den Eindruck, dass sowohl internationale Zusammenarbeit wie humanitäre Hilfe an einen Wendpunkt gelangt sind. Veränderte weltweite Machtverhältnisse schaffen neue Herausforderungen. Die zentrale Herausforderung bleibt jedoch die Armut. In keinem Fall wird es eine adäquate Antwort sein, mit lokalen Projekten zu reagieren oder zu versuchen, Entwicklung zu planen oder Armut zu verwalten.

Zukunftsorientierte Entwicklungszusammenarbeit erweist ihre Echtheit, indem sie Veränderungen bewirkt, die sowohl für das Leben der Menschen in Armut wie auch für unsere eigene Zukunft wichtig sind. Dabei stehen vernetztes Denken und Handeln an erster Stelle. Entwicklungszusammenarbeit muss Staaten und Bevölkerungsschichten befähigen, ihr Schicksal selber in die Hand zu nehmen. Angesichts globaler Vorgaben wird die Schweiz – und das ist eine weitere Erkenntnis – nicht mehr darum herumkommen, sich auch über eine Erhöhung ihres finanziellen Engagements Gedanken zu machen. Das bedingt eine offene Auseinandersetzung über Verantwortung und Solidarität in einer globalen Welt. Vor 60 Jahren hat die Schweizer Bevölkerung in einer konkreten Situation ihre Verantwortung wahrgenommen; in einer globalisierten Welt stehen wir vor einer ähnlichen Entscheidung, denn alle sind wir einander Nachbarn geworden.

Ernstpeter Heiniger, Kreuzbuchstr. 44, CH-6006 Luzern (Switzerland); epheiniger@bluewin.ch

Book Note
Buchhinweis

English edition

Judith Butler, Jürgen Habermas, Charles Taylor, Cornel West, The Power of Religion in the Public Sphere, edited and introduced by Eduardo Mendieta and Jonathan VanAntwerpen, Afterword by Craig Calhoun, New York, Columbia University Press (A Columbia/SSRC Book [Social Science Research Council]), 2011, 137 p.

This extraordinary book is due to a public event that took place in the Great Hall of New York City's Cooper Union, held 22 October 2009. These four eminent and renowned philosophers and thinkers met for nearly five hours to engage in an intensive dialogue on various aspects of the general theme before an audience of over a thousand people. The editors praised the result of this event as follows: "This book is a testament to the vitality of the public sphere, in its uniquely American incarnation" (viii).

The contents of the four main chapters are:

- Jürgen Habermas, "'The Political': The Rational Meaning of a Questionable Inheritance of Political Theology", 15–33;
- Charles Taylor, "Why We Need a Radical Redefinition of Secularism", 34–59;
- Judith Butler, "Is Judaism Zionism?" 70–91;
- Cornel West, "Prophetic Religion and the Future of Capitalist Civilization", 92–100.

The book includes the dialogues held in between the presentations of the authors' papers:

- Dialogue: Jürgen Habermas and Charles Taylor (led by Craig Calhoun), 60–69;
- Dialogue: Judith Butler and Cornel West (led by Eduardo Mendieta), 101–108;
- Concluding Discussion, J. Butler, J. Habermas, Ch. Taylor, Cornel West (led by Craig Calhoun), 109–117.

The readers not quite familiar with contemporary social and political theory as discussed mainly Europe and Northern America might find most helpful both the «Introduction» by the editors (E. Mendieta and J. Van-

Antwerpen) and Craig Calhoun's Afterword: "Religion's Many Powers".
The latter focuses on the socio-religious context of the US where plain
evidence of the "power of religion" in public life with reference to the past
as well as to the present is documented.

Edición en castellano

Jürgen Habermas, Charles Taylor, Judith Butler, Cornel West, *El poder de
la religión en la esfera pública,* Edición, Introducción y Notas de Eduardo
Mendieta, Jonathan VanAntwerpen, Colección: Estructuras y Procesos.
Serie Filosofía, Madrid, Editorial Trotta S.A., 2011, 152 p.

«En los últimos años, en medio de una extendida recuperación del
interés por la relevancia pública de la religión, son las categorías mismas
de lo religioso y lo secular las que se reexaminan, reelaboran y replantean.
Es lo que hacen, en esto libro, cuatro destacados pensadores y representantes de la filosofía política y social contemporánea: Jürgen Habermas,
Charles Taylor, Judith Butler y Cornel West.

Se recogen aquí sus intervenciones en un coloquio sobre ‹el poder
de la religión en la esfera pública›, tanto sus propias exposiciones como su
posterior diálogo mutuo. Cada uno de ellos en su peculiar estilo intelectual y, traspasando los confines de las disciplinas académicas, desde un
fuerte compromiso público. Juntos representan algunas de las voces filosóficas más originales e influyentes de hoy, y abarcan el espectro de la
teoría crítica más reciente, de pragmatismo y el posestructuralismo a la
teoría feminista y la teoría crítica de la raza, la hermenéutica o la filosofia
del lenguaje.

La presente edición española se completa con un conversación entre
Jürgen Habermas y Eduardo Mendieta sobre la relevancia filosófica de la conciencia postsecular y la sociedad mundial multicultural.» (www.trotta.es/pa-
gina.php?cs_id_pagina=13&cs_id_contenido=29567; accessed 27.03.2013.)

Deutsche Ausgabe

Religion und Öffentlichkeit, hg. von Eduardo Mendieta, Jonathan VanAntwerpen, aus dem Englischen von Michael Adrian, Frankfurt am Main,
edition suhrkamp 2641, 2012, 196 S.

Seit dem 17. September 2012 liegt nun auch eine deutsche Übersetzung des international beachteten Kolloquiums in New York vor. Die hochkarätigen Dialogpartner stellten sich den vieldiskutierten Fragen um Religion in einer säkularisierten pluralistischen Gesellschaft, dies vor dem Hintergrund des Wiederauflebens der Religion in der Öffentlichkeit und ihrer Einflussnahme auf sie sowie der Migration und des sich vor allem in Europa etablierenden Islam. Das fordert die heutigen Denker und Denkerinnen, die sich profiliert in der Öffentlichkeit engagieren, heraus, neu darüber nachzudenken und im interdisziplinären Gespräch zu diskutieren, was die Begriffe «religiös» und «säkular» und die öffentliche Rolle der Religion bedeuten.

Wie Eduardo Mendieta in der Einleitung feststellt, repräsentieren die hier auftretenden Gesprächsteilnehmenden ein breites Spektrum zeitgenössischer Forschungsrichtungen wie z. B. Kritische Theorie der Frankfurter Schule, Pragmatismus, Poststrukturalismus, Feministische Theorie, Hermeneutik, Sprachphilosophie.

Der Begriff «Öffentlichkeit» geht auf die politikwissenschaftliche Habilitationsschrift von Jürgen Habermas (*1929) *Strukturwandel der Öffentlichkeit. Untersuchungen zu einer Kategorie der bürgerlichen Gesellschaft*, Neuwied/Berlin, 1971, 5. Auflage (1962) zurück. In der englischen Übersetzung *Structural Transformation oft the Public Sphere*, Cambridge, MIT Press, 1989, wird dieser Begriff mit «public sphere» wiedergegeben und hat vermutlich nachher als «Öffentlicher Raum» Eingang in den deutschen Sprachgebrauch gefunden wie analog dazu als «l'espace public» in den französischen.

Dr. Paul Stadler, Wolfganghof 18, CH-9014 St. Gallen, Schweiz
pablomm@hispeed.ch

Bartolomé de Las Casas (1484–1566).
Ein Missionar als Pionier des Völkerrechts.

Patrick Huser: Vernunft und Herrschaft. Die kanonischen Rechtsquellen als Grundlage natur- und völkerrechtlicher Argumentation im zweiten Prinzip des Traktates *Principia quaedam* des Bartolomé de Las Casas, LIT Verlag, Wien 2010, 266 S.

D ie historische Bedeutung des spanischen Dominikanerbischofs in der Neuen Welt wurde lange verkannt und die Rezeption seines Wirkens einseitig zu einer katholisch-papistischen Denkrichtung degradiert. In der Folge der Auseinandersetzung mit *500 Jahre Conquista* sind in den letzten zwei Jahrzehnten wissenschaftliche Untersuchungen verschiedenster Disziplinen vorgelegt worden, die den Blick auf ein genuin eigenes Denken des «Vaters der Indios» öffnen, dies auch im rechtsgeschichtlichen Bereich.

Bartolomé de Las Casas lässt sich auf verschiedene Weise rezipieren. So hat zum Beispiel der peruanische Befreiungstheologe Gustavo Gutierrez 1992 eine theologische Studie über das Denken und Wirken von Las Casas verfasst. Der in Freiburg (CH) dozierende Theologe und Kirchenhistoriker Mariano Delgado gab neben einer Werkauswahl auch mehrere historische Schriften über Las Casas heraus. Patrick Huser, Theologe und Delegierter des Internationalen Roten Kreuzes, legte 2010 an der Theologischen Fakultät der Universität Luzern eine Dissertation mit dem Titel «Vernunft und Handeln» vor, die sich mit den Rechtsprinzipien befasst, die der grosse Kämpfer für die Verteidigung der Rechte der Indios ausgearbeitet hatte. Der Verfasser grenzt seine Untersuchung auf die kanonischen Rechtsquellen im zweiten Prinzip des Traktates *Principia quaedam* von Las Casas ein und hebt vor allem deren völkerrechtliche Bedeutung zu Gunsten der Indios hervor.

Gegen die Ideologie der Superiorität
Die Dissertation liest sich wie ein Stück europäische Rechtsgeschichte

und korrigiert viele verstellte und zu optimistische Sichtweisen von Gleichheit und Volksrechten, die durch den aufgeklärten Geist propagiert wurden. Bacon, Hume, Montesquieu, Voltaire, de Paw und viele andere waren der Auffassung, dass «alle Nationen jenseits des Polarkreises oder zwischen den Wendekreisen im Vergleich zum übrigen Menschengeschlecht minderwertig sind» (Hume), und rechtfertigten so die Versklavung der Indios. Auch der spanische Humanist Juan Ginés Sepúlveda (1490–1573) – er war Jurist, Historiker, Philosoph und Berater von Karl V. – beharrte auf der aristotelischen Philosophie von der natürlichen Sklaverei (natura servi) und vertrat im Namen des Christentums eine koloniale Herrenmoral (natura domini). Hier setzt die Dissertation an: mit einer Verlagerung des Diskurses von der politisch-philosophischen auf die rechtliche wie kirchenrechtliche Ebene.

Las Casas' Position

Nach einer Kurzbiografie über Las Casas kommt der Autor zuerst auf die spanischen Klassiker des Naturrechts wie Francisco de Vitoria, Francisco Suárez und eben de Sepúlveda zu sprechen und schildert den berühmten Disput von Valladolid (1545 oder 1546). Vor einer Jury anerkannter Gelehrter legten die beiden Kontrahenten, Sepúlveda und Las Casas, ihre Positionen dar. Las Casas pochte auf das Selbstbestimmungsrecht des Individuums und auf ein naturrechtliches Rechtsverständnis. Dieses sichert eine auf das Heil des Menschern angelegte Gerechtigkeitsordnung und schliesst jegliche Versklavung aus.

In der Dissertation folgen dann lange Exkurse, die das lascasianische Denken über das Naturrecht und das Römische Recht darlegen. Diese beiden Rechte bilden die tragenden Säulen für sein völkerrechtliches Argumentationsgebäude. Im Unterschied zu seinen Gelehrtenkollegen, die vom Schreibtisch und von der Universität aus reflektieren, führt der Advokat der Indios an vorderster Front einen engagierten, aber fairen Kampf mit den damaligen tonangebenden Akteuren (spanische Krone, Konquistadoren, Gelehrte, Ordensleute, Heiliger Stuhl usw.).

Principia quaedam

Das Herzstück der Dissertation bilden die Textanalyse und der Kommentar zu den Rechtsquellen im zweiten Prinzip des Traktates *Principia quaedam*. Dessen genauer Titel lautet: *Einige Rechtsprinzipien, nach welchen vorzugehen ist in der Untersuchung zur Darstellung und zur Verteidigung des rechtlichen Status der Indios.* Casas legt darin folgende rechtliche Schlüsselbegriffe dar: Herrschaft (dominium: alle Menschen haben Recht auf Besitz von Gütern der Erde), Leitungsamt (officium: in einem freiheitlichen Akt soll Leitungsgewalt vom Volk auf den Souverän übertragen werden), Freiheit (libertas: sie liegt in der vernunftbegabten Menschennatur) und Wohl der Menschen (bonum hominum: das Gemeinwohl liegt im Aufbau einer Freiheitsordnung). Das Interessante dieser Untersuchung liegt in der Begründung all dieser Prinzipien auf der Grundlage der damaligen kanonischen Rechtsquellen. Dieser entscheidende Einbezug des kanonischen Rechts in seine Verteidigungsschrift zum Wohle und Schutz der Indios macht den unermüdlichen Theologen, Juristen und Bischof Las Casas zu einem schöpferischen wie originellen Vordenker des Völkerrechts und der Menschenrechte.

Schade ist, dass die Lektüre dieser hervorragenden Dissertation durch zu viele Wiederholungen und Zusammenfassungen manchmal ermüdend wirkt. An deren Stelle wäre ein Schlusskapitel über die Wirkungsgeschichte der *Principia quaedam* wünschenswert gewesen, im Sinne, dass Las Casas' Stimme weiterhin gehört werde, wenn im Kampf gegen Unterdrückung nach Hilfe geschrien wird.

Paul Vettiger, Oberseeburghalde 38, 6006 Luzern, Schweiz;
vettiger@hispeed.ch

Books received/
Liste eingegangener Bücher

Tamim Ansary, *Die unbekannte Mitte der Welt. Globalgeschichte aus islamischer Sicht,* aus dem Englischen von Jürgen Neubauer, Frankfurt/New York, Campus Verlag, 2010, 367.

George Dardess and Marvin L. Krier Mich, *In the Spirit of St. Francis and the Sultan: Catholics and Muslims Working Together for the Common Good,* Maryknoll, New York, Orbis Books, 2011, 205.

Félix Mutombo-Mukendi (éd.), *Exégèse, Théologie, Pastorale & Mission. Dix ans aus service du Seigneur en Europe:* Institut Biblique et Théologique de Bochum [IBTB], Bochum, Editions IBTB Presses, 2012, 494.

Helmut Schmidt, *Religion in der Verantwortung. Gefährdungen des Friedens im Zeitalter der Globalisierung,* Berlin, Propyläen/Ullstein Buchverlage, 2011, 251.

Karsten Schmidt, *Buddhismus als Religion und Philosophie. Probleme und Perspektiven interkulturellen Verstehens,* Stuttgart, Verlag W. Kohlhammer, 2011, 320.

Martin Üffing SVD (Hg.), *Mission seit dem Konzil* (Studia Instituti Missiologici SVD, Band 98), Sankt Augustin, Steyler Verlag, 2013, 228.

David Van Reybrouck, *Kongo. Eine Geschichte,* aus dem Niederländischen von Waltraud Hüsmert, Berlin, Suhrkamp Verlag, 2012 (3. Auflage), 783.

Huaqing Zhao, *Die Missionsgeschichte Chinas unter besonderer Berücksichtigung der Bedeutung der Laien bei der Missionierungsarbeit (ca. 16.–19. Jh.)* (Studia Instituti Missiologici SVD, Band 97), Sankt Augustin, Steyler Verlag, 2012, 308.